Free Trade
Free World

THE
LUTHER
HARTWELL
HODGES
SERIES

ON
BUSINESS,
SOCIETY,
AND THE
STATE

William H. Becker, editor

Free Trade
Free World

THE ADVENT OF GATT

Thomas W. Zeiler

The University of North Carolina Press
Chapel Hill and London

© 1999 The University of North Carolina Press
All rights reserved
Designed by Jacquline Johnson
Set in Monotype Bembo
by Running Feet Books
Manufactured in the United States of America

Publication of this work was aided by a grant included in the
Eugene Kayden Faculty Manuscript Award of the University
of Colorado.

The paper in this book meets the guidelines for permanence and
durability of the Committee on Production Guidelines for Book
Longevity of the Council on Library Resources.

Library of Congress Cataloging-in-Publication Data
Zeiler, Thomas W.
Free trade, free world : the advent of GATT /
by Thomas W. Zeiler.
p.   cm. — (The Luther Hartwell Hodges series on business,
society, and the state)
Includes bibliographical references and index.
ISBN 0-8078-2458-5 (hardcover : alk. paper)
1. General Agreement on Tariffs and Trade (Organization)—
History.   2. International trade—History.   3. Cold War.
I. Title.   II. Series.
HF1379.Z45   1999
382—dc21   98-22832
CIP

03   02   01   00   99   5   4   3   2   1

To Rocio

Contents

Illustrations

Acknowledgments

Over the five years that this book was in the making, I was fortunate to have the support of people too numerous to give them their fullest due credit. But here is a partial attempt.

For financial support, I am indebted to the University of Colorado at Boulder Graduate School for its array of grants and fellowships, the Harry S. Truman Library, the Carl Albert Center of the University of Oklahoma, and the American Heritage Center.

Colleagues in this country, and beyond, vastly improved this book. Randall Woods must be singled out for giving an early draft a close reading. As I have come to expect over the past seven years in Boulder, Robert Schulzinger cut right to the core of what I wanted to say but did not always manage to convey. Alfred Eckes, who introduced me to trade theory, history, government workings, and even some of the players, reminded me that there are sound alternatives to established dogma. From England, Razeen Sally kindly sent copies of his work that helped me with theory, Alan Dobson patiently allowed me to sound off for a few days in Glasgow, and Kathleen Burk cast a shrewd eye on my interpretations. The Contemporary History Institute at Ohio University invited me to discuss a part of this book; the experience was invaluable. Thanks to the graduate students there, especially Yong Lee, as well as Chester Pach, Alfred Eckes, and Alonzo Hamby. And, of course, my colleagues in the Department of History have always been supportive, but I especially thank Pat Murphy for her constant help with the computer.

There are archivists to appreciate; there are others who go well beyond the call of duty. Simon Davis in the Australian Archives befriended us during our stay in Canberra. Liz Safly and Dennis Bilger are special people, as any researcher who has worked at the Truman Library knows. Alf Aerlandsson graciously opened up the IMF Archives. And Michael Divine of the

American Heritage Center gave me the run of the wonderful holdings at the University of Wyoming, as well as stimulating conversation about foreign policy. Thanks also to Patrick Bova, Jeremy Cauchi, Mary Ellen Chijioke, Gould Colman, Margaret Cook, David Hays, Anita Heavener, Todd J. Kosmerick, Michael Nash, Marjorie NcNinch, Jessica Randolph, Mark Rinovitch, Nancy Shawcross, Christina Shevnik, Carol Staus, and Cassandra Volpe.

The University of North Carolina Press is simply wonderful, in all aspects of publishing. Thanks to Lewis Bateman, Ron Maner, and Stevie Champion for their advice, suggestions, and many, many improvements.

Now to single people out. Haroldine Helm provided the comforts of home in Independence, Missouri. My gratitude also goes to Cecilia Calvo in Washington, D.C., for her good cheer and cheerful accommodations. Anna Hearder and her children in London offer the best in hospitality. I only wish the late Professor Harry Hearder, a model for historians, could be around to assess this book. And then there is our dear friend—really a family member—Corinne Templer, who put up with me for weeks on end as I worked at the British Public Record Office. Her wit, her caring, her generosity are boundless, and I thank her deeply.

As for family, my sisters Jeanie and Diana made life easy, even with the teasing, during my research visits when they resided in Washington, D.C., and Tempe, Arizona, respectively. Having a brother like Doug in New York City was a godsend, even if he has fled since then. Thanks also to Elly and Harvey Falit of Ann Arbor for their kind hospitality. And my parents know how much they mean to me because of, above all, their moral support and advice that is truly the most sensible found on earth.

This book is dedicated to my wife, Rocio, simply my rock and that of our family in Colorado. During my endless research and writing, she endured many trials, not least of which was tolerating me and my absences in the midst of having two children and carrying on her busy work schedule. A mere dedication is but meager thanks for her love, but I hope it is a start.

Free Trade
Free World

Introduction

Benjamin Franklin once mused that just as the counties of England of his time did not ruin each other by protectionism, one day "neither would the nations."[1] That dream endures, yet it reveals an underlying tension long a trait of international trade relations. This is the debate between protectionists and the global business leaders and government officials who seek a commercial regime unfettered by barriers. During and after the Second World War, this standoff influenced policymakers in the United States and the British Commonwealth of Nations, who devised a liberal trade order in the hopes of reconstructing a global economy that lay in ruins and that many observers blamed for promoting economic strife and eventually war in the 1930s. Their efforts transformed the world trade system, the global economy, and the very nature of international relations.

The era encompassed by this study, 1940 to 1953, witnessed a shift in world power that occurs rarely in history. In the global economy, the change took place among friends. After centuries of presiding over the economic system, Europe fell in line behind the new superpowers, the United States and the Soviet Union. A major result in the trade order was a changing of the guard from British rule making to American attempts to push its ideology and policy to the fore during the Second World War. As Europe adapted to its dependent status, efforts to configure the commercial system were subsumed, first, under the vast project of restoring global order and then, under the seismic transformation in international politics caused by the Cold War.[2]

GATT, or the General Agreement on Tariffs and Trade, arose during this epoch. Planned by Anglo-American officials during the war, this tariff forum swept aside a grand fantasy called the Charter for an International Trade Organization (ITO). Visionary internationalists, economic theorists, and pacifists dreamed that commerce could be guided by a code of univer-

sally applicable rules and principles. They assumed that multilateral cooperation to lower trade barriers would bring balance to the global economy,
thereby ending war and poverty. The idea had no logic in the unstable circumstances of the 1940s, however. GATT, initially a mere appendix to the
ITO to guide tariff negotiations, proved more adaptable to the demands of
wartime sustenance, recovery, economic restoration, and, above all, the
Cold War.

The harnessing of trade for political and diplomatic ends is the interpre-
tive thrust of this study. Actually, decisions about trade in the United States
were largely *not* about economics at all. From the 1920s to the 1970s, exports and imports of merchandise, in total, never climbed above 10 percent
of gross production. To be sure, imports affected some sectors and America
netted a hefty trade surplus. But for an economy that produced hundreds of
billions of dollars in goods and services, foreign trade was insignificant.
Considering just one year—1947—gross national production stood at $231.3
billion, but the value of foreign trade (goods, gold, and silver) amounted to
a mere $22.5 billion.[3] This was not inconsequential, but it also was not a de-
termining factor in the economy.

Trade was, however, integral to the U.S. political agenda. In the tense
times of world war and cold war, economics came second to ideology,
which was expressed in the politics and diplomacy of trade policy. Thus,
this study argues that GATT was designed to ensure American values and security, not just profits.

Three elements support the notion that a political rationale for free trade
drove U.S. commercial policy.[4] One concerned the nature of American
capitalism. Free-traders, especially in the big business sector, assumed that
an open, competitive exchange of goods would preserve America's way of
life. Joined by conservatives in Congress, business leaders were concerned
about the rise of big government. This interventionist "state" manifested itself in the New Deal, the regulated economies of Western Europe, and communism. All of them threatened principles and practices of private enterprise,
guided by the free market. Free trade was a hallmark of this market capitalist system, which was the basis of the U.S. economy and was considered
a foundation of American democracy.

The second political element of trade was protectionism, defined as the
imposition of trade barriers by the government to shield domestic producers and workers from competitive foreign goods. All nations engaged in
protectionism. Some countries "discriminated" in commerce, favoring the
products of certain nations or groups of nations over others' goods. That is,

discrimination prevented equal access into national markets. Others raised barriers against everyone. To obtain protection, interest groups lobbied political representatives. Thus, policy in all nations, and in GATT itself, reflected political pressures.

The third element essential to the political rationale of U.S. policy related to diplomacy. This was the contribution of Secretary of State Cordell Hull, who served Franklin Roosevelt, and other idealists in the State Department. They crusaded for free trade to encourage peace. Nations that exchanged goods would naturally cooperate in the political sphere, they claimed. This was the underlying foundation of the pursuit of a universal code of trade rules embodied in the ITO Charter.

Unfortunately for the free-traders, the constant pressure for protectionism and the ideological battleground of the Cold War shifted America's trade objectives from peace to security. Realism and national security, not idealism and economic theory, took precedence in decisions. GATT revealed the tension between free trade and protectionism, capitalism and communism, private enterprise and regulatory socialism. In short, ideology and politics entered the world trade arena, where they shaped the contours of GATT.

America's aims and role in the development of such pragmatic trade policy relates to the debate over protectionism and free trade. Some critics have accused leaders of selling out U.S. producers and workers in a headlong drive to aid wartime and Cold War allies. This perspective stems from concerns about recent high levels of imports that worsened the U.S. trade deficit and prompted job loss overseas. This diverse group also is contemptuous of elitism; entrenched bureaucrats and global business leaders spouted free trade dogma while the policy process excluded Congress, leaving the State Department free to encourage imports. Reducing barriers with little regard for the impact on domestic interests has supposedly been the rule in U.S. policy since the 1930s, conclude these critics.[5]

Others have claimed that American trade policy was a selfish product of predatory business leaders and imperial-minded officials who shut out imports but forced in exports abroad. In this view, the government worked with international bankers, merchants, and investors, in tandem with efficient elements of the labor, farm, and industrial sectors, to determine policy. Seeking to overcome production gluts at home and control markets abroad, this "corporatist" juggernaut dominated the world economy, stunted development in poor nations, and created an elite political system unresponsive to the popular will. A neomercantilist trade policy, they argue, built a global empire after the Second World War that dominated friends and oppressed the weak.[6]

Both arguments ignore important aspects of U.S. policy. The first group of critics err because protectionism remained such a major part of policy that leaders were forced to adopt a modified program of "multilateralism," or the simultaneous reduction of barriers by nations. Thus, *freer*—not free— trade prevailed. And the Left neglects the effectiveness of America's trade partners to shape international trade and commercial rules along lines compatible with their own interests. Indeed, these countries often blocked American designs.

Both arguments also tend to elevate economics over politics. It is a mistake that gives a skewed picture of trade policy, for politics dictated U.S. decisions as well as GATT rules. In sum, theory regarding the nature of trade relations and the "state" shows that domestic and global politics compelled the United States to place protectionism under an umbrella of trade liberalism.

In the American state, Congress, under the Reciprocal Trade Agreements Act (RTAA), gave the president power to cut tariffs. Passed in 1934, the RTAA enabled a cautious lowering of tariffs but required concessions from foreigners. Congress extended the law periodically, often attaching protectionist restraints. The president beat back some of the more pernicious amendments, but he accepted others to obtain authority to negotiate in GATT. Thus, the executive branch dominated the policy process but interest groups and their representatives in Congress had their say. This compromise, the heart of U.S. trade policy, opened the way for the liberalization of world trade barriers in GATT. Free trade, in short, was never an alternative in American policy.[7]

GATT also reflected protectionist demands. Liberalism prevailed but only after GATT rules allowed for protectionism so that leaders could respond to domestic pressure. In other words, mercantilist instincts tempered the free market. Loopholes in rules allowed nations to "escape" from commitments to lower trade barriers. GATT's guiding multilateral principles—most-favored-nation treatment (or the extension of concessions to all GATT parties), tariff reduction on a nondiscriminatory basis, and equal treatment— were joined by a litany of escapes. These included import quotas for farmers and fisheries, national security and balance-of-payments escape clauses, and waivers for discriminatory customs unions. Economic and political pressures necessitated this compromise.

Integrating protectionism into a trade system designed to lower tariffs,

GATT, like U.S. policy, did not embrace free trade orthodoxy. Like the Reciprocal Trade Agreements Act, GATT was pliant enough to let policymakers maneuver around or assuage protectionists. This melding of inherently contradictory elements—multilateral trade liberalization tempered by economic nationalism—embedded protectionism in the overarching drive for freer trade.[8] Nations pursued multilateralism, with exceptions, and thus squared market capitalism (free trade) with regulatory demands (protectionism).

It is a central argument of this study that by liberalizing trade while protecting domestic economies—a bargain consistent with U.S. trade law, practice, and history—GATT facilitated American foreign economic and diplomatic objectives. Visionary wartime plans for free trade, and hopes that the ITO would complete the trinity of postwar reconstruction (the other two elements being monetary reform under Bretton Woods and security under the United Nations) were constrained by political compromise at home and then erased by Cold War strategists. The flexible GATT promoted American ideology, trade interests, and the strength of the Western alliance. The tariff forum was, in sum, suited to the self-interested behavior of nations and compatible with the times. This is the story of how GATT adopted the free trade–protectionist compromise in a time of conflict and change. And in this process, so influenced by history, lies the reasons why GATT endured.

CHAPTER I

War and Peace
1940–1943

On September 1, 1939, Nazi Germany invaded Poland to touch off the Second World War. Six days later, Adolph Hitler's forces were halfway to Warsaw. The blitzkrieg then turned west. Starting in April 1940, Nazi tanks rolled through Denmark, Norway, Holland, Belgium, and Luxumbourg, skirted French defenses, and then captured Paris on June 22. Germany now readied for an assault on Great Britain, the sole remaining western European democracy.

The United States watched the Nazis and marauding Japan in China with growing unease, yet the American public did not wish to send American soldiers to stop these aggressors. President Franklin D. Roosevelt knew better, but he could do little more than revise the country's neutrality laws in a way that would allow him to provide military supplies to the Allies. He choked off trade with Tokyo and prodded Americans toward intervention in Europe. Roosevelt, however, had his hands full with isolationists at home who opposed his efforts.

In foreign affairs, the president naturally focused on the war. Foreign trade policy was not a priority; only direct aid would rescue the Allies. Anyway, unlike his State Department, FDR was not an enthusiastic free-trader. He did realize, though, that America could boost British morale with the hope of a better postwar world, which included the promise of an open global trade system. Thus, Roosevelt lobbied for renewal of the Reciprocal Trade Agreements Act, which he had inaugurated in 1934. The RTAA signaled a vigorous internationalism, showing the Allies that America would not retreat under the cover of protectionism and into a shell of isolationism. To be sure, the administration was willing to accommodate moderate protectionists to ease the bill's passage. But lobbying for the law in 1940 and 1943 stressed foreign policy. In the midst of the war crisis, American officials enlisted trade policy in their service.

The notion that freer trade served foreign policy interests was not revolutionary. Tariff protection had been a hallmark of national policy since the nation's birth, but by the twentieth century both political parties advocated cautious reciprocity treaties to boost global cooperation, as well as exports. The rise of liberal internationalism under President Woodrow Wilson during the First World War had linked diplomacy and peace to freer trade. With the onset of the Great Depression and the passage of the Smoot-Hawley Tariff Act of 1930, protectionism was increasingly viewed as detrimental to global solvency and to peace.

Smoot-Hawley was not the sole cause of poverty and trade friction, but its symbolism was tremendous. The Democrats, eyeing the White House in 1932, blamed the law for worsening the Great Depression, prompting foreign trade retaliation, and weakening democratic friends abroad. Protectionism was simply ill-timed, as world trade plummeted by 60 percent between 1929 and 1932. Trade provided no stimulation to employ the one-quarter of the jobless workforce. Furthermore, because nations viewed Smoot-Hawley as an economic blockade, they retaliated by raising barriers to American exports. The Reciprocal Trade Agreements Act of 1934 took a stab at reversing this cycle of protectionism, at least giving the impression that the United States preferred an internationalist trade policy.

Prodded by Secretary of State Cordell Hull, Roosevelt sent the RTAA to Congress to halt the international trade war, promote exports, and encourage a reciprocal lowering of tariffs. Yet the law's significant impact was on the policy process. No longer would Congress set tariff rates. Instead, the State Department was free to negotiate down tariffs after Congress renewed the law. A former Tennessee congressman who pursued the South's traditional policy of free trade and export expansion as a key to agricultural prosperity, Hull messianically opposed protectionism and coaxed Roosevelt to endorse his views. Hull became particularly renown not for the free trade argument but for drawing parallels between protectionism and war. To illustrate his point, he liked to tell a story about neighbors in Tennessee who hated each other. One man's mules went lame just before plowing; the other ran out of corn for his hogs. After talking, the first man traded his corn for the second's mules. Cooperation led to prosperity, as both realized their mutual dependence, and peace reigned in the neighborhood. Attacked by protectionists in the 1940s because the RTAA had not averted war, Hull retorted that no nation that signed a trade agreement fought America,

Secretary of State Cordell Hull (fourth from left) observes as Roosevelt signs the
repeal of the arms embargo in November 1939. In their continued focus on aid to
the democracies, both called for Congress to renew the Reciprocal Trade Agreements
Act a few months later. (Courtesy Franklin Roosevelt Library)

and those that did were mostly aligned against the Axis powers.[1] Hull steadfastly defended the trade-peace rationale.

But trade relations in the 1930s hurt Hull's campaign for free trade. Of
top concern were America's major trade partners: the British Commonwealth of Nations. Britain, its dominions of Canada, Australia, New Zealand, South Africa, and a number of colonies had turned to protectionism
to retaliate against Smoot-Hawley, which denied them access into the large
American market, and to combat the Great Depression. Canada and the
United States signed a trade agreement in 1935, yet an Anglo-Canadian
accord in 1937 maintained imperial tariff preferences under the Ottawa
Agreement of 1932. Tariff preferences lowered or eliminated duties within
the empire but raised them against nonmembers. This discriminatory network placed U.S. traders at an unfair disadvantage in empire markets. As
Britain's top export market, America responded by refusing to lower tariffs

until the pernicious Ottawa system was abolished. A circle of retaliation characterized Anglo-American trade relations in the 1930s.[2]

An important trade agreement between the United States and Britain in 1938 revealed the difficulty of cooperation, but it was also noteworthy for exhibiting the influence of diplomacy in trade relations. Over a year in the making, the accord was consummated because of Hitler's march through Austria and Czechoslovakia. Winning more concessions than it gave, Britain, under the watchful eyes of the southern dominions (Australia, New Zealand, and South Africa), barely lowered preferential Ottawa tariff rates. Yet Hull focused on the benefits of building unity among the democracies rather than on improving a bad deal. Roosevelt went along, though he doubted that boosting British exports would ensure world peace.[3] Still, the Anglo-American accord opened the way for closer political relations between the two nations.

Clearly, however, the groundwork had yet to be laid for a multilateral trade system, under which nations would reduce barriers in a fair and simultaneous fashion. When war began in 1939, Hull hoped to secure a more lasting network of free trade arrangements. He banked on the war to convince Congress that the RTAA was a prerequisite for postwar peace. He expected the president to use this argument when confronting protectionists, who refused to subordinate trade to world politics.

Roosevelt never viewed trade matters with Hull's dogmatism. He backed freer trade because it benefited his New Deal. Liberal trade was a means to help struggling farmers and workers augment their exports. A pragmatic politician, Roosevelt would not be pinned down to the theory behind free trade principles. He was an experimenter in domestic relief programs, but he was not prone to fantasizing, like the State Department, that deliverance lay in abolishing tariffs. As an elected official, he would not hang out core supporters like labor in the winds of the free market. Thus, FDR never endorsed the vision of a worldwide tariff truce or other universalist dreams. He even ignored Nazi behavior and approved a barter deal in 1934 that swapped raw cotton for cheap German goods. In 1936 the president only tepidly endorsed the Democratic plank on the RTAA. But as war erupted, he knew that support for multilateralism was important to the Allied cause.[4]

Elevating the RTAA to the level of diplomacy was also a tactic to get the legislation through Congress. As the "Great Debate" over intervention in the war raged in the United States in early 1940, Roosevelt sent the RTAA extension bill to Capitol Hill. Commentators predicted that the stage was set for a tough fight. Roosevelt was vulnerable to pressure, as he aimed for reelection later in the year. Led by isolationist Senators Arthur Vandenberg of Michigan and Robert Taft of Ohio, the Republicans also sniped at the Hull program. Worried advisers urged the president to compromise and return the power to ratify agreements to the Senate. FDR agreed to suspend negotiations of new accords yet he asked for a three-year extension of the RTAA, leaving his autonomy over tariff rates intact. Tariff cuts, he argued, would help defeat fascism.[5] Protectionists did not buy that explanation.

Protectionists—Republicans and Democrats alike—preferred to focus on the economics of trade. RTAA accords would increase unemployment, they claimed, by exposing producers to unfair competition. Furthermore, they would not use Americans as guinea pigs for the State Department's free trade experiment of handing over domestic markets to foreigners. In addition, some held that the RTAA placed too much power in the hands of the executive. In an era of fascism, the law gave Roosevelt unrivaled power over the people's representatives on Capitol Hill. Protectionists charged that FDR had bypassed Congress's tariff, tax, and treaty authority. And they joined columnists Dorothy Thompson and Walter Lippmann, as well as historian Charles Beard, in ridiculing the notion that freer trade ensured peace and goodwill.[6] Protectionism was a major force in trade politics.

Protectionists could make a good case for import restraints. Trade had had little ameliorative effect on the Great Depression, as Roosevelt well knew. Even State Department statistics showed meager returns. Doubling the U.S. trade surplus between 1932 and 1939 through agreements with twenty-three countries, the RTAA still had not raised exports above the 1929 level of $5.24 billion. Exports accounted for less national production than ten years before—just 3.5 percent—and as a percentage of farm income had actually fallen from 15 percent to 8.4 percent. Ranging from textile makers to unions and small farmers, protectionist interest groups rolled out impressive statistics that blamed economic dislocation on Hull's trade program. Ironically, the nation suffered its first trade deficit in goods and services since the nineteenth century in 1934, the very year the RTAA became law. A huge outflow of gold and silver was the reason, but by 1940 imports of merchandise and precious metals shot to $7.4 billion, while exports still lagged. The ratio of imports to total U.S. output was tiny—a mere 2.6 percent—but protectionists preferred to point out, correctly, that 93 percent of production was consumed at home. Thus, they claimed, protection of the home market for American interests was in order.[7]

The administration took the protectionists seriously. The RTAA had been altered over the past few years to give producers more access to the Committee for Reciprocity Information, which informed top officials of whether tariff increases were needed. Opinion polls also revealed meager support for freer trade. A majority of Americans welcomed the RTAA as a tool to aid the Allies, but there was general apathy, skepticism, or opposition to the drive for higher imports. Protectionism thrived in the Midwest and the West, bastions of a partisan Republican Party that had long led the charge against free trade. But it also existed in regions where livestock, lumber, mining, glass, pottery, and oil interests feared competition. In fact, a large percentage of retailers, manufacturers, farmers, and workers in all states—from one-quarter to two-thirds polled—either viewed imports as a threat to their livelihoods or were uninformed about the RTAA.[8]

The average citizen and politician understood the economic logic of protectionism. For instance, the government packaged reciprocal trade as a boon for agricultural exports. According to the farm press, however, the sole beneficiaries were rich producers in agribusiness. The National Grange, an organization that had long represented small farmers against big business, lamented the rise in imports and opposed the RTAA. The American Farm Bureau Federation, a spokesman for big agriculture, backed the law but demanded that constituent agencies in the Departments of Commerce and Agriculture be consulted during tariff negotiations. The farm sector had been in crisis since World War I, faced with surplus production that the Roosevelt administration had tried to remedy by government purchases of commodities and payments for fallow land under the New Deal's Agricultural Adjustment Act. Wartime demand reduced the surpluses, but farmers feared that they would recur. They sought income guarantees from the government and did not count on exports to alleviate the gluts, which competitive imports would undermine by lowering prices. Farmers hoped for a sane system of tariffs and the continuation of import quotas.[9]

Protectionism was particularly strong in the industrial sector. The National Association of Manufacturers (NAM) had never officially announced a position on the trade agreements program, but this body of seven thousand conservative small business leaders largely opposed it. Howard Young of the Tariff Committee demanded amendments before NAM would back the law. In January 1940 he told North Carolina's Congressman Robert Doughton, who chaired the Ways and Means Committee that oversaw the legislation in the House, that these must include Senate ratification of accords, compensatory duties if exchange depreciation lowered the price of imports, and the deletion of unconditional most-favored-nation status for trade partners, which granted them the benefits of agreements even if they were not parties to negotiations. NAM backed freer trade, wrote Young, but not at the expense of U.S. producers.[10]

Aware that free trade ideology did not predominate in American society, protectionists enjoyed leverage in Congress. Republican politicians, many representing inefficient and small industries, led the way. But Hull's agenda also posed a problem for Democrats. Voices of protest were raised in Democratic strongholds in the South, a traditional bastion of free trade, and along the Atlantic seaboard, where dependence on shipping ostensibly created a natural ally for lower tariffs. An example was the textile industry, which wanted limits on imports and drew on backing by both parties. Democrats would fall in line behind the RTAA, but many endorsed cautious tariff cuts to protect constituents. Clearly, passage of the Reciprocal Trade Agreements Act of 1940 was no sure bet in Congress. Indeed, Secretary of the Interior Harold Ickes noted that "no one had a very hopeful feeling about the situation, the president least of all."[11]

Republican protectionists in Congress took the offensive. They identified with isolationists, particularly Senator Robert Taft. Like his father, the former president William Howard Taft, the Ohio senator proposed that the nonpartisan fact-finding body, the U.S. Tariff Commission, set prices at the level of domestic products. This would even out the competitive edge of nations with wages so low that they enjoyed a significant cost-of-production advantage. The idea appealed to many critics who blamed imports for problems in their districts. The New Deal had built up wage rates and thus raised production costs, they noted. But then Roosevelt nonsensically had let in low-cost imports that destroyed the very producers he had tried to save. High tariffs were the solution to such competition.[12]

A conservative hatred of big government under the New Deal underlay the GOP attack. To them, the welfare state and federal activism intruded in the private sector, subverted individualism, and endowed the president with unconstitutional powers. The New Deal promoted deficit spending, handouts to the needy, support for the rights of unions to bargain with business, and regulation of industry and banking. It had created a bloated bureaucracy, sympathetic to FDR, that controlled domestic and foreign policies and regimented the economy. Such "statist" structure epitomized fascism and communism. Thus, for the Right, the RTAA was another example of a "dictatorial, arbitrary, and secretive" measure that commandeered policy from "duly elected representatives of the people" and handed it to "bureaucrats," claimed two Republican congressmen in February 1940.[13] Reeling from a recent recession and his ill-fated attempt to pack the Supreme Court, Roosevelt was vulnerable to these attacks.

Antistatism was not the ken of the GOP. Senator Joseph O'Mahoney, a Wyoming Democrat, warned of the "economic disease" of centralism that let the president bypass Congress's authority over commerce. Raymond Moley, a former member of Roosevelt's brain trust in the early New Deal, believed that Congress should have the final say over trade. At stake, he announced after breaking with the administration, was nothing less than the cherished doctrine of the separation of powers. Conservative lawyers had tested the RTAA's constitutionality in the Supreme Court. The Court had upheld the law, asserting that because Congress retained the right to renew the legislation, the Constitution had been served. But O'Mahoney and GOP legislators now sought Senate ratification of the law.[14]

By doing so, they hoped to constrain State Department negotiators, who supposedly gave away tariff concessions in trade agreements with impunity. Protectionists disdained the preachy Cordell Hull and his apparent neglect of domestic interests. And diplomats always seemed to get suckered in bargaining. America leveled its tariff barriers, but the British nations obviously did not adhere to such a policy for they maintained their imperial preferential tariffs. Faced with the RTAA of 1940, therefore, protectionists proposed higher tariffs on many goods and congressional oversight of agreements. They hoped to defy the Will Rogers quip that the United States never lost a war or won a conference.

What lost protectionists their case was the isolationism of the extremists. Hull's notion that free trade was a form of peace insurance was certainly questionable. Interdependence led as much to rivalry for markets and resources as did friendship. Japan and China, as well as Germany, France, and Britain, had traded intensely but ended up fighting. Permeable trade frontiers might also render importing nations more vulnerable to foreign economic disturbances, thus destabilizing a country and beginning the downward spiral to political strife that had allowed fascism and militarism to take hold abroad. Hull's theory stretched the empirical data. But a course other than trade liberalization seemed detrimental to the Allied cause. So skeptics went along with Hull, leaving the protectionists hanging.

By hammering away at internationalism, as the European democracies teetered on the brink of oblivion, protectionists appeared as outmoded isolationists. New York congressman Daniel Reed exemplified the extremism that mocked legitimate protests against imports. This Republican graphically described how the Soviet Union was using U.S. exports of munitions, oil, and machinery against defenseless Finnish villages. Three years later, at the next renewal of the RTAA, he blamed Japan's devious attack on Pearl Harbor on American scrap and petroleum sales. That no trade agreements existed between the United States and either Russia, Japan, or Germany was lost on Reed. That cutting off exports would not have deterred these aggressors (as the Japanese case demonstrated), or that America was at war with no nation with which it had signed a trade accord, was irrelevant to him. Reed plunged ahead, accusing Hull of having invented the "pious peace argument" to please civic associations and disguise the fallacies of free trade economic theory.[15] Hull could not have done a better job of discrediting protectionism as the preserve of crackpots.

As the voice of the liberal traders, the State Department patiently countered the protectionist attack by framing the extension bill of 1940 in terms of national and international interests. The argument that trade bred peace was not the only debating point available. Hull and his compatriots defended themselves from every protectionist parry. But ultimately, the winds of war that blew through Congress won the day for the Reciprocal Trade Agreements Act.

Under questioning before the Ways and Means Committee for a day and a half, and the Senate Finance Committee for a full day, Cordell Hull responded to complaints about the RTAA. He began with the economic arguments. Negotiators had cut tariffs on hundreds of items, but concessions still covered only 15 percent of total imports. Thus, claimed Hull, low duties had little effect on corn, peanut, and cattle prices, and minimal impact on hog and dairy farmers, who still controlled 99 percent of the domestic market. Protectionists were hoodwinking farmers so that they would turn against Roosevelt in the election of 1940. In any case, producers would do better to focus on exports, argued the secretary of state. Three-quarters of farm exports, and almost half of the country's nonagricultural goods, had been granted concessions or assurances that tariffs would be frozen at current levels. The postwar era promised new and expanding foreign outlets.[16]

Although their health did not depend on export expansion, many interests were receptive to this argument. Farmers hoped to sell some of their surpluses overseas. Organized labor remained neutral on the law, split by unions opposed to the RTAA. Yet the Brotherhood of Railroad Trainmen, for one, looked to exports to generate jobs. So did such big manufacturers as automakers. And consumer and civic associations, led by women's groups, claimed that low tariffs reduced prices at home, high exports raised the standard of living, and free trade encouraged international cooperation. All took issue with protectionists. Northeastern shoemakers claimed, for instance, that the U.S.-Czech trade agreement of 1938 had ruined them. Yet imports from Czechoslovakia amounted to a mere 1 ¼ percent of the footwear industry's total domestic output. If protectionists were right, declared the *Boston Herald*, then Yankee ingenuity had disappeared, "and our shoe manufacturers are playboys among the tombs of their ancestors."[17]

One of the most effective weapons used to combat opponents of Roosevelt and Hull was partisan denunciation of the Republican Smoot-Hawley Act. Americans certainly did not want to return to the worst days of the Great Depression, when high tariffs had nearly wrecked the nation. The *Iowa Register* of Des Moines contrasted the GOP's "Mr. Elephant," mired in the protectionist muck of the past that enriched only special interests, with "Mr. Sense," who symbolized the Democrats. Such attacks were unfair to Republicans who worried about their constituents. But many commentators feared that protectionists would block the growth necessary for postwar domestic health and reconstruction in Europe. Even the Republican editor William Allen White warned his party not to make the "sad mistake" again of adopting "an old-fashioned, high-tariff-platform policy."[18]

Administration officials also countered their image as uncaring bureaucrats who undemocratically opened American markets to salivating foreigners. By setting limits on the duration of executive branch power over tariff policy, Congress reserved its constitutional prerogatives over commerce, they explained. In addition, after producers received a fair hearing, the State Department undertook the technical job of determining tariff concessions. Trade delegations were truly full of hardheaded and stingy negotiators who adhered to modest, practical trade liberalism. Thus, Congressman Doughton of the Ways and Means Committee denied that the RTAA was a "Santa Claus policy" for imports.[19]

Yet above all other arguments stood internationalism, that is, the pivotal role that trade played in diplomacy. Opponents simply failed to grasp that economics and diplomacy were intertwined. There were no alternatives to the RTAA except the "growth of national economic isolation, with all its disastrous results for the peace and prosperity of nations," argued Hull. That rhetoric was relevant now that Hitler was on the move, but it also had salience in the context of postwar planning. Colossal problems loomed in the future, especially the immense chore of economic restoration in the wake of wartime destruction. Only sound trade relations that put people to work would provide the stability necessary for peace.[20]

The peace argument prodded Congress to pass the bill and earned Roosevelt's strong endorsement of the RTAA for the first time. Choosing his words carefully in an election year, the president dodged voter concerns over imports. The law would help the U.S. economy, but "what is more important," he declared, "the Trade Agreements Act should be extended as an indispensable part of the foundation of any stable and enduring peace."[21]

Wartime attitudes simply proved too much for the protectionists. Indeed, they lost but were not routed. After beating back several protectionist amendments, the House extended the RTAA for three years by a fairly close vote of 218–168 and the Senate by a slim 41–35 tally. Roosevelt signed the Reciprocal Trade Agreements Act in April 1940, as the Nazi blitzkrieg stormed across Europe. The RTAA was a bright hope in the dark early days of World War II. Indeed, Republican presidential candidate Wendell Willkie supported it to promote peace. But because his accord with this and other internationalist policies did not distinguish him from FDR, voters saw no reason not to reelect Roosevelt.[22] The circumstances of war also doomed the protectionists, now tarred as narrow-minded isolationists.

Protectionists were in an even deeper hole by the time of the next renewal of the Reciprocal Trade Agreements Act, in 1943, for the United States was then at war. The administration had edged toward conflict in September 1940 by sending Britain some old destroyers. Roosevelt then persuaded Congress to authorize billions of dollars in assistance to the British under the Lend-Lease Act of March 1941. Meanwhile, Britain had heroically held off the Nazi invasion, and a frustrated Hitler turned east to attack the Soviet Union in June 1941. Aiding the Allies in every way short of war, the president also confronted Japan's advance in Asia with growing determination. Trade sanctions were imposed throughout 1941. Hull had tried to use commerce as a diplomatic tool by offering the Japanese a trade agreement in return for their withdrawal from China. Transmitted to Tokyo on November 26, 1941, the effort failed. Less than two weeks later, the Japanese attacked Pearl Harbor, thrusting the United States into the Second World War.

The administration's attention over the next few years was directed toward mobilizing the economy and public for war and holding back the Nazi and Japanese onslaught. What little attention it paid to the reciprocal trade program came in the form of a handful of trade agreements, signed to maintain momentum for the multilateral idea once the war was over. Mid-level officials in the State Department also busied themselves with plans for a postwar free trade system. Such discriminatory trade practices as imperial preferences and restrictive import quotas, both key elements of British policy, were targeted by Harry Hawkins. This State Department planner was chief of the Division of Commercial Policy and Agreements and Hull's right-hand man on RTAA issues. He also helped devise a set of universal trade principles that offered an alternative to the autarchic trade blocs endorsed by the Nazis.[23]

By 1943 free-traders referred even more than before to the relationship between internationalism and low tariffs. Still, protectionist foes made life difficult. Congress had grown more conservative since 1940. A bloc of southern Democrats, set on scaling back the New Deal, now dominated major committees. More ominous for the administration, however, were Republican gains in Congress. In the 1942 midterm elections, they had picked up forty-four House seats (just seven votes short of a majority) and nine votes in the Senate. Thus emboldened, Republicans and conservative Democrats had become watchdogs over wartime spending and New Deal programs. The GOP had also pledged to clamp down on unfettered postwar internationalism.[24]

Although the public had a greater appreciation for the economic bases of peace, protectionist interest groups and legislators asked for a tariff freeze and limits on imports until the war came to a close. Protectionism resonated for the average citizen, of modest education and income living in the heartland of the country. Of the two thousand people surveyed in October 1942 and January 1943, pollsters found half in favor of self-sufficient, national industries to replace imports. Over three-fifths spurned peace as a rationale for admitting foreign goods. And a majority still had no knowledge of the RTAA, trade agreements, or even who made trade policy. The Republicans' hope of retreating "back into comfortable pre-war patterns" of protectionism, wrote Joseph Jones of the State Department, seemed realizable.[25]

During the 1943 RTAA renewal battle, protectionists reared up to confront the administration. They denounced the concept of a postwar multilateral trade order. Anglo-American plans to increase U.S. imports by a universal lowering of tariffs, they protested, sold out domestic interests. To show their disdain, several Republican opponents boycotted the RTAA vote. Senator Eugene Millikin, of Colorado, a new and articulate voice of protectionism, and a rising star within the GOP ranks, criticized "the new propaganda to surrender our home market" for the illusionary hope of peace. Like many of his colleagues, he could not understand how the country could survive low-cost imports. Returning servicemen and workers leaving defense plants after the war would be victims of this free trade order, designed for foreigners by the generous State Department that uttered stirring slogans with little practical meaning.[26]

Critical to the debate was Republican Senator Arthur Vandenberg, positioned between isolationists who foolishly hid behind a tariff wall and free trade "global zealots." An emerging supporter of internationalism in foreign affairs, Vandenberg nevertheless ridiculed the administration's argument that the RTAA would determine the fate of the postwar world. He thus had repudiated Cordell Hull before his Senate Foreign Relations Committee. Now the RTAA had taken on "the magnitude of The Sermon on the Mount," and he would not stand for such dramatics. Vandenberg backed the bill because it played a role, however small, in promoting Allied unity. But he wanted it limited to two years. He also proposed an amendment to have the Tariff Commission set tariff rates based on standards laid down by congressional statute. Trade policy would thus be returned to congressional control, allowing Congress also to engage in foreign policy decisions.[27]

Vandenberg internationalists gave the administration an opening. Trooping to Capitol Hill once again, Hull and his allies looked beyond economic issues to warn that American global leadership was at stake in the RTAA renewal. The United States must end discriminatory trade practices, fulfill postwar dreams of world security and prosperity, and act properly as the world's creditor by buying sufficient amounts of imports. The RTAA was the acid test of America's intentions. The country must not only win the war, said House Speaker Sam Rayburn of Texas, "but we are going to do a man's part in trying to keep the peace of the world after this war is over" by ensuring that the era of Smoot-Hawley and isolationism was over.[28]

War and postwar concerns clinched bipartisan support for the RTAA of 1943. Molding a compromise, Ways and Means chairman Robert Doughton got the law extended for two years (Hull wanted three) but managed to cancel many protectionist amendments. After FDR agreed, the bill sailed through the House with the help of 145 Republicans. It then hit a wall of resistance in the Senate. Republicans proposed an amendment to terminate all trade agreements six months after the war in order to reassert congressional authority over commercial policy. The provision passed the Finance Committee by a vote of 11–10, but Democratic heavyweights weighed in and it went down to defeat on the Senate floor by a 51–33 tally. Vandenberg's Tariff Commission amendment also failed by a close vote, as did another that provided for Senate ratification of agreements. Eighteen Republicans then joined the Democrats to renew the law by a large margin. The vote showed that Congress now sought "practical international collaboration now and for the future," exalted Hull in June, when Roosevelt signed the legislation.[29]

Hull's statement was a typical exaggeration by a free trade multilateralist whose optimism outran his realism. Yet he can be excused, for he was already lobbying for a code of universal free trade principles for the postwar years. It was a vision with boundless possibilities. By 1943 victory in World War II seemed assured. The Nazi advance had been halted, and Germany suffered under a relentless barrage of Allied bombs. Japan had turned to defense a year before, as the American navy pushed toward Tokyo. At home, despite the increased strength of conservatives, protectionism had been overwhelmed by sentiment that demanded a vigorous U.S. role in international affairs. Multilateralists thus flourished in Washington, D.C.

Two successful renewals of the Reciprocal Trade Agreements Act revealed the protectionist undercurrent in policy-making, while at the same time they gave free-traders great hope. These idealists now looked abroad, to Great Britain and the Commonwealth, to draw up a blueprint of their sweeping vision. Hull dreamed that these allies would engage in negotiations to create a free trade order, abolishing all forms of discrimination in world commerce and agreeing to a code of rules and principles that would enshrine market capitalism in the international trade system. The British soon brought him down to earth.

CHAPTER 2

Defending the Empire
1941–1944

Because of wartime destruction, the British Commonwealth had different ideas than America about a postwar trade order. Hurt by the Great Depression, then battered by the Axis, Great Britain faced a future of decline and hardship. Its once predominant global position, fortified by an expansive empire, lay in tatters. Spending for the war had exhausted the treasury and forced a sell-off of many overseas assets. The British now depended on military and economic aid from their dominions and colonies, as well as from the United States.

This dire situation led Britain to refuse to subject its economy to competition. Britain would engage in planning a postwar commercial order with the United States. But free trade multilateralism was out of the question, and by and large the rest of the Commonwealth agreed. It was not that the British nations opposed universal principles to liberalize world trade. They just conflicted with the U.S. idealists on how to achieve this end. British planners sent out clear signals during wartime negotiations with the United States that a modification of the American vision was in order.

The interwar years had convinced the British that economic security must take precedence over high profits. Regulated, rather than American-style market, capitalism was required. The great economic thinker John Maynard Keynes believed that the government had to harness profit making to maintain consumption levels and assure full employment. He had long criticized the notion that reducing restrictions on imports promoted a favorable balance of trade. From his perch in the Treasury Department, Keynes represented a varied group of economists and politicians who supported trade and exchange discrimination, including imperial preferences, quantitative (quota) controls on imports, and trade financed in sterling, not dollars.[1]

20

John Maynard Keynes (right), advocate of trade regulation, with U.S. secretary of the Treasury Henry Morgenthau. (Courtesy Franklin D. Roosevelt Library)

The Commonwealth had developed this discriminatory system over the past decade. The "sterling bloc" was a main element. In this arrangement, trade was financed by sterling accounts that could not be converted into dollars to buy nonempire goods. Britain purchased food from the dominions, which used their receipts to buy British manufactures. Trade thus remained within the empire. Americans complained that this network curbed their exports and violated free trade principles, as did Canada, which refused to participate in the arrangement. But by war's end the sterling bloc accumulated a balance of 3 billion pounds that could not be used for imports from the United States.

Furthermore, despite the Anglo-American trade agreement of 1938, the Commonwealth upheld the Ottawa Agreement of 1932. This accord had created the system of preferential tariffs that discriminated against nonempire traders. Unfortunately for the United States, its two largest export markets, Britain and Canada, had led the way in creating a "margin" between the favorable rates applied to the empire and those tariffs raised against outsiders. Imperial preferences hurt U.S. food exporters. Their livestock, meat, and wheat could not compete with dominion meat, grains, and fruit that now enjoyed comparatively lower tariffs and thus a lower competitive price. For instance, Australia cut into U.S. sales by selling to Britain much of its butter, meat, apples, and dried fruit. Such trade discrimination dropped U.S. exports.[2]

Preferences also had political value. Conservative Party imperialists—"empire isolationists"—cherished the Ottawa Agreement. Their rural base led them to embrace tariff margins to encourage Commonwealth food production. Most, however, viewed Ottawa as an emblem of empire unity, independence, and strength. The British nations had banded together to fight Nazism and the Japanese. Solidarity was tested by war. American power posed another challenge. Proclaimed the secretary of state for India, Leo Amery, Cordell Hull's free trade plans could "very well succeed as a policy for breaking up the British Empire and reducing it to an American Lebensraum or Mandated territory." Fellow Conservative prime minister Winston Churchill disdained such views, but he was careful, for Amery's allegiance was critical to his wartime coalition government. The prime minister also reasoned that Britain's postwar salvation lay in regulated, not free, trade.[3]

That position was supported by Labour Party members of the War Cabinet. Although opposed to discrimination and the colonial taint of the imperial trade network, Labour viewed preferences as necessary safeguards for

industry and workers. A drastic cut in barriers would speed economic dete-
rioration, undercut employment plans, and render the Commonwealth vulnerable to wild fluctuations in the American economy. As Board of Trade
president Hugh Dalton of the Labour Party explained, "I believe neither in
free trade nor in protection but in planning." The ascendant Labourites
spoke for mainstream opinion across the Commonwealth.[4]

Britain would have to take special protectionist measures to balance its
international accounts and pay for imports necessary for civilian and military consumption. A trade surplus, built by quotas and preferences, would
help. So would a dramatic lowering of U.S. tariffs. Once Britain was secure
from a German invasion by late 1940, Churchill turned to postwar reconstruction. This hinged on replenishing financial reserves by curbing domestic consumption, expanding exports, and maintaining protectionism. The
British prepared to modify free trade designs.

Meanwhile, Churchill encouraged cooperation with the United States.
Prodded by the proposals of Foreign Office counselor Owen Chalkley in
November 1940, the War Cabinet sought to work with America on a postwar economic order. Chalkley advocated little more than commodity disposal, for the war precluded discussions about more extensive plans. Yet the
British could not deny their reliance on America for their survival. Collapse
was imminent by early 1941, as Treasury reserves stood at less than $100
million and the supply of gold had dwindled to less than $50 million. Not
surprisingly, England eagerly welcomed the Lend-Lease Act of March 1941,
which provided billions of dollars in war materiel. But this came with strings
attached, namely an understanding that the Commonwealth would repay
the United States by embracing the trade principles of Cordell Hull.[5]

Lend-Lease provided the first forum to plan the commercial regime. In late
1940 and 1941 State Department trade adviser Harry Hawkins proposed to
halve U.S. tariffs in return for the elimination of Ottawa preferences and
sterling bloc exchange controls. Sweetening the pot, he announced that
Britain could defer its side of the bargain until the war ended. London would
not deal. Empire isolationists and wary dominions suspected the Americans
of conniving to capture Commonwealth markets. Keynes also ridiculed the
plan, for Britain could not commit to ending controls without regard for
postwar conditions or freedom over economic policy. Besides, aid allayed
the need for concessions on preferences. Hawkins was alarmed that Britain
considered resort to discriminatory trade practices after the war.[6]

The drafting of the Mutual Aid Master Agreement, which set the terms for Lend-Lease, and the formulation of the Atlantic Charter in August 1941 gave the Americans a chance to address this concern. Remembering the friction over World War I debts, Roosevelt and Churchill agreed on compensation for Lend-Lease in political, military, and economic principles rather than money. But State Department idealists wanted clear British commitments to eliminate preferential tariffs. They would never realize that ambition. Keynes bypassed them and went directly to Roosevelt to discuss his draft of Article VII of the Master Agreement in June and July 1941. Article VII dealt specifically with Anglo-American trade relations. Keynes offered a skeleton draft that ended trade discrimination, but only "as circumstances allow."[7]

The British simply would not accept free trade doctrine. Meeting with Keynes, Undersecretary of State for Economic Affairs Dean Acheson believed that Article VII demanded British adherence to nondiscrimination, although he would not bind them to ending preferences. Keynes was angry. He wished to protect Churchill's political flank and to retain leverage in negotiations, but he also philosophically differed with the Americans. Only laissez-faire dogmatists—and Roosevelt was not one of them—would force the downtrodden British to abandon their protectionist lifeline. Free trade was destructive. Nondiscrimination was a "cover behind which all the unconstructive and truly reactionary people of both our countries would shelter," he told Acheson.[8]

Still, few British officials sought a skirmish with the United States. The Americans might retreat back to isolationism or lower barriers only to dominion trade, thus breaking up the empire. Even to Keynes, the request to modify the Ottawa system, at the least, seemed reasonable if America slashed its tariffs. Yet Britain could not unilaterally abrogate margins; the dominions' consent was required. And the dominions demanded greater access to the American market as a substitute for the loss of exports within the empire, which were assured by preferences and bulk-purchasing agreements. Thus, the entire Commonwealth hinged its support for multilateralism on substantial U.S. concessions.[9]

But State Department ideologues wanted much more. Although sympathetic to Britain's plight, they sought a commitment to end discrimination and grant fair entry to U.S. exports. Without this, Congress would pressure Roosevelt to retaliate, with dire consequences for trade and political relations. Temporary controls were permissible, but the long-term principles of Article VII must promote free trade. But this was too rigid for the presi-

Roosevelt and Churchill at the Atlantic Charter Conference in August 1941.
(Courtesy Franklin Roosevelt Library)

dent. Concerned about showing the Axis powers that the democracies were unified, Roosevelt was unwilling to nail British coattails to the wall of free trade multilateralism.[10]

On board the president's ship off the Newfoundland coast in mid-August 1941, FDR and Churchill issued the Atlantic Charter. They conferred about goals and military strategy, producing a statement similar in meaning to Roosevelt's recently enunciated four freedoms. Supporting collective security and condemning territorial expansion, the Atlantic Charter advocated global democracy and prosperity. It epitomized universalist concepts that liberal internationalists had long endorsed. Except, that is, for Point Four of the document, regarding the commitment to liberalize postwar trade.

Essentially, the earlier Keynes-Acheson talk was duplicated. Britain's draft of Point Four blandly called for "a fair and equitable distribution of produce," whereas America's demanded equal access (nondiscrimination) to markets and raw materials. Redrafting occurred, but Undersecretary of State Sumner Welles argued that phraseology was not the issue. If Britain prevailed, then nations "might as well throw in the sponge and realize that one of the greatest factors creating the present tragic situation in the world was going to be permitted to continue unchecked in the post-war period." Point Four urged equal access, but Churchill inserted the saving phrase "with due regard for our present obligations" as a means of maintaining preferences. Roosevelt sided with Acheson, whom Keynes had persuaded to oppose free trade policies. The president preferred to place the immediate needs of the Allies above broad principles. Anyway, he was satisfied that Churchill had conceded more than initially expected.[11]

Point Four disgusted State Department idealists. For one thing, trade policy toward Britain was political dynamite at home. As research chief Leo Pasvolsky warned, protectionists welcomed the resistance to free trade. It heightened their Anglophobia and economic nationalism. Second, the saving phrase might deter Congress from renewing Lend-Lease. Isolationists were already angry that Britain was reexporting Lend-Lease goods to South America to build dollar reserves, rather than using them for the war effort. Third, Churchill had deprived Point Four of meaning and specificity. Not even the experts could explain whether and when the saving phrase applied to preferences.[12]

The British were just as successful in negotiations over the Lend-Lease Master Agreement that resumed in the fall of 1941. The United States resolved that Article VII must pave the way for a nondiscriminatory trade system. Agreeing in principle, Churchill would not accept the U.S. vision in practice. As America entered the war in December 1941, he requested an exemption for preferences from the Master Agreement. At first, even Roosevelt reacted unfavorably. The president protested that British reservations would sow discord in the alliance at the darkest time of the war. But the very enormity of the crisis brought out the realist again in Roosevelt. Attacking the Ottawa system at this juncture would unnecessarily undermine Anglo-American cooperation.[13]

Placing military objectives above idealism, FDR informed Churchill that he would not compel Britain to trade preferences for Lend-Lease aid when they signed the Mutual Aid Agreement on February 23, 1942. Article VII called for an end to commercial discrimination and for the reduction of trade barriers. But a saving phrase watered down this commitment. It required "mutually advantageous economic relations" as a precursor to any agreement to reduce tariffs and preferences. That elastic term allowed the British to determine when economic relations were mutually beneficial. They could be parsimonious, withholding concessions on preferences until they deemed the situation favorable.[14]

The look on Hull's face best expresses the disappointment of
accepting British terms for trade discrimination in the Atlantic Charter.
(Courtesy Franklin Roosevelt Library)

Point Four and Article VII let Britain slow down the free trade drive, but
planners proceeded anyway to the next step of formulating a code of principles and rules to guide a commercial institution. Suggestions were heard
from academics, journalists, business leaders, and government officials. After
the First World War the League of Nations had neglected to create a trade
forum, with disastrous results. That mistake would not happen again. The
United States and Canada contemplated a customs union to encourage
cooperation, while another idea emerged for an Anglo-American body to
promote trade, common cultural ties, and the surrender of sovereignty in
economic affairs. Such grandiose schemes for supervision of the world
economy thrilled State Department planners like researcher Leo Pasvolsky
and his assistant, Harley Notter, who collaborated with the like-minded
Percy Bidwell of Yale University.[15]

The British were already well ahead in the planning process, however, and they did not envision a free trade order. In early 1941 the scholar Arnold Toynbee of Oxford University broached to Pasvolsky an idea for a global economic authority that would merely mediate between national tariff commissions. The War Cabinet's Official Committee on Postwar External Economic Problems and Anglo-American Cooperation, known as the Hurst Committee, then concluded in August 1941 that the realities of U.S. power and British weakness compelled acceptance of Hull's "visionary" multilateral idea. Timid answers would undermine the war and reconstruction efforts. But most officials preferred a compromise between unilateralism and free trade universalism.[16]

On July 31, 1942, James Meade offered the compromise in the form of a commercial union to complement Keynes's financial union scheme. An academic now working in the Economic Section of the War Cabinet Secretariat, Meade won later fame for framing Britain's full-employment policy. He is less heralded for his commercial union idea, which served as the foundation of the International Trade Organization, the ancestor of the current World Trade Organization. He endorsed multilateralism but demanded that the United States act like a creditor by augmenting its imports and providing loans to needy trade partners.

Britain's stake in world trade required multilateralism, modified by regulatory mechanisms, held Meade. Dependent on food imports bought by exports of manufactures, the country had "a powerful interest in the general removal of restrictions in international commerce." He would not abandon the fixtures of British protectionism, including import and sterling controls. His plan, moreover, called for equal treatment for private and socialistic systems. But it did seek to expand trade. Thus, while he sought to modify free trade multilateralism, Meade shunned excessive forms of discrimination.

A "Charter" of rules, reflecting British interests, formed the heart of his proposal. One rule forbade preferential tariff treatment, except for nations grouped by political affiliation (like the Commonwealth). A second put limits on such protective devices as subsidies and quantitative barriers, but a third rule exempted a nation (like Britain) with a demonstrable balance-of-payments deficit during a difficult "transitional" period from a duty to ease up on these measures. An International Commerce Commission would decide disputes and would be empowered to sanction members guilty of noncompliance with the rules. The charter placed the burden of sacrifice on solvent countries (America) and let vulnerable nations (Britain) hold on to protectionism. Yet it represented a middle way between empire isolationism and U.S. free trade dogma.[17]

Hugh Dalton, president of the Board of Trade, enthusiastically handed the Meade plan to the cabinet in November 1942 after adviser Hugh Gaitskell redrafted it. Dalton noted that the idea buried autarchy, braced the monetary union, and considered problems in the current atmosphere of collaboration. Hull would be impressed, while the internationalist wing of the Republican Party would have evidence of British cooperation and thus steer away from protectionism. And, of course, the code would expand British exports. A backstop to the Atlantic Charter, Meade's agenda, concluded Dalton, would "help to keep trade good and keep men bold."[18]

But many officials gave the proposal a cool reception. The projected adverse trade and payments balance led Chancellor of the Exchequer Kingsley Wood to frown on the plan. Britain needed freedom to restrict imports. Others called the idea unrealistic. Why should a code work now when cooperative endeavors had failed in the past? Furthermore, U.S. and British objectives diverged. E. W. Playfair of the Treasury Department noted that America sought open competition, whereas the British wanted to limit that aim. Britain would be better served by regulating commerce, not encouraging the "nineteenth century conditions" of laissez-faire in which only powerful U.S. producers would thrive.[19]

To sell Meade's plan to the War Cabinet, Foreign Secretary Anthony Eden convened a Committee on Postwar Commercial Policy under the venerable permanent secretary of the Board of Trade, Sir Arnold Overton. The committee reported on January 6, 1943, folding Meade's plan into guidelines for lowering trade barriers. Included were provisions to halve preference margins, prohibit new ones, and cap ad valorem tariffs at 25 percent, while allowing for quotas when needed. Subsidies, quotas, and export taxes would be constrained. State trading would be permitted to coax the Soviet Union into joining a commercial union. A trade institution would oversee the rules.[20] The Overton Report was bound to pique a range of cabinet members but appeal to the Americans.

A sweeping, concrete plan, the Overton Report challenged the Americans. The United States negotiated tariffs on specific items, with one nation at a time, and then generalized concessions to those most-favored nations that granted America equal tariff treatment. That approach was ponderous and piecemeal, subject to pressure from vested interests and resulting in moderate tariff cuts. The Overton Report recommended cutting duties by a percentage reduction across entire sectors. U.S. protectionists would throw tantrums, but Overton hoped to "strike the American imagination" by offering a "radical diminution of Imperial Preferences" as a lure. The dominions would go along, trading preferences for significantly lower U.S. tariffs. And the British would appear as visionary as Cordell Hull.[21]

Traps for the Overton Report actually lay in Britain, not the United States. To be sure, other proposals for regulating and balancing international trade appeared in Britain in 1943, including a World Trade Alliance Organization backed by industry and labor and collaborative networks with U.S. industrialists.[22] But the Overton Report was the focus. Socialists feared for their planning agenda, which was guarded by trade discrimination. Conservatives defended the Ottawa system of tariff preferences, and moderates were simply unwilling to expose producers to competition when the economic circumstances were stacked against Britain. In short, the Overton Report ended up being the most forward advance for free trade policy in Britain.

The Treasury Department was a major force behind halting the Overton plan. Socialist Hubert Henderson wrote an opposition report. By proposing to sweep away barriers, Overton backed the "higgling of the market," which undercut employment, production, and social security policies. Henderson preferred protectionism. To be sure, America was to lower its tariffs across-the-board, as well as abolish its preferential networks with the Philippines and Cuba. But for its part, Britain must be very careful.[23]

Significantly, Keynes agreed because of the deteriorating payments balance. "I have more sympathy for protection than you do," he wrote Meade. Britain would be deceitful if it pledged to eliminate discriminatory barriers, for they would likely increase after the war. Anyway, Roosevelt would not accept automatic cuts in tariffs at risk of an eruption in Congress. In sum, the report had an ungrounded faith in free trade dogma. Keynes posited that the Overton proposals would be unacceptable to all nations.[24]

There was also the issue of imperial preferences. Tariff negotiator John Stirling noted that Roosevelt wanted to lure the empire into a formal dialogue that would put Article VII into practice. But "blind Ottawaphobia" had seized the U.S. public and the State Department. In addition, because the Republicans had gained seats in Congress by 1943, it was unlikely (and, as it turned out, true) that the renewal of the RTAA that same year would grant FDR more authority to cut tariffs. Furthermore, Congress would rebel at Britain's attempt to bargain with preferences after it had agreed to end discrimination under Article VII. And neither Britain nor the dominions would budge on adjusting the Ottawa accord until America offered adequate concessions on its tariffs. The Overton Report gave the erroneous impression that Britain was ready to abolish imperial preferential tariffs.[25]

Yet because the expansion of British exports was a national interest, Keynes and other "modified multilateralists" sought a positive approach to Article VII and the preference issue. They proposed that instead of the Overton plan, Britain seek an arrangement with the United States to cut preferences and tariffs simultaneously, keeping British economic circumstances under close scrutiny. Along with a tariff ceiling and pledge to end quotas as soon as possible, exploratory talks would be undertaken with the Americans on trade policy. But Keynes was clear that British interests would be served. Without "a more robust—if you like, a more selfish—policy, we are sunk," he concluded.[26]

Still, a cabinet majority supported the Overton Report out of a concern for friendly relations with America. Keynes was too alarmist, they said, whereas the potential gain from U.S. tariff cuts outweighed the losses from narrowing preference margins. In addition, the cabinet feared that the dominions, which eyed America as a postwar market, might part company with Britain if Churchill balked at Article VII. Harcourt Johnstone of the Department of Overseas Trade even thought the report too timid. By permitting import controls for two years, he argued, the plan would prompt nations to block the export drive demanded by British merchants, manufacturers, and unions. In any case, Article VII obligated British cooperation. And Roosevelt would wave the report in response to GOP charges that he coddled the imperialistic British. Wrote Nigel Ronald of the Foreign Office, the report listed the "sort of things we and the Americans and others will have to swallow if we are to attain the sort of better world which we profess to be seeking to promote."[27]

So, Winston Churchill accepted the document in April 1943, but only with a major modification. He agreed with Lord Cherwell, his staunchly anticommunist adviser, that multilateralism would counter Soviet power after the war. Trying to dominate Europe, Russia would undersell competitors by using slave labor and state monopolies. Article VII would build a capitalist alliance of America, the Commonwealth, and Western Europe as a counter. Yet the prime minister covered his flank within his coalition cabinet. He accepted a Treasury amendment that preserved the right to impose import controls. He also still had the saving phrases regarding imperial preferences. These qualifications clamped down on free trade multilateralism and protected the economy from U.S. competition. Armed with the Overton Report, the British prepared to compel the United States to shoulder the burden of multilateralism.[28]

The outcome of the Overton Report debate thrust the British into a role of both friend and opponent of American free-traders. The Americans lauded Churchill's readiness to uphold Article VII, regardless of the saving phrase. They were less happy about reducing duties on a percentage basis, which might be a violation of U.S. tariff law. In any case, both nations had scheduled exploratory talks in Fall 1943 to discuss trade and monetary issues. While Roosevelt labored to renew the RTAA, the British consulted the dominions on the Overton Report.

The dominions held sway over Commonwealth policies, and not only as key trade partners of the British. Under the terms of the Ottawa Agreement, their permission was required to alter preferences. They had been left out of Article VII talks, but now Britain hoped to align them behind the Overton Report at a meeting in London in June 1943. The dominions understood the obligation of Article VII but only Canada, because of its dependence on the U.S. market, backed Hull's multilateral idea. Empire isolationists existed in all nations. Preferential tariffs, moreover, gave the southern dominions secure access to empire markets. Australia sold nearly 55 percent of its exports to Britain; 70 percent stayed in the empire. The abandonment of preferences for the uncertainties of the free market would be costly.

Australia typified dominion ambivalence to free trade. The ruling Labour Party disdained market forces. That Canberra would be "required to dismantle its protective tariff and preferential trading policies sent cold shivers up many Australian spines," noted Herbert Coombs, a top official in the Ministry of Postwar Reconstruction. As a developing nation, Australia was highly protectionist, seeking to curb imports in competition with such infant industries as motor vehicles, paper, machine tools, textiles, and pharmaceuticals. Built in the 1930s to ease the reliance on primary commodities, such "secondary" production could not cope with mature British and U.S. industries. Thus, Australian tariffs were prohibitive. Yet because manufacturers sought to obtain capital equipment from America and Europe, the Ottawa Agreement had to be adjusted so that Australia was not forced to buy only from Britain. Food producers, moreover, counted on the U.S. market after the war.[29]

Though loyal to Britain, Australia had a stake in American power. Export growth was paramount to pay for Labour's social programs. After the war, the United States would replace the impoverished Britain as the main buyer of Australia's major commodities, wool and meat. Australia hoped to use preferences, which covered one-fifth of Australian exports, as a bargaining lever to win large American tariff cuts. Thus, Canberra had endorsed Article VII in a Reciprocal Aid Agreement with the United States in September 1942. Yet development worries, full employment concerns, a predicted balance-of-payments deficit after the war, and the failure to conclude a trade agreement with the United States in 1943 led Australia to accept the Overton Report only in principle.[30]

For the dominions and India, multilateralism came second to internal development and reconstruction after the war. Except for Canada, they wanted to retain preferences for the short run and hold on to quotas, domestic subsidies, and state trading over the long haul. But all agreed with the broad goals of the Overton Report, recognizing that Commonwealth discrimination impeded trade with the booming United States. Thus, the dominions welcomed Anglo-American planning.[31]

As the Commonwealth meeting ended, Roosevelt signed the RTAA of 1943 and the State Department turned to the Overton Report. Anglo-American jockeying was about to begin. Britain insisted that the United States jettison high tariffs to set an example to the world. Open to a bold approach, the Americans asked Britain to end its caginess and honor the spirit, not just the letter, of Article VII. All barriers, including preferences, must fall. In September 1943 British minister of state Richard Law arrived in Washington, D.C., ready to set an agenda for formal discussions of a host of postwar economic issues. A monetary system was the top priority, but trade planning was also high on his list.

Richard Law carried an aide-mémoire that presented the Overton Report as a more appropriate means than the timid RTAA to fulfill the intentions of Article VII. The Overton Report explicitly called for tariff cuts in broad sectors, a method that would benefit British exports but provoke protectionists in Congress. Perhaps the Americans would agree to a tariff ceiling. In return, the War Cabinet would offer to halve preference margins. That would guard some semblance of the Ottawa system but meet the multilateral requirements of Article VII and make Roosevelt's job easier in Congress.[32]

Law and Keynes instructed Percivale Liesching, a veteran Board of Trade negotiator who oversaw trade matters for Britain at the Washington talks, that British goals were to reduce U.S. tariffs, allow import controls, and connect trade to Keynes's monetary plans. America was to take responsibility for postwar reconstruction. Officials broke off into a Subcommittee on Measures for Stimulating Commerce, where Liesching handed the Overton Report to Harry Hawkins, who led the U.S. experts. The report was transformed into the "Illustrative Outline on Commercial Policy" that guided the talks.[33]

America supported the goals of the Overton Report but not the philosophy behind it. Multilateral tariff negotiations, full employment goals, and integration of nations into a commercial union appealed to Hull. Yet conflicting economic doctrines came into play. Whereas the Americans endorsed multilateralism as an end in itself to promote private enterprise and prosperity, the British cared only that trade volume increased. For the British, regulation of commerce was the safe route to growth.[34] Soon, the Americans edged closer to the British view.

Compromise arose on many issues. For instance, the United States sought precise limits on state traders and cartels, which enjoyed price advantages over merchants left unsheltered from government aid or global combines. Britain welcomed large-scale organizations as long as they did not discriminate. Besides, the Soviet Union would insist on government monopolies. The experts left the extent of freedom allowed for cartels and state trading undetermined, but clearly, America would have to give way.

Britain then pointed out that U.S. agricultural export subsidies were interventionist and provided protection not enjoyed by British farmers. True, replied the Americans, but they were necessary because the New Deal had raised domestic prices above world levels. Subsidies closed the gap so that farmers could compete abroad. Unlike tariffs and quotas, they were visible and would end once domestic and world prices merged. In any case, no nation was ready to abandon price supports. Both sides agreed that international commodity agreements would help solve the problem of price differentials, but the United States remained under pressure to phase out export subsidies.[35]

Both nations frowned on quantitative barriers, but Britain wanted more liberal resort to them. Considering the British payments imbalance, the Overton Report called for an objective test to set the duration of quotas. Liesching sought them for two years after the war and then progressive reduction over the next three years unless circumstances dictated otherwise. But Hawkins demanded a one-year grace period, banking on the plans for

monetary union being debated by Treasury officials to limit quotas. Yet during the commercial talks, he moved closer to the British stance. To protect financial reserves and farmers, quantitative barriers would be acceptable. Liesching grew even tougher, however, seeking to package British quotas with tariffs as a bargaining ploy to win U.S. concessions. Hawkins balked but Britain's intention to impose quantitative barriers with minimal constraints became a priority from then on.[36]

Debate on tariffs and preferences exemplified the blending of protectionism into the multilateral idea. Both sides sought simultaneous, rapid, and broad tariff cuts, but they differed on method. Hawkins refused to cut tariffs across sectors, for the RTAA required a selective process. He also shied from placing a ceiling on tariff levels. The technical challenge of converting tariffs to ad valorem rates, then valuing these to conform with other countries, would be too complex. Liesching, however, insisted on percentage duty reductions. He also countered that rough uniformity could be obtained by using the tariff of one nation as a yardstick for each product. Hawkins was unconvinced but would keep exploring options for duty reduction.[37]

British diffidence on preferences matched American reserve on tariff reduction. Ending discrimination was Britain's aim, but not by reneging on the Ottawa accord. Liesching had a bargaining strategy in mind. Without greater access to the U.S. market, British nations could not phase out preferences. Again, the Reciprocal Trade Agreements Act was inadequate to the task of postwar multilateralism. Convinced that all nations must sacrifice, Liesching demanded that America adopt the sectoral method of duty reduction. The formula was simple: radical U.S. tariff cuts would render preferences obsolete. Liesching offered to halve preference margins as a starting point for negotiations.[38]

But the Americans recoiled at the linkage of tariffs to preferences. They were simply "different in kind," said Hawkins. No doubt, tariffs were harmful, but preferences were worse because they were discriminatory. They targeted U.S. exports of dried fruit, tobacco, apples, wheat, typewriters, refrigerators, and cars. And preferences politicized international trade. They could jeopardize postwar relations by encouraging closed trade blocs. As well, even moderate liberal traders in Congress would rebel against indiscriminate tariff cuts across sectors. Furthermore, the fifty-state customs union of the United States was based on economic intimacy and geographic proximity; empire unity was largely artificial. Only the eradication of preferences warranted substantial duty reductions on America's part.[39]

Liesching countered that Britain, too, had political factors to consider. Parliament, the press, and producers defended the Ottawa system. There was also the issue of empire unity. Hard for an outsider to comprehend, this "special relationship . . . went very deep in the life and thinking of the British people." Besides, Ottawa was a global version of the preferential network among the American states. Liesching believed his offer to halve margins was generous and that the Americans must make allowances for existing preferential systems. Hawkins argued that other nations would protest such a deal as an Anglo-American plot. Besides, it would incur the wrath of Congress.[40]

As the Washington discussions came to a close in mid–October 1943, the United States made a significant concession. Liesching reported to London that the Americans had become more realistic by accepting token preferences if an overhaul of the RTAA did not materialize. Indeed, Hawkins was more beaten than convinced. At great risk to his career, he agreed to devise a tariff reduction formula based on sectoral cuts. No higher authority, including Cordell Hull, had endorsed this plan. It was doubtful that Roosevelt would revise the RTAA to accommodate across-the-board reductions. Yet Hawkins believed that he had found a way to abolish Ottawa preferences.[41] In fact, however, Liesching had managed to safeguard that very system because he knew that the Americans would likely never agree to sectoral tariff reductions.

On October 21, 1943, the meetings ended. A report combined the work of the commercial subcommittees with the centerpiece financial discussions. Included in the trade report was the Meade/Overton plan for a commercial union and a broad convention to allow each nation to mold its trade policies with those of other countries. The joint report left all subjects open for future discussion. Hawkins reported that the trade talks "had made remarkable progress," with disagreement more on "technique or method rather than of policy." Both delegation heads commended the development of an agenda that lay a foundation for prosperity and peace.[42] The momentum toward trade universalism had quickened, though not in the direction of free trade.

Liesching had every reason to be satisfied. The Americans had adopted the Overton Report as the agenda for future talks, and Hawkins would try to gain acceptance of the sectoral approach to tariff reduction. He was further heartened after briefing the Canadians, who welcomed the prospect of large U.S. concessions. Prime Minister Mackenzie King pursued a full employment program that relied on the expansion of international trade. U.S.

tariff cuts would swell exports for Canada, the world's third largest trading nation. Like Britain, Canada hoped to convince the United States to shoulder the burden of trade liberalization.[43]

On the American side, the Special Committee on Relaxation of Trade Barriers viewed the exploratory talks as an invitation. Unilateral reductions were out of the question. But by promoting trade liberalization, the United States "would provide strong leadership for a world movement to create conditions favorable to a great expansion of international trade, on a private basis, and thereby contribute to American material welfare and security against war." Now was the time to act, before nations resorted to restrictive policies due to unemployment and reconversion pressures.[44] Secretary of State Cordell Hull went into action.

The Washington talks catalyzed the State Department. The British had presented a plan for U.S. leadership over the postwar trade regime. But Hull now determined to reshape the proposals in the image of his free trade dreams. He seized the initiative, informing Britain, Canada, the Soviet Union, and China of his readiness to discuss trade issues. The 1944 election would slow talks, but the State Department forged ahead. Indeed, America emerged as the proponent of planning when Churchill's cabinet deadlocked over whether to endorse the Washington proposals.

That is, the British got cold feet. The main problem came from the Treasury and empire isolationists. There were also fears that Roosevelt would either lose his reelection bid in 1944 or face a Republican House, and maybe Senate, full of protectionists. Thus, even Liesching sought to delay more discussions with the Americans until the political situation was clearer. James Meade was livid, warning that if Britain placed the Washington proposals in "cold storage," they would suffer a "death by refrigeration." The dominions would retreat to protectionism, and the world would be left with no guidance on trade matters once the war ended. Americans would lash out at Britain's sly game of publicly endorsing multilateralism while privately retreating to empire protectionism.[45] But most of the cabinet disagreed.

Empire isolationists, the Labour Party, and business leaders charged that the Washington plans would return the world to a jungle of unregulated competition beneficial only to U.S. imperialism. Eyeing the rising power of the Labour Party, Leo Amery warned his fellow Conservatives to make a stand on imperial ideals. But the Labour Party also hoisted a warning flag.

Privy Council Clement Attlee and Minister of Aircraft Production Richard Stafford Cripps sought freedom over state purchasing, import and exchange controls, and tariff preferences. Britain was susceptible to an inevitable American economic collapse, said the socialist Cripps, and should be "wary of being manoevred into making further concessions upon the points not yet agreed in the hope of satisfying the demand for a free-entrance ticket for American capitalism into every market in the world." The British business community was also apprehensive of a trade policy based on unfettered capitalism.[46]

Britain, desirous of regulation, was headed to the Left. Considering the impact of imports and exports on employment, Sir William Beveridge of the Liberal Party proposed to tie government stimulation of the economy to trade expansion. The Beveridge Plan of 1944 lay the groundwork for the landmark White Paper on Employment of the following year. It advocated Article VII as an elevator for prosperity but held on to the fire escape of trade discrimination in case of British difficulties. Multilateralists like Meade, Law, and Lord Cherwell were alarmed by such thinking. Refusing to budge on trade preferences and import controls would be a "Declaration of War" on the United States and economic suicide for Britain. But in early 1944 they were cries in the wilderness of protectionism.[47]

The dominions revealed this to be the case. To be sure, they had loosened the bonds of empire since World War I, making their own decisions on domestic and foreign policies. Canada, New Zealand, and Australia were now as close to U.S. policy on matters of defense, diplomacy, and economic development as they were to Britain. They even refused British attempts to unify the empire around a common foreign policy in 1944 as "sentimental indulgence in nostalgic mammy songs" by a declining nation. Having survived Japanese aggression with U.S. aid, Australia and New Zealand planned a regional security system and expanded trade networks that counted on American leadership.[48]

Yet the need to prop up Britain and curb U.S. dominance led the dominions, even Canada, to hesitate on the Washington report. Preferences were meaningless in light of the loss of British purchasing power and the beckoning American market. But nobody wanted to toss aside the imperial life buoy. Thus, the southern dominions counseled caution. Australia demanded that nations agree to elevate full employment and social security above free trade. Without these foundations of Labour Party doctrine, warned one official, Canberra "would wash her hands of the whole business" of multilateralism. Along with New Zealand, Australia called for a world conference on employment—not just trade—to push regulatory policies to the fore in trade planning.[49]

Winston Churchill decided in February 1944 to halt commercial planning in Britain until he digested the full implications of the Washington report. He asked Chancellor of the Exchequer John Anderson to chair a committee to study the Washington proposals, but he refused an "abandonment of Imperial Preference unless or until we are in [the] presence of a vast scheme of reducing trade barriers in which the United States is taking the lead." Trade cooperation was his goal, he told the House of Commons in April 1944, but considering the "limiting words" of the Atlantic Charter and Article VII, Britain was, "in every respect, so far as action is concerned, perfectly free."[50] These were ominous words for free-traders in the United States.

Churchill's decision, motivated by politics as much as economic philosophy or foreign policy concerns, was not so much a reversal as a retrenchment. As World War II wound down, he worried about Britain's economy and deteriorating position overseas. But he also had electoral considerations in mind. His coalition cabinet would break apart once the impetus of war was gone. The Labour Party's spending platform appealed to the people, who were apprehensive about reconversion to a peacetime economy and the recurrence of depression. In 1944 Labour was ascendant, threatening to take over the country. Churchill tried to unify the Conservatives and soothe voters by, among other things, pledging to protect British trade interests.

Yet the British cabinet debate and discussions with the United States since 1941 showed that Churchill's decision of 1944 to defend discriminatory trade practices was not new. Military necessity had driven Britain to coauthor the Atlantic Charter and the Lend-Lease agreement. But the British needed to protect their economy by curbing America's seemingly excessive concerns with market capitalism and by asserting a regulatory approach in international trade affairs. This arena provided a battleground between ideologies, between the British idea of government intervention and America's defense against such intrusion.

Free trade frightened the British. Their economy was in shambles and the sun was setting over the empire. Most officials—and not just empire isolationists—hoped to slow the decline. This was the reasoning behind the qualifications in Point Four and Article VII of the Lend-Lease Master Agreement. The Overton Report advocated liberalization but by a different means and in a more distant time than desired by America. The route that Britain and the Commonwealth would take to a free trade world wended its way around state controls, protectionism, and a requirement that America shoulder an inordinate share of the tariff reduction burden.

The Commonwealth put the United States on notice that a regime of free trade was unacceptable, but regardless, American officials forged ahead. They sought to assuage British concerns while pursuing their multilateral dreams. Their determination was strong, but so was the resistance at home and abroad to their vision.

CHAPTER 3

Modified Multilateralism
1944–1945

In 1944 progress on the postwar planning front coincided with impressive military victories. In June, the Americans closed in on Japan and the Allies swept toward Berlin from the east and west. By this time, Anglo-American officials had created an international monetary system. A charter for collective security under the United Nations organization soon followed. Universal ideals flourished in the economic and political arenas.

At home, Franklin Roosevelt experienced rougher going. He had been debilitated by an attack of influenza in late 1943. Politically, strikes, fears of renewed race riots, and public contempt for wartime wage freezes, price controls, and consumer shortages bolstered the appeal of his GOP critics. The conservative coalition of Republicans and southern Democrats had reduced some New Deal public works programs and had passed a tax bill over his veto in 1944 that curbed government revenues. But Roosevelt still called for an economic bill of rights and passed the GI Bill, which provided financial benefits for the fifteen million returning veterans. He remained popular enough to seek a fourth term in office and win, although he did so by his smallest margin ever.

Euphoric over wartime gains, the administration drafted its commercial plans. Free-traders wanted the Reciprocal Trade Agreements Act (RTAA) renewed with authority to cut tariffs across sectors, as Britain had demanded. They also overhauled the Overton Report in anticipation of discussions with the British, talks that outlined the International Trade Organization (ITO).

In mid-1944 FDR's reelection occupied the administration, but trade planning continued in the vacuum caused by British stalling on the Washington report. This effort tapped rising internationalist sentiment in the country. At home, the result was victory both for Roosevelt and for the free-traders.

In January 1944 Secretary of State Cordell Hull's assistant, Harry Haw-kins, broadcast that trade policy "will be an important factor in determin-ing whether we will this time win and retain the peace or blunder headlong into another bitter, costly world war." Republicans, including presidential candidate Thomas Dewey, agreed. Yet although the GOP platform lauded ef-forts to remove barriers, it backed Hull's trade program only after Dewey revised the plank. For their part, the Democrats dealt with trade liberaliza-tion, expansion, and cooperation in their presidential platform. To be sure, FDR's reelection did not turn on trade issues, but multilateralism won him bi-partisan support. For instance, businessman William Clayton, who usually voted Republican, cast his ballot for Roosevelt because old guard protec-tionists still shaped GOP policies.[1]

In regard to trade, foreigners were much more of a burden for the pres-ident than domestic critics. Britain's response to the Washington report was worrisome; multilateralists like James Meade could not budge the cabinet. Also, the *Economist* posited that a bloc of empire and European nations would likely gang up to discriminate against the Americans after the war. The jour-nal was noted for reflecting official British opinion. Meanwhile, Parliament upheld discrimination to protect British interests. Explained Conservative Walter Elliott of Glasgow, the United States was "the paradise of hard-shell private enterprise" whereas the Soviet Union was "the paradise of hard-shell Communism." But Britain was the "vertebrate, we are a soft-skinned coun-try, with our bones inside" and thus required protectionism.[2]

Such views, and the cabinet's apparent inability to make up its mind on the Washington report, angered the Americans. Hull complained that Win-ston Churchill no longer cared about liberalizing trade. The chill in rela-tions prompted Richard Law to visit Hull and request that Article VII talks be discontinued until later in the year, when Britain's economic forecast be-came clearer. After lecturing on the benefits of free trade, Hull gave in. With the cabinet's review of the Washington report mired in debate through Fall 1944, he had no other choice.[3]

The holdup did not stop his own bureaucracy of planners from proceed-ing. In early October 1944 a Committee on Trade Barriers handed a draft of a trade code—Articles of Agreement for a Proposed Multilateral Conven-tion on Commercial Policy—to the new interdepartmental oversight body, called the Executive Committee on Economic Foreign Policy, which Hawkins headed. The articles offered options for ending discrimination, su-pervised by a trade organization, and called for the resumption of Anglo-American talks to fulfill the goals of Article VII. They aimed to provide a 10 percent duty floor and narrow preference margins and to permit limited quotas. The document also presented two ways to halve tariffs.

One involved sectoral cuts on a percentage basis. The Executive Committee preferred this "horizontal" approach, a centerpiece of Britain's Overton Report, because it provided a precise obligation by all nations to lower tariffs. The other method called for bilateral accords among pairs of nations to be extended to a "nuclear" club of major nations. This technique was consistent with the reciprocal trade program. It compelled tariff reductions on selected items and limited them to principal producers. It was the method that would be adopted by the General Agreement on Tariffs and Trade (GATT).[4]

The planners viewed the horizontal approach as the key to free trade. It would sweep aside barriers and lend clarity as to the extent to which countries would ease their protection. Also, the current process of horse-trading on each bilateral accord gave legislators too much input into policy; a multilateral pact gave them (and interest groups) one shot at negotiators. An indiscriminate slashing of tariffs would not subject sensitive industries to unfair competition, argued the State Department, as an escape clause would provide them with an exemption from any concessions that might prove injurious. The articles made clear, however, that only America's bold leadership would end foreign discrimination and stave off worldwide protectionism. They were also just the sort of unilateral revisions in American trade policy sought by Britain.[5]

Handing British planner James Meade the plan in November, Hawkins assured him of a U.S. commitment to cut tariffs dramatically. He would ask Roosevelt to implant the horizontal method in the RTAA extension bill of 1945. That pledge showed Meade that the United States had finally decided to grant large-scale concessions following the prescriptions of the Overton Report. The articles also conceded the need for including employment, quota, and preference policies in a trade convention. The outline, wrote Meade, put "commercial policy on the map again," to Britain's advantage.[6] He urged his government to restart the Article VII talks.

Yet his government did not agree. Britain would close some preferences and ease some quotas if America dropped its tariffs. But discriminatory controls and targeted, bulk-purchasing agreements with Australia, Canada, Argentina, and Brazil would continue. John Maynard Keynes frowned on the escape clause, moreover, because it would protect the U.S. market. It also confirmed to him that Americans had more faith in timid reciprocity than in bold action. Hawkins left England taken aback by British obstructionism.[7]

British skepticism carried into the new year. In January 1945 the *Economist* issued such a reproach of U.S. trade policy that the State Department alerted Roosevelt. The journal demanded that the RTAA bill, being readied for Congress, include authority for sectoral tariff cuts. If it did not, Britain would balk on Article VII talks. Furthermore, Australia, New Zealand, and Britain, preparing their White Papers on Full Employment, had asked for a conference on employment policy in conjunction with Article VII planning. The State Department was not adverse to the suggestion but did not want to elevate domestic agendas over trade liberalization. Planners urged the president, as he left for the Yalta conference in February, to persuade Churchill to restart the Article VII discussions promptly.[8]

Planning could not proceed until Congress authorized tariff reductions under the RTAA. Roosevelt's reelection in November 1944 and support from the private sector gave him leverage to drive for multilateral trade. But a major revision of the law, by sectoral reductions, would be extremely difficult. And, as it turned out, politicians pulled back from the free trade dogma of the bureaucracy and business.

To be sure, free trade had backing. Business leaders and organizations from fifty-one nations had recently met at the Westchester Country Club in Rye, New York, to back a code of nondiscriminatory trade rules. Particularly vocal were American corporate heads, bankers, industrialists, and peak associations like the Chamber of Commerce and the National Foreign Trade Council. By upholding Article VII, they hoped to open Britain's regulated economy to their exports and investments and combat the trend toward big government intervention. These globe-trotting business leaders were free trade purists who sought a competitive system unhindered by protectionist restraints. Earlier, they had formed the Committee on International Economic Policy, under the Carnegie Endowment for International Peace, which called for a United Nations Economic Organization to administer free trade rules.[9] They also sloughed off their Republican Party loyalties to endorse the president's internationalist trade policies.

William Clayton's appointment as assistant secretary of state for economic affairs in December 1944 also bolstered the free trade forces. This entrepreneur ran the world's largest cotton-exporting firm. Hailing from Tennessee (like Cordell Hull), he held a southerner's hatred of high tariffs, which were blamed for poverty in the region. Clayton had risen to power in the business community, fending off criticism from liberals for his domination of the cotton market and for his conservative economic views. He disliked New Deal intervention in the economy, but he had created a minor stir in 1936 by voting for Roosevelt. He explained the shift as a vote for free trade principles. After serving in the Commerce Department, he joined the State Department. The sixty-six-year-old Clayton soon assumed the retired Cordell Hull's mantle as free trade ideologue.[10]

This "evangelist in the cause of multilateralism," writes Randall Woods, did not concern himself with the domestic impact of free trade. Clayton envisioned liberal trade as an end in itself. Pragmatists like Dean Acheson, however, viewed trade as a diplomatic weapon. They accepted protectionism, for a doctrinaire insistence on free trade would weaken the economies of allies and, during the Cold War, they soon argued, would undermine the front against communism. Protectionism abroad and at home could not be eradicated, no matter how principled one was. But Will Clayton never learned that lesson.[11]

As a politician who shied from free trade, FDR listened to the pragmatists. He did tell Prime Minister Churchill at Yalta that he would sponsor a multilateral convention once the United Nations had been established in Spring 1945. Yet Roosevelt resisted efforts by Clayton to incorporate the horizontal tariff-cut method into the RTAA. A fear of losing bipartisan support for his foreign policy initiatives motivated this stance.[12]

At the end of March 1945, when Roosevelt sent the Reciprocal Trade Agreements Act to the House, the Bretton Woods monetary agreement was before Congress and the United Nations conference in San Francisco was about to open. Thus, Democratic Party chiefs—Majority Leader John McCormack, House Speaker Sam Rayburn, and Ways and Means Committee chairman Robert Doughton—reined in the planners. McCormack had relented on his idea for a permanent extension of the RTAA because it would have converted trade agreements into treaties, subject to Senate ratification (and protectionist pressure). Instead, FDR's version called for a renewal of the RTAA for three years and a halving of tariff rates. Anticipating a fight with protectionists, the politicians refused the State Department demand for sectoral tariff cuts.[13]

Despite the isolationist brand, opponents of the RTAA did not stay silent. Americans looked inward, so impervious to trade that a scant 9 percent had heard of the trade agreements program when hearings were under way in May 1945. The State Department claimed that a "revolution in American thinking on the tariff" had occurred, but a National Opinion Research Center poll found that 61 percent of the respondents opposed an increase in imports, even if it helped the United Nations. Even veterans, with their awareness of global problems, split down the middle. Senator Robert Taft thus proposed a one-year extension without new authority to cut tariffs. That scheme would deny claims of GOP isolationism yet slow liberalization until normal economic patterns allowed a sober determination of policy. Many legislators and interest groups agreed.[14]

Extreme protectionists were defiant. GOP congressman Harold Knutson of Minnesota was outraged that Clayton appeared at House hearings on behalf of the new secretary of state, Edward Stettinius. Republicans grilled Clayton for a day, riled when he confessed, ironically, that his cotton firm had profited from high tariffs. They then argued that low costs abroad necessitated protection of the U.S. market, leveled charges of unconstitutionality at the bill, questioned the State Department's ability to negotiate fair trade accords, and ridiculed the notion that Roosevelt could attain his goal of creating sixty million jobs when imports put workers on relief rolls. The National Watch Workers Union sent a petition from sailors on the USS *Hermitage*—a ship loaded with timing devices made by union members—urging Congress to "protect their job opportunities while they sacrifice their lives if necessary to preserve democracy." To Clayton's shock, the Republicans then defended the notorious Smoot-Hawley Act of 1930.[15]

Protectionists doubted that Article VII talks would usher in a new era of peace. Congressman Carl Curtis, a Republican from Nebraska, learned from the Library of Congress that between 1838 and 1920 Britain—even as a low-tariff country—had engaged in 35 continental and colonial wars, with only 17 years of peace. Free trade did not cause wars, Curtis deduced, but neither would it magically bring peace. The RTAA had not ended imperial trade preferences, and now sterling bloc restrictions loomed as additional obstacles to U.S. exports. Churchill had opted to guard the empire, and the Soviets would keep an iron hand on Eastern Europe. Republican Bertrand Gearhart suggested that America also look after its own interests and protect its markets.[16]

Yet again the logic of internationalism undermined these arguments. The RTAA proved to be Harry S. Truman's first test in Congress after he assumed the presidency in early April 1945. British observers wondered whether a politician who had focused on domestic issues and hailed from the isolationist Midwest would embrace multilateralism. The concern was misplaced. Truman had advocated the merits of freer trade in high school debates. As a Missouri senator, he had backed all of the RTAA extensions. He believed in an internationalist foreign policy and the New Deal; thus he backed protectionism when needed but freer trade as a rule. But he assured Speaker Rayburn that on the way to lowering trade barriers, he would not "trade out" producers by subjecting them to unfair levels of imports.[17]

The press, exporters, labor, producers, consumer advocates, churches, academics, peace groups, and Democrats helped Truman with the renewal of the Reciprocal Trade Agreements Act. Business leaders organized the Committee on International Economic Policy and the Committee for World Trade to aid the cause. Mississippi congressman William Colmer's Special Committee on Postwar Economic Policy and Planning also lobbied for a trade code after Colmer had toured the world and country to investigate economic conditions. Free trade would, moreover, provide fuel for Roosevelt's economic bill of rights, which sought full employment to prevent a postwar depression. In his book *Sixty Million Jobs*, Secretary of Commerce Henry Wallace argued that if Americans regarded "imports as being just as important to us as exports," full employment at good wages could be achieved without the sort of state interventionism in vogue in the British Commonwealth.[18]

Socialism, poverty, and war could be curbed by intelligent leadership over trade, contended the free-traders. Possessing half the globe's industrial capacity and most of its gold, money, and technology, the United States controlled the economic fate of its trade partners. Opening its doors to imports, the world's largest consumer could speed British recovery, which would then resume purchases of American goods. Protectionism merely forced nations toward socialism and even communism, as the current trend in Western Europe revealed. Headed for a clash with capitalism, these systems might doom a durable peace.[19]

That worry, coming at the end of the war in Europe, proved too much for the protectionists. Convening the United Nations at San Francisco in March 1945, Secretary of State Stettinius warned that security depended as much on fair economic dealing as on political accord. The RTAA, echoed Assistant Secretary of State Dean Acheson, showed that America would "preach in San Francisco" what it "practice[d] everywhere." Swamped by the wave of internationalism, Republicans were warned by journalists not to endanger the United Nations by misguided economic isolationism.[20]

Beyond the backing for the RTAA, good leadership gave Truman a victory, though not a rout. The omission of the horizontal method of tariff cutting and the inclusion of escape clauses for defense industries turned out to be wise decisions, for the Ways and Means Committee approved the bill by just three votes. Partisan debate broke out on the House floor in May. The GOP minority reintroduced sixteen protectionist amendments that Doughton's committee had rejected. They met defeat, but some by close margins. Sending a letter beseeching both parties to accept the bill, Truman helped block the protectionists. The RTAA of 1945 passed the House with the help of thirty-three Republicans, 239–153. Leading Democrats gathered in Rayburn's chambers to drink whiskey and call the retired father of the trade agreements program, Cordell Hull, with the good news.[21]

The celebration was premature. The Senate Finance Committee had just accepted the international monetary system, but then it approved Senator Taft's amendment against halving tariffs by a 10–9 margin. Free-traders fumed as seven Republicans and three Democrats forced the issue to the Senate floor. But after a week of debate, enough defecting Republicans canceled out Democrat deserters to rebuff this and other protectionist measures, albeit some very narrowly. The RTAA passed 54–20 in June, aided by fifteen Republicans in an unexpectedly easy win.[22]

The administration erred, however, when it claimed that passage rang the death knell for protectionism. Certainly, the victory brought more adherents to the internationalist wing of the GOP. So did the realization that the end of the war in Europe required the United States to take a global leadership role and not close itself off by protectionism. But many Republicans had joined with a growing number of Democrats from states outside the traditional free-trading South to oppose the Reciprocal Trade Agreements Act. A current of dissent ran under the free trade platform.

The RTAA of 1945 came under attack in London, and years later from historians, for its modesty. Critics argued that trading the horizontal tariff method for votes encouraged protectionism, scaled back free trade designs, and undermined British recovery. The British added that they lacked the personnel to negotiate numerous bilateral agreements in what would prove to be a time-consuming process. The Anglo-American accord of 1938, after all, had taken ten months to finish. Future negotiations would include fifty nations under the RTAA method.[23] The law was just too timid.

Yet these critics ignored trade politics. No president would forsake producers; neither Congress nor the public would let him. Free-traders strove to take advantage of nascent internationalism to gain approval for their ideals. But politicians prudently set their sights lower. A defeat for the RTAA, in whatever form, would have ruined the foreign economic policy of the Truman administration and harmed British economic prospects.

Besides, the extension was a step forward. The law prompted significant reductions in U.S. tariffs a few years later in GATT. It also facilitated approval of the articles of the trade convention and their conversion into the Proposal to Establish an International Trade Organization. The RTAA of 1945, along with the proposal, marked progress toward multilateral goals. And not all British observers were critical. Truman had "scored a Congressional victory of the first magnitude," concluded Ambassador Halifax in Washington. And in London, James Meade believed that the extension would now jump-start Article VII talks.[24]

Prodded by the passage of the RTAA, the British returned to the Article VII table, although with some trepidation. This was a very difficult time for Britain. The European war had left victors and vanquished alike with huge economic problems. The British, moreover, were engaged in an election campaign in June and July 1945 that led to the ousting of Winston Churchill from office. And officials in London remained split over trade policy, particularly the American ITO proposal.

A staggering 4 billion pound debt and the loss of half its overseas assets jeopardized Britain's social security at home and its power abroad. Projecting an annual import budget of 1.5 billion pounds, the government oversaw an export drive to boost overseas sales by 50 percent over 1938 levels. This effort targeted new markets, especially the "dollar-fat" United States. For example, the Hambro Plan aimed to open marketing offices in over a dozen U.S. cities. One bureau in Dallas already displayed British wares. Yet British exports remained at only 36 percent of prewar levels. Discriminatory trade and exchange controls would persist, but officials noted that Article VII planning was necessary to boost exports and lift the economy out of its doldrums.[25]

Politics and diplomacy pushed the British toward the U.S. outline of the ITO convention. In the election campaign, the rivals Churchill and Clement Attlee of the Labour Party pledged to uphold Britain's freedom over trade and financial policy to reverse the payments deficit. Yet both also sought cooperation with the Americans. Still, tension was apparent. Commentator Walter Lippmann complained to Keynes that the two nations had "no corresponding union of ideas and feelings" on trade matters.[26]

The British frowned on the ITO proposal because it placed principles above pragmatic domestic concerns. The usually supportive Meade criti- cized it for this reason. It indicated "a very dangerous trend of thought in the U.S.A., of which Will Clayton in the State Department may be taken as the symbol, that the way to cure unemployment is to have stable exchange rates and free trade rather than" expansionist domestic policies. Keynes also wanted employment discussed before free trade, not vice versa, and pro- tested the American restraints on quantitative barriers and state trading en- tities. Labor and industry agreed with the government that combating protectionism was not the issue. Rather, regulating commerce in a way that brought equilibrium in imports and exports of all nations must be the cen- tral doctrine.[27]

The rest of the Commonwealth also objected to the draft. Canada and America, awaiting the outcome of the British elections in July 1945, dis- cussed the ITO plan. Ottawa recognized that the ITO would undercut pro- tectionism, counter the extreme Australian demand that nations commit to maintaining full employment as the basis of a multilateral trade convention, and end the sterling bloc that Canada had refused to join. But the selective approach to tariff reduction closed off the U.S. market, Canada's main ex- port source, and intensified resistance in the Commonwealth to ending im- perial preferences and other discriminatory measures. Canada urged the United States to trade more freely.[28]

The two nations did manage to devise a means of negotiating tariffs. Canada suggested that a dozen or so "nuclear" nations offer concessions si- multaneously at a conference. The group would include the major European and Commonwealth countries, the United States, and the Soviet Union. This nuclear club accounted for over half the world's imports and com- prised all types of economies. A handful of nations from Latin America, Asia, and the Middle East would be invited to ensure the inclusion of the developing world. Adhering to the constraints of the RTAA, item-by-item tariff bargaining among pairs of nations would occur but would then.be gen- eralized to the entire nuclear group. Tariffs, preferences, and quotas would be discussed. The approach thus took into account U.S. trade law, yet it comprehensively attacked tariff barriers. This bilateral-multilateral process was adopted by GATT in 1947.[29]

By the time the procedure had been explored, Clement Attlee had become prime minister. The State Department hoped that the usually international-minded Labour Party would begin a dialogue on the Ameri- can proposal and thus resume Article VII talks. At one level, Britain had no choice, as a debtor needful of foreign aid. Although the leftist Attlee would maintain import controls, he also disliked cartels and British imperialism. Therefore, Foreign Secretary Ernest Bevin announced that as long as other nations would cooperate to lower trade barriers, the new government would reconsider the Ottawa system of preferences. The cabinet decided to send a delegation to Washington, D.C., in September 1945 to discuss trade and financial matters at the Stage III talks of the Mutual Aid Agreement. Britain's intention was to obtain a large loan first and then address the ITO proposal.[30]

Yet Attlee's triumph did not clear the path for free trade. One indication was Richard Stafford Cripps's appointment as president of the Board of Trade. In 1939 he had left the Labour Party, opposed to a coalition with the Conservatives. But he remained in the public eye. During the war Cripps visited India, China, and Russia in a semiofficial capacity. He sowed an Anglo-Russian rapprochement, failed to negotiate independence for India in 1942, and worked brilliantly as minister of aircraft production. Austere and uncompromising, a superb and intelligent administrator, the socialist Cripps was reinstated in the Labour Party before the 1945 elections. Determined to regulate the British economy, he became William Clayton's nemesis in demanding protection from free trade forces.

Cripps knew that the British economy faced huge problems. His oversight of Indian independence had revealed to him an empire in decline. Answers to the country's misery lay in stricter controls and, above all, in U.S. generosity. Because America would not agree to sectoral tariff cuts, Cripps declared that Britain would not sacrifice its own defenses, namely Ottawa preferences. In charge of Britain's trade negotiators, Cripps vowed to scrutinize the ITO proposal and cleanse it of laissez-faire dogma.[31]

Uncertainty gripped the British delegation as it embarked for the United States in September 1945, two weeks after atomic bombs ended the Second World War. Attlee sought a large loan on easy terms and hoped to assure the Americans that he was not a socialist. Yet Meade bet that the State Department would tie a loan to Article VII. The new chancellor of the Exchequer, Hugh Dalton, warned that "doctrinaire Willy" Clayton would blackmail Britain into ending the Ottawa system. Keynes comforted them that there was no reason to expect the United States to twist their arms. Still, the British were coming with hat in hand, giving the United States leverage. And they were wary of the American proposal for the International Trade Organization.[32]

The British had finally returned to the planning table after two years. The commercial discussions were led again by Percivale Liesching and Harry Hawkins. Bent on defending their trade principles, Cripps and Clayton gave the orders to their respective delegations.

America hinged success in Washington on coaxing the British to abolish imperial preferences. Some officials preferred a tough line. Why not use the loan being negotiated under the Anglo-American Financial Agreement as leverage against the empire, asked Harry Dexter White of the Treasury Department? He worried that Congress would reject the loan without a British pledge to end preferences. Hawkins knew that such a hardball tactic would not work, however. That the British showed up in Washington to talk meant they would end preferences, he argued. And Cripps would look at credit on such terms as blackmail. Clayton, who leaned toward White's position, demanded a clear commitment to abolish margins. Eventually, Secretary of the Treasury Fred Vinson decided not to dangle the loan before the British, but the principled Clayton so pontificated against the Ottawa system that Keynes later remarked, "I used to think the *Mayflower* sailed with lawyers aboard, but now I realize it must have been filled with theologians."[33]

Clayton was willing to slash U.S. tariffs to buy progress on preferences. Half of Britain's imports from the empire were favored over those of outsiders. A small percentage had modest margins, yet over a third entered duty-free and thus enjoyed a large competitive edge over U.S. exports. Fifty-nine percent of empire imports into Canada got similar treatment. A halving of American tariffs, authorized under the RTAA, would drop U.S. rates to the Underwood Act levels of 1913. That should earn the abolition of preferential margins, believed Clayton.[34]

For the British, free trade multilateralism was unrealistic. Clayton's ambitions neglected the breakdown in the distribution of and payment for trade in Europe. A dogmatic attack on preferences would induce an austerity program and controls far beyond those now envisaged by Attlee. Thus, Cripps announced his support for the ITO convention on the condition that protectionist and regulatory safeguards were included. The Americans would also have certain obligations, like cutting export subsidies and tariffs. The entire Commonwealth agreed on these points.[35]

From the first commercial policy meeting on October 1 to the last on December 1, 1945, therefore, the battle was joined. For his part, Clayton warned that Congress might not ratify the loan agreement without movement on preferences. America had also proven its generosity by its willing-

William Clayton (left) confers with Richard Stafford Cripps.
(Courtesy United Nations Photo Library)

ness to halve duties under the Reciprocal Trade Agreements Act of 1945.
Furthermore, he spoke of the ill will generated by the Ottawa system and
its potential negative effect on a postwar trade.

But Britain stayed firm. Preferences, Liesching countered, were no worse
than high U.S. tariffs, which would now not be cut by sectors, as America
had pledged at the 1943 Washington talks. An inequity existed. Britain was
to terminate, permanently, its valuable trade system whereas America's concessions would be modest and temporary, guided by the selective tariff-
reduction method and lasting only three years until the RTAA was considered by Congress again. Who knew how strong protectionists would be by
then? The British were committed to liberalization, but the U.S. proposal

"could hardly be considered as 'mutually advantageous' in the language of Article VII," he concluded.[36]

The split on preferences centered on timing and priorities. The British refused to jump off the cliff, unconvinced that the benefits of free trade were at the bottom. Whereas the Americans pursued immediate adjustment of preferences, the British wanted a gradual approach. Clayton's free trade plan was better suited for a more distant time when the British economy would be healthier. Britain feared that Clayton's attitude "might easily wreck the whole negotiation."[37]

Ultimately, the Financial Agreement dealt with preferences. They would be reduced or eliminated if the United States granted large tariff cuts. There were two caveats, however. First, the benefits accrued to both sides must be "mutually advantageous," a phrase so elastic that Britain could refuse to reduce margins regardless of American concessions. Second, the dominions had to give their consent, and, as before, that might be difficult to obtain. Although they were ambivalent toward the Ottawa system, industrialization, full employment, and healthy payments balances depended on the protection the dominions got from preferential tariffs within the empire. The loan accord would prove troublesome for the free trade idealists.[38]

The commercial plan incorporated the terms of the Anglo-American Financial Agreement. The Americans would be allowed to cut tariffs selectively and insert escape clauses in agreements. Britain would seek to eliminate preferences and neither create new ones nor increase margins. But the Washington proposals deleted the demand for an immediate abolition of preferences and made British action contingent on substantial U.S. concessions. Clayton had surrendered ground. The compromise so worried his delegation that the tariff preference formula was kept vague to disguise his acquiescence to Commonwealth discrimination. The British saw a good bargain. No unilateral abandonment of the Ottawa system would occur. Once action was required, the Commonwealth would profit from the halving of U.S. tariffs.[39] Imperial protectionism would live on.

A host of other issues were addressed at the conference. Quantitative barriers were a flashpoint. The Americans wanted quotas limited to cases of severe difficulties, worried that they would replace preferences as protectionist devices. They wanted the terms of the transitional period determined by an objective test given by the International Monetary Fund (IMF). Such "automaticity" was impossible to achieve, replied the British, who preferred the ITO to sit in judgment, not the miserly IMF. A subcommittee proposed that the IMF and the ITO have a common membership and incorporate the exchange principles of the former. But the British had just begun to contest this issue.[40]

Britain was also irritated by the assault on government stimulation of the economy in the American proposal. The tenuous link of employment to trade was a problem. In preparation for reconversion to peacetime production, Congress had begun to seek limits on social spending for full employment. This minimalist approach was unacceptable to the Commonwealth governments and producers. Interventionism, deficit spending, and planning were in order. The proposal also inhibited state trading, but the British government directed food trade. The Americans gave way, permitting non-discriminatory state trading but requiring Soviet-style complete monopolies to commit to a purchase commitment under which they would buy and sell on a commercial basis.[41]

Meanwhile, America sought to eliminate income subsidies that helped British farmers compete, but retain export payments that aided U.S. farmers abroad. Liesching refused. Deficiency payments maintained incomes in rural areas of Britain and thus were important to politicians. Inefficient production added to world surpluses and price problems, he conceded, but all nations subsidized farmers. American negotiators admitted that quotas, tariffs, and export subsidies had dumped surpluses overseas at competitive prices. But Britain should relent, for it was not a commodity exporter and did not possess a huge farm sector. A subcommittee worked out an arrangement in which subsidies would be allowed, but export payments could not be used to maintain domestic prices above export prices. Limited intergovernmental commodity agreements would expand consumption and thus unload burdensome surpluses.[42]

The British were successful in defending export taxes imposed on foreigners who bought raw materials from the colonies. Britain had spent an enormous sum to advance the colonies toward dominion status. Export taxes reduced these expenses that drained the British budget by channeling commodities to local processors, thereby encouraging development. But the Americans objected that the taxes could not be limited like tariffs. Foreigners, with no way to protest the taxes, consumed these goods. Britain countered that tariffs punished foreigners, too. U.S. smelters could impose duties on processed tin imports, for instance, while Malayan ore exporters were denied such protection. Export taxes solved the dilemma. As both tariffs and export taxes enabled domestic industries to survive, argued Keynes, both should be allowed. America retreated, accepting "selective negotia-tion" of export taxes in the same manner as tariffs.[43]

The proposal also denounced cartels, an issue rooted deeply in U.S. po-litical and economic history. During the trust-busting days of the Progres-sive Era, reformers had blamed depression and political instability on these restrictive practices. "Not only are cartels an economic menace but they are loaded with sinister political implications," said Assistant Attorney General Wendell Berge. Antitrust laws corralled domestic monopolies but foreign combinations had flourished. Roosevelt had viewed such global collusion as a trade barrier. Cartels drove exporters out of foreign markets, as German chemical makers had done after World War I, and were tools of aggression, as the Nazi experience later attested. America was not an innocent, but the nation looked to a future in which the destructive regimentation of mar-kets, by price-fixing and strict allocation of exports, would cease.[44]

Mocking Treasury Secretary—and former attorney—Fred Vinson, Keynes remarked that the Americans advocated antitrust policy because it had been a boon for lawyers. In all sincerity, though, Keynes argued that no country could expose its economy to American exports. Anyway, when compared to U.S. trusts, British cartels were benevolent. International combinations were not always evil, claimed the Board of Trade in an opinion backed by dozens of British firms and associations. As long as they were efficient and fair, they should be welcomed as a means to stabilize prices and business conditions. Overarching principles could not be laid down, for each na-tions' courts would rule differently on their legality. Cartels could be prop-erly addressed by building a body of case law under the ITO, which would hear complaints and suggest remedies.

The plan was unworkable, responded Vinson, for the ITO would be sad-dled by thousands of cases. Better for members to outlaw certain practices and not leave the trade body to decide with vague criteria, counseled Berge. But that recommendation was too inflexible for Keynes. He feared that rigid U.S. antitrust laws would prevail. The British revised the proposal so that cartels would be investigated by the ITO on a case-by-case basis, not limited by strict rules.[45]

This compromise epitomized Britain's success in reshaping many aspects of the proposal. Standing in for Clayton, Clair Wilcox, a Swarthmore Col-lege economics professor who now headed the State Department's Office of International Trade Policy, exalted that "[w]e are busy writing new lyrics to the song of nineteenth century liberalism and we shall no doubt get them sung back to us—while we pay out dollars." Wilcox, a free trade idealist, viewed the Washington Proposals, as the commercial plans were now called, as a further step toward his vision of free trade universalism.[46]

The Washington Proposals had not, however, honored America's prior intention of universalism. Trying to head off charges in Congress that he had been whipped, Clayton announced in November 1945 that the British had committed themselves to ending preferences. That was erroneous. Keynes was convinced that Clayton was posturing to sell the loan and trade package to Congress. But the claim so stunned Attlee's cabinet that it demanded a reconsideration of the Washington Proposals. The southern dominions were furious that Britain had supposedly not consulted them, a violation of the Ottawa Agreement. Just before the meetings adjourned in December, British negotiators inserted moderating language into the proposals that guarded the Ottawa system from extinction. Then, and only then, Britain announced that the Washington talks had been fruitful.[47]

The Washington meeting had not given Britain all that it wanted. Progress toward fulfilling Article VII had ensued; the British were to try to eliminate discriminatory practices. The Americans could be content. Postwar planning had restarted after a two-year hiatus. Britain could have balked at Article VII discussions or delayed further. And the Americans might have abandoned the multilateral project entirely. In the fall of 1945, as the United States, Britain, and the Soviet Union struggled to restore peace to the world, commercial planning might have been placed on a back shelf of diplomacy. It was not.

Yet Prime Minister Attlee also had good reason to be satisfied. British trade interests had been upheld and America's doctrinaire free trade ideas stymied. To be sure, Roosevelt and Truman had pulled back the free-traders by refusing to adopt the method of sweeping away tariffs by entire sectors in the RTAA. Thus, America had modified multilateralism even before sitting down at the table with Liesching and Cripps. Britain continued the process. Facing a determined free-trader in Will Clayton, the British had arrived in Washington with little leverage, for they needed the loan. But they managed to stand their ground. This was especially true for the big issues of empire preferences and quotas. The Americans simply would not push their closest ally any closer to the brink of collapse.

Clement Attlee had taken up where Churchill had left off. During the war, Churchill had conceded very little in substance on trade issues while he had backed American designs in rhetoric. Roosevelt would not disrupt

the wartime alliance over commercial principles. Anyway, Britain was on
record for having endorsed Article VII and having joined the United Nations and monetary system. Attlee got the loan while his negotiators helped
forge an outline for a commercial convention. Truman, mindful of Britain's
importance in the postwar world and increasingly wary of Soviet expansion, would not push Brtain too far. And all the time, in war and now in
peace, visionary free-traders in the State Department had beaten a slow but
inexorable retreat. They would continue to do so during the early Cold
War.

CHAPTER 4

Planning in the Cold War
1946

When the Washington talks ended in late 1945, the context for trade planning had changed. With the end of the war, the Grand Alliance against the Axis that had bound the United States, Great Britain, and the Soviet Union crumbled. During 1946 the two capitalist nations eyed communist Russia with increasing suspicion, and the Soviets returned the favor.

World War II had disguised fundamental differences between the United States and the Soviet Union. The Americans held to a vision of universalism, in which cooperation would guide the world toward peace and the United States toward great prosperity. Joseph Stalin had other ideas. The Russian leader's policy reflected his paranoia toward enemies at home, tremendous Soviet losses in the war, a historic expansionist thrust, and the Marxist pursuit of proletariat revolution. Rather than universalism, the Soviets sought a balance of power and spheres of influence, expanding their control around their borders.

The Cold War arose from divergent aims and approaches. In February 1946 Stalin asserted that communism would triumph over capitalism. A month later, as President Truman looked on, former prime minister Winston Churchill urged an Anglo–American alliance to prevent the Soviet iron curtain from falling over Western Europe. It was clear that the division wrought by ideology and geopolitics had no room for one-world universalism.

Economics reflected this fact. The Americans increasingly judged aid and trade policies in terms of their benefits to the Western powers. Anglo-American planners met in London in late 1946 to refine the Washington proposal for the International Trade Organization (ITO). They also designed a tariff protocol, the General Agreement on Tariffs and Trade. In both instances, Commonwealth regulatory protectionism remained a focus, but the specter of the Cold War now hung over the deliberations.

⚭

That global security and economics were linked was apparent in Congress's passage of the Anglo-American Financial Agreement, the $3.75 billion credit to England negotiated at the Washington talks. In exchange for the loan, Britain had agreed—under Article 9—to prohibit discrimination, end the sterling bloc within a year to allow the conversion of pounds into dollars, and negotiate on imperial preferences. The concessions provoked British Conservatives. The agreement represented an "economic Munich," a sellout of the empire "for a packet of cigarettes" that stripped England of its wealth.[1] Even less hysterical voices viewed the terms as onerous. Most likened the United States to Shylock, a pernicious money-lender preoccupied with export profits. America neglected the need for equilibrium in the world economy, refusing to act as a responsible, sympathetic creditor.

Prime Minister Attlee and Parliament heeded the advice of Chancellor of the Exchequer Hugh Dalton, Keynes, and Churchill to accept the loan as a necessary evil to save the economy. Attlee had sent an emissary to Washington to inquire about easier terms for currency convertibility, but the Americans refused him. Yet Keynes was upbeat. He marveled that the Americans would rehabilitate a competitor. And Churchill noted that the accord did permit Britain to hold on to imperial preferences, even though the nation was obligated to negotiate on them.[2]

This was not the message when Congress considered the deal in early 1946. Will Clayton implied that the loan was Britain's reward for promising to abolish preferential tariffs under the terms of Article VII. Without it, Britain would rely on the empire, rather than outsiders, to supply its imports. The rest of the administration denied that the money was remuneration or a gift, though President Truman claimed that "progress toward multilateral trade" would "be in itself sufficient warrant for the credit." Thus, there was an assumption that Britain would curb discriminatory trade practices.[3]

Because that was not Congress's reading of the Financial Agreement, proponents conjured up the image of Soviet expansion to get the accord ratified. They referred to Stalin's speech of February 1946 when he had rejected the compatibility of capitalism and socialism. Having dominated Eastern Europe, Stalin evidently had imperialistic designs in Asia, the Middle East, and Western Europe. Attlee's further regimentation of the British economy might turn the nation toward socialism and thus place Britain in the Russian orbit. The loan would encourage market capitalism instead. In

July 1946 fear of communism and big government statism won the loan over isolationist and protectionist protests.[4]

The Soviet Union was a factor in trade planning as well. At the end of 1945, the Americans drew up a list of the countries to discuss the Washington Proposals and then proceed to a United Nations conference, where the ITO code would be completed and tariff rates negotiated. Fifteen nations were chosen, based on their commercial importance and diverse economic systems. This nuclear club included America, Russia, and the Commonwealth nations of Britain, Australia, New Zealand, South Africa, Canada, and India; Europeans France, Holland, Luxembourg, Belgium, and Czechoslovakia; Cuba and Brazil from Latin America; and China. All but the Soviet Union accepted invitations.

International trade policy became enmeshed in administration debates over the proper approach to the Russians. The Soviet Union was reluctant to subscribe to principles that would govern its economy and strengthen its capitalist enemies. Averell Harriman, the U.S. ambassador in Moscow, played down this ideological struggle but counseled against encouraging Russian participation at planning sessions. He believed that the Soviets merely wanted freedom to dominate Eastern Europe. Harriman doubted that they would show up at trade talks that might lead to Western economic penetration in areas that they prized.[5] Stalin's politicization of trade ran counter to multilateral ideals.

The Russians had also refused invitations to discuss their system of state-run monopolies at the Article VII talks. According to Harriman, Stalin backed free trade only when these monopolies profited. Tariffs were used to prevent importers from selling foreign goods at lower prices than Soviet products. For example, duties had been levied on Lend-Lease aid to promote Soviet manufactures. Harriman concluded that it was pointless to negotiate tariffs with the Russians. He advised that the Soviets be denied membership in the nuclear club until their intimidation of Eastern Europe stopped and they cooperated in solving the European supply problem in an open, "non-political" way.[6]

Such a tough stance worried other members of the State Department. Stalin's status as one of the Big Three powers was a reason to invite him into the nuclear club, held Dean Acheson. As the world's top state (government-directed) trader, moreover, the Soviet Union would have a big role in the ITO. Acheson demanded that Russia consent to purchase some goods on a commercial basis to ease pressure on Eastern Europe and help Stalin's image in the United States. But more demands were inappropriate. Anyway, as a major consumer and exporter, Russia would likely be enticed into the planning talks. Acheson instructed Harriman to invite the Soviets to the nuclear meeting and to advise them to prepare a tariff reduction schedule. But by late December 1945, Stalin had not responded.[7]

Silence from Moscow led George Kennan, the chargé d'affaires in the U.S. embassy, to try to discuss the Washington Proposals with the Russians, this time with the people's commissar for foreign trade, Anastas Mikoyan. He got nowhere. Like Harriman, Kennan noted that Soviet aims were politically driven. Faced with Stalin's stalling, Secretary of State James Byrnes announced in mid-February 1946 that the nuclear club would meet without Russia. With the Soviets compelling their satellites to reduce trade with the West—Bulgaria had exported $11 million to the West in July 1945, but sales had fallen to $2.2 million by the following February—it was clear that Moscow did not wish to cooperate in the multilateral exercise.[8]

In the meantime, U.S. planners readied the ITO proposals for the nuclear club conference. This was complicated by the looming congressional midterm elections in November 1946 and preparations for the presidential election in 1948. Revising the proposals into a Suggested Charter for the ITO proved taxing, but the dawning of the Cold War stimulated the effort. The United Nations expanded the nuclear club to eighteen countries, adding Chile, Lebanon-Syria, and Norway, which would convene in London to discuss the Suggested Charter by October 1946.[9]

This first session of the ITO Preparatory Committee would also append a tariff protocol, called the General Agreement on Tariffs and Trade (GATT), to the Suggested Charter. Because of the enormous number of products and the complexity of selective duty cuts, each member of the nuclear club would propose tariff schedules that set maximum rates for every item. The schedules would then be incorporated into the GATT protocol, under which concessions negotiated in bilateral agreements would be extended to all participants at a world conference. Failure to conclude a bilateral agreement would not hold up the broader multilateral accord because GATT would encourage countries to continue bargaining. In sum, the tariff concession process would entail round-robin negotiations, applied in a multilateral fashion to ensure optimum liberalization. Delays in completing or ratifying the Suggested Charter would not prevent tariff cuts from going into effect. And it was planned that GATT would be eventually subsumed under the Suggested Charter.[10]

Timing influenced arrangements for the tariff negotiations. Under the Reciprocal Trade Agreements Act, proposed concessions in the GATT protocol had to be made available for public hearings. Sure that protectionists would pressure the administration for exemptions, Secretary of State Byrnes postponed the GATT talks until 1947, after the November elections. British officials complained that the decision would delay U.S. tariff cuts. Clayton and Harry Hawkins were also upset. The move might discourage multilateralists and cast doubt on America's faith in freer trade. In addition, the 1948 presidential election would come into play. Lengthy tariff talks would push trade issues into the political spotlight, susceptible to protectionist pressures. Besides, negotiators would have to hurry before the RTAA's tariff-cutting authority expired in 1948. The president would be risking too much in a narrow, politically charged time frame.[11]

Top administration officials were more concerned about the congressional elections. Polls predicted that the GOP would pick up seats; bad tariff bargains might win them even more. Thus, the State Department asked nuclear nations to focus on the Suggested Charter but only work on preparing tariff lists and put off negotiations until later. Clayton acquiesced, for electoral politics took precedence. As *Time* magazine pointed out, Truman and Byrnes were two former senators who "knew that when a Congressman scratches a constituent, even a world-minded one, he finds a high tariff interest. They did not want to do any scratching before elections."[12]

Domestic support was a worry. Protectionists were active, of course, but business crusaders for free trade also criticized the trade plans. The Cold War, a struggle against an archenemy of private enterprise, rallied them around market dogma. These free trade perfectionists stressed that high levels of productivity, not employment, would increase wages and purchasing power. The National Association of Manufacturers (NAM), the National Foreign Trade Council, and the U.S. Chamber of Commerce sought tighter rules on cartels, import and exchange controls, subsidies, and state trading, as well as protection for overseas investors. The Washington Proposals had failed to prevent statism and therefore, noted a General Motors executive, "were not revolutionary" in the least.[13]

Business purists looked to government only to trigger, not regulate, exports. Truman had responded in 1945 by revamping the Commerce Department's commercial services and seeking to raise exports by $10 billion. Despite congressional efforts to bar exports of consumer goods in short supply, the $7 billion in U.S. exports in 1946 and seemingly limitless demand overseas made that goal attainable. Yet ideology also entered these calculations. William Jackson, president of the Chamber of Commerce, warned that "another totalitarian system is extending its dominion over large portions of Europe and Asia bidding for territory, economies, and the mind and soul of humankind everywhere." Only an invasion of dollars and goods would contain this invidious cancer. Only an ITO that embraced free trade and free markets would help quarantine communism, contended Jackson.[14]

The public seemed to understand that trade cooperation, because it bolstered internationalism, was a national interest. Since the world "is getting much smaller," said a Missouri housewife in mid-1946, "trade is a good method of understanding each other." A trucker warned that protectionism would lead to another war. Several polls still found Americans leaning toward protectionism, unaware that the United States enjoyed a favorable trade balance. Thus, Truman championed the ITO plan as a way to unify friendly nations. The government extolled advocacy groups like the World Trade Foundation, which promoted this view at the community level. The foundation's two-month "Operation New Brunswick," for example, included interviews with over a thousand people divided into age groups. The foundation then urged stores to sell import merchandise, sent information to companies showing how industries and products were dependent on imports, held quiz programs with high school students, and broadcast on radio.[15] Such campaigns sought (in vain) to make trade policy less obtuse to the public at large.

Domestic considerations influenced the Executive Committee on Foreign Economic Policy's revision of the Washington Proposals into the Suggested Charter during the summer of 1946. Scholars have meticulously explored this document, having concluded that the draft was the last opportunity to stamp free trade doctrines on the postwar order before the nuclear club pressured for changes. In recognition of British needs, there was no requirement for automatic abrogation of preferential tariffs, although no margin was to expand after July 1, 1946, and no new preference would be imposed. That held for U.S. arrangements with Cuba and the Philippines as well. The Executive Committee also called for mutually advantageous tariff cuts. Prior notice, in writing, had to be given before a nation could invoke an escape clause.[16]

The escape clause issue exhibited the free trade bent. U.S. military advisers demanded a liberal construction of the national security escape clause, for example. They wanted a free hand to stop shipments of goods, raw materials (particularly fissionable products), and technology to the communists. But the Executive Committee refused to let an escape clause be invoked at any time the military saw fit. The Suggested Charter permitted an escape for the preservation of essential resources, sales of arms and fissionable materials, war or crisis situations, stockpiling of strategic materials, subsidies for security industries, and financing major overseas projects. But planners would not allow a loophole so large that nations could pull back from multilateral commitments on everything except luxury goods.[17]

Other sections of the American Suggested Charter stressed free trade. They allowed quantitative barriers to aid reconstruction, end balance-of-payments deficits, overcome food surplus or shortage problems, and for development. But the Treasury Department prevailed over the final provisions. In a section bound to provoke the Commonwealth, the rigid International Monetary Fund (IMF) would have the last say over the terms of exchange controls. The planners also softened language on cartels yet still sought limits on them, as well as on subsidies and state traders.[18]

Provisions for intergovernmental commodity agreements were the only significant divergence from multilateral idealism. Leslie Wheeler noted that his Department of Agriculture disliked the tone of this chapter, for it implied that such accords were inherently restrictive. But food producers at home and abroad feared chaos in global markets without them and would demand high subsidies for protection in their stead. The Executive Committee agreed that commodity agreements could regulate consumption and production. The Suggested Charter was revised to treat them as regulatory, rather than restrictive, measures, supervised by the ITO. Agreements would run for five years, however, during which time the trade body would determine if a surplus burden could not be better solved by the normal play of competitive forces.[19]

In July 1946 the planners completed the seven chapters of the Suggested Charter, including one regarding the administration of the ITO, and readied it for other nations. Seeking to avoid the appearance of having acquiesced to the document, Britain asked that it remain confidential until the Commonwealth had met to discuss its provisions. The Americans agreed. Meanwhile, the State Department sounded out all nuclear nations except for the Soviet Union. Supportive, they all confronted the free trade crusade nonetheless. From the Czechs to the French to the Brazilians, the United States learned that each nuclear nation, in its own way, sought latitude for trade discrimination. Hoping to change their minds in London, the Americans awaited the end of the empire talks before publishing the Suggested Charter on September 20.[20]

Meeting before the nuclear club convened, the Commonwealth complained about America's Suggested Charter. The policy of the British nations was frozen in its mold of the past few years. The multilateral effort would receive their backing as long as regulatory and protectionist safeguards qualified free trade.

Britain sought a common front to present to the Americans. The Empire Parliamentary Association had already vowed to defend preferences. In addition, the dominions realized that tariff margins could be used as leverage in the GATT negotiations. Like Britain, the southern dominions also counted on quantitative barriers as a protective weapon. Willing to trade off preferences for U.S. tariff cuts, the Commonwealth would seek freedom in the ITO Charter for preferences, quotas, bulk-purchasing agreements, and other discriminatory measures.[21]

Canada was the only firm supporter of the U.S. plan. To be sure, engaging in free trade with America was a risk, as the United States was susceptible to depression and protectionism. Canada, therefore, would hold on to exchange controls in case of sudden changes in the American economy. Ottawa was also less likely to disparage state trading, for it had just developed its own Commercial Corporation to aid business. As a major food exporter, it would also not criticize commodity agreements. Still, the nation praised the assault on barriers of all kinds, including preferences. In November 1945 free trade interests had compelled the Liberal government to cancel two tariff hikes to demonstrate support for the Washington Proposals. Canada sought vigorous constraints on cartels and wanted to go much further than the Americans in decontrolling commodity trade. Canada agreed with most of the Suggested Charter.[22]

That was not the case with the southern dominions. They worried about losing their British market for food. South Africa had expressed little interest in the proposals but agreed with other dominions that minimal preference margins were imperative. New Zealand and Australia approved of commodity accords to boost exports. New Zealand in particular wanted to end U.S. export subsidies. As 84 percent of its exports went to Britain, moreover, this dominion required a market assured by preferences. Both Australia and New Zealand sought to strengthen the employment provisions and aid for industrializing nations in the Suggested Charter. They

Masters of trade regulation: Australian minister of external affairs Herbert Vere Evatt and prime minister Benjamin Chifley meet with Labour compatriot, British prime minister Clement Attlee. (Courtesy National Library of Australia)

were so serious about their demand for freedom to resort to discrimination that they had not yet signed the Bretton Woods accord to protest IMF restraints on trade controls.[23]

Australia, the most powerful southern dominion, had problems with the U.S. charter. Prime Minister Benjamin Chifley agreed with its intentions but not its lack of attention to domestic concerns. Hailing from the ranks of organized labor, Chifley valued American friendship but would not sacrifice the Labour Party's regulatory program to free trade ideals. Full employment was crucial to his nation's modernization and social security, as well as his political future. Thus, on reviewing the Suggested Charter, Chifley concurred with Herbert Coombs of the Department of Postwar Reconstruction that the draft had inadequacies.[24]

Chifley might lower Australia's high tariffs, and he would certainly take part in the ITO drafting discussions. Officials understood the importance of multilateral principles and sought a major role in postwar global diplomacy. Seeking markets outside of the empire, he would also trade in preferences on items like dried and canned fruits. But abolishing margins for vital wool, meat, butter, and fresh fruit exports was out of the question because he hoped to shore up his political base in rural areas. Thus, on preferences, Australia felt that Britain had already conceded too much to the Americans.[25]

Typical of developing nations, India also sought freedom to discriminate. This new dominion was a supplier of raw materials, with great industrial and consumer potential. A target of Soviet penetration, destabilized by internal fissures, and Anglophobic, India posed challenges for Commonwealth unity and multilateral cooperation. A Muslim minority chafed at regulations set by the Hindu majority, threatening to ignite the country into turmoil. Moreover, India lacked financiers to stimulate output, technicians to organize industrialization, and large-scale energy output to maintain expansion. A payments crisis loomed, for the nation's population had shot up 10 percent since 1939, prompting a higher demand for food imports. India would limit foreign trade and investment until domestic needs had been met. Its tariffs were moderate but there were plans to increase rates on consumer goods.

The Federation of Indian Chambers of Commerce, the United Provinces Chamber, and other business organizations frowned on the Suggested Charter. To be sure, preferences were detested symbols of imperialism. But business groups opposed the notion of equal access to markets and raw materials. Cartels and tariffs blocked predatory foreign firms that would pillage this fragile, infant economy. India "would like to have rewritten [the] entire draft Charter," reported R. K. Nehru, a trade official in the Commerce Department. America, Indians contended, was stampeding the developing world into accepting rules suitable only for rich nations. India must equip itself with all the necessary instruments of regulation to combat the big powers. Nobody was sanguine about Indian cooperation on the Suggested Charter.[26]

The Commonwealth talks also revealed that Britain itself would contest the document. Empire isolationists had called the potential curbs on the Ottawa Agreement "the Boston Tea Party in reverse," disastrous for the colonies. Manufacturers and exporters also balked at undermining the Ottawa system until the United States had cut tariffs. And preferences were a matter of "domestic" interest to the empire, not subject to decisions by outsiders. Supportive factions of the Labour Party still vowed to check market trends by guiding imports and exports. Most interest groups that backed multilateralism also protested the inadequate remedies for unemployment and payments problems and the lack of burden on creditors, particularly the United States, to correct these ills. Indeed, America appeared as an unwilling buyer that would freeze out imports. Freedom over quotas had to be retained in the transitional period and an escape clause granted for concessions on preferences, just as U.S. tariffs would enjoy.[27]

The Commonwealth talks revealed the lure of protectionism. The southern dominions, except for regulatory foe South Africa, were protectionist. Australia demanded a chapter for employment and the creation of an Industrial Development Commission to give technical assistance. The southern dominions aimed to convert tariff preferences to quota preferences and wanted freedom from IMF restrictions. When Australia and New Zealand demanded import controls as instruments of long-term policy, Britain and Canada objected. Yet dominion obduracy restrained the British, who were hesitant liberal traders anyway.[28]

Such diffidence confirmed for American observers that the London Preparatory Conference would threaten their Suggested Charter. Destitution and mountains of protectionist constraints abroad, Cold War tensions, and predicted Republican Party gains in the upcoming elections would spook nuclear nations from market capitalism. Discrimination was rampant the world over, as shown by the Benelux customs union, Swedish-Soviet and British-Argentine trade agreements, an Anglo-Canadian wheat accord, and a Russo-Swiss oil arrangement. There was, in short, no support for free trade. Even the Twentieth Century Fund, packed with advocates of freer trade, viewed the Suggested Charter as unrealistic. Once congressmen understood its implications, they would denounce it. The document was naive, undermined by diverging Russian, British, and American trade policies.[29]

By the time the first session of the Preparatory Committee of the ITO opened in London on October 15, 1946, the international climate was not conducive to free trade, much less to the universalism that harkened back to Cordell Hull's tenure in the government. The Soviets did not even appear. The Truman administration pressed on, convinced that it could sell its Suggested Charter as a guide for commercial relations. The nuclear club nations pondered the document and welcomed American ideas. They just defined their aims differently than the United States.

Confronting the skeptics, the administration and its allies championed their multilateral blueprint in London. As Truman informed the United Nations that a trade code would "complete the postwar structure of peace," the Preparatory Committee convened. Clair Wilcox, chief of the State Department's international trade division, headed the thirteen-member U.S. delegation. This Clayton deputy steeped in free trade doctrine took on the critics. The Suggested Charter was a working document that America would modify if deemed too harsh. Trade could be linked to domestic economic policies, Wilcox pledged, but exceptions to free trade must be limited and multilateral principles upheld.[30]

Others did not echo Wilcox's enthusiasm. The Europeans, Canada, and Cuba supported the Suggested Charter, but critics Australia, India, and Lebanon attracted other developing nations to their cause. Disturbingly, Britain was cautious. Stuck between its commitments to the United States under Article VII and Article 9 of the Financial Agreement, but pressed by the Commonwealth, the British would not champion the American cause. Like other free trade idealists, Wilcox had mistakenly concluded that the Commonwealth had assented to ending the Ottawa system before the meeting. On the topic of quantitative barriers, moreover, the Americans conceded ground. Indeed, the Suggested Charter exited London with most American aims intact. But the session was a hollow victory.[31]

Wilcox had a tough time, particularly with Australia. Herbert Coombs, the Australian delegation chief and an acolyte of regulation, was nicknamed "Nugget" due to his small stature. But he had big-time influence. Charged with supervising the country's modernization, he got assurances from Wilcox that the trade organization would focus on employment and development, compel creditors to spend, and halt commodity price fluctuations. And Coombs vowed that preferences would remain, at the least, as a bargaining tool in the GATT negotiations. He believed that "the Americans had finally learned that laissez-faire economics have many limitations."[32]

Respectful of Coombs's influence with the developing nations and Australia's leverage in Commonwealth circles, Wilcox had him preside over the committee that studied the commercial policy chapter. Coombs proposed a commission on industrialization that would permit discrimination. Wilcox blocked him, fearful that this body would override the ITO. Yet he agreed to draft a new chapter on economic development to allow import quotas for poor nations. Wilcox claimed that it was the only major concession made by the United States during the meeting.[33]

That was not true. The United States also backed down on the general use of quantitative barriers. The International Monetary Fund had limited the transitional recovery period to the end of 1949, after which nations resorting to import controls to stabilize their exchange positions would have to seek approval from the ITO. France and Britain sought a longer transition and less stringent criteria for imposing restrictions. They opposed the need to consult the ITO except on the subject of new or intensified controls.

They succeeded in revising the Suggested Charter along these lines; the United States found itself alone in the battle to eliminate quotas. An exception to the rule of nondiscrimination broadened their scope in the event of declining or low currency reserves. As one scholar has noted, "the exceptions represented major departures from the full rigour of multilateral principles."[34]

Other U.S. concessions smoothed the way in London. Cartels would enjoy more leeway. In a show of compromise, Wilcox decided to let the ITO prove the perniciousness of monopolies. He did reject amendments for more restrictive commodity accords, and he turned against the regulatory measures of a World Food Board (backed by all other exporters) then under consideration by the United Nations Food and Agriculture Organization. Rules governing the entrance requirements for commodity accords were eased, however, so that the ITO could better moderate prices. The chapter on the organization's administration was altered very slightly. In addition, Wilcox toned down a "large quantity of big talk into a small number of innocuous generalizations acceptable to the United States" by adding a chapter on employment that voiced regulatory principles but did not allow the ITO to endorse interventionism as its main goal.[35] The Commonwealth would fight this another day.

On November 26, 1946, the Preparatory Committee reached agreement on 74 of 89 articles of the Suggested Charter. The nuclear club left such technical issues as tariff valuation and administration for an interim committee to discuss at Lake Success, New York, in early 1947. The New York delegates would also ready alternative drafts of contested articles for a second Preparatory Committee conference in Geneva, to convene in Spring 1947 along with the GATT negotiations. Nuclear countries would then turn over the Geneva draft of the ITO Charter to a gathering of the United Nations in the fall.

The articles of the Suggested Charter were approved by almost all of the nuclear club. Except for India, the eighteen nations had compromised on all matters of substance. They completed a trade charter faster and with more agreement than anyone had believed possible. "All of the countries here now have our grand design clearly in mind," Wilcox exclaimed as the meeting wound down. The result, he declared, "was not only an improvement on the U.S. draft but a document that made no important concessions on any matter of fundamental principle."[36]

Wilcox was either too exhausted to comprehend the inroads on America's plans or he ignored the compromises in order to meet expected criticism from business purists and the new Republican Congress. The "London Charter," as the Suggested Charter was now called, marked a high point of U.S. influence in planning. Wilcox had gotten a blueprint for the ITO. That was a major accomplishment in a world rife with protectionism and divided by the Cold War. But he had failed to prevent what Richard Gardner has described as "crippling exceptions on quantitative barriers and employment that aborted free trade principles." Wilcox admitted that import quotas might replace tariffs as protective devices. And though he argued that concessions on employment were more apparent than real, emboldened regulatory protectionists in foreign delegations left London to rally against market influences.[37]

Had the United States succeeded in London? Yes, if one takes the view that a document that embraced multilateralism of any kind was better than no document at all. No, because the revised provisions of the London Charter corrupted free trade ideals and thus undercut the State Department planners.

The foreign response drove home this point. The British, including even the king of England, lauded the London Charter. They welcomed it both as a catalyst to lowering barriers and as a stimulus to employment. Britain's Cabinet Trade Negotiations Committee resolved that the London draft was a "[c]onsiderable improvement over the Suggested Charter, for it granted greater flexibility to deal with balance of payments difficulties." The Labour Party and the press backed the London Charter only because it stepped around free market capitalism.[38]

The revised plan was also acceptable to the British because of developments in American politics. The Republican seizure of Congress in November 1946 likely meant that America would not embrace free trade in coming years. Opposition leader Winston Churchill believed that to be the case. As a consequence, he counseled that neither should Britain. Truman might persuade the Republicans to proceed with the Geneva conference, but preferences must cover Britain just as high tariffs would protect the United States. Thus, sixty members of Parliament, supported by an array of British export and import interest groups, joined Churchill on November 12 to defend the Ottawa system.[39] British trade policy would stay the protectionist course.

Australia's reaction also revealed the American compromise. A marked improvement on the Suggested Charter, the London draft, wrote Herbert Coombs, "gave an entirely new twist to the basic philosophy underlying the Charter." Planners now paid attention to domestic requirements rather than to the international system. "What once had been a legalistic document had gained elasticity permitting nations to prove that particular practices were in fact justified from a national viewpoint without being unduly inimical to the international interest." The ITO would be more flexible without condoning the indiscriminate protectionism that had embittered trade relations in the past. Australia would have to make concessions, but at least the London Charter was consistent with regulatory, interventionist principles.[40]

Whether the Republicans would stomach these revisions and the tariff cuts under GATT was a major concern for foreign observers. Predicting that the election would have a greater bearing on policy than when the GOP controlled Congress in 1918 and 1930, the Canadian embassy in Washington, D.C., warned that House isolationists might ruin the multilateral project. Indeed, as the pro-Republican *Chicago Tribune* claimed, the Preparatory Committee talks had "insulted the American people, who had just voted to rid their economy of governmental controls. Yet in London, dozens of global planners had forged a trade system wilder than any ever dreamed up by the New Deal."[41] Stumbling blocks and crises loomed in the future for American free-traders.

A tumultuous year, 1946 culminated in setbacks for the Truman administration. The Republican triumph in Congress was the most visible. Not so obvious was the London Charter. A product of various pressures, it had veered from U.S. designs. The Preparatory Committee meeting epitomized a struggle between the United States and its trade partners over economic ideas. The British Commonwealth had slipped in revisions of the Suggested Charter that blocked major American objectives. And the lack of participation by the Soviet Union could not be overlooked. Russia's absence forced an abandonment of hopes for a universalist trade order. In short, a battle raged in the international arena over economic principles and policy.

Clair Wilcox knew that the nuclear club would junk the London Charter if America refused it or balked at GATT. Thus, he determined to muffle the GOP in order to proceed with large tariff concessions. This was the only way, he believed, to coax trade partners toward free trade multilateralism. Managing domestic and foreign protectionism would be challenging, for the wartime aura of universalism that had effectively countered protectionists had disappeared.

The global arena had grown more tense as the Cold War took shape in

1946, but the home scene became positively divisive. Memories of wartime cooperation dwindled as Americans turned inward. The Cold War came to bear as government officials and business leaders debated the future of capitalism and the American way of life. And politics stood on the brink of an era of partisan conflict not seen since after the First World War. Such circumstances undercut idealism in trade planning and injected realism into the policy process. The Truman administration set out on a wholly pragmatic approach to international commerce as Democrats squared off with the empowered Republicans in Congress to contest trade policy at the very dawn of GATT.

CHAPTER 5

The Republicans Strike Back
1946–1948

An activist federal government had reshaped the American economy during the New Deal and Second World War. Democrats held that liberal planning, undergirded by government, could maintain prosperity in the postwar era. Yet in 1946, a majority of the country criticized such regulation as statist regimentation. The Republican Party benefited from this backlash.

The GOP won both houses of Congress in November 1946, riding the tide of dissent against the New Deal. The rejection of a full employment bill revealed the unpopularity of the regulatory approach. Furthermore, anti-inflation curbs on the economy riled Americans. Business leaders hated price constraints, workers chafed at wage controls, and consumers complained about shortages, high prices, and inadequate services. Conservatives blamed Truman for these problems. They also lashed out at internationalism in foreign affairs, targeting free trade doctrine and the coddling of the regulatory state abroad.

In particular, Republicans wanted to slow or halt the drive toward lower tariffs. The administration feared that years of commercial planning would unravel, thereby undercutting economic cooperation and the effort to contain communism. As a result, pragmatism prevailed in the highest ranks of government. By compromise, persuasion, and even confrontation, Truman managed protectionism to preserve his broad objective of freeing trade.

The administration went to work even before the Republican Eightieth Congress convened in January 1947. The State Department sought to rally liberal traders around the idea of large tariff concessions and the London Charter. Both would strengthen and unify the bloc of capitalist nations.

The Committee on Trade Agreements, an interdepartmental body responsible for overseeing tariff negotiations, prepared a list of concessions to present at the planned GATT meeting. Wisely issued after the election, it included 13,000 products covering 80 percent of U.S. duties eligible for tariff cuts and the binding (freezing) of rates at current levels. So extensive were the concessions that they "would, in effect, amount to a revision of the Tariff Act," concluded Winthrop Brown. This former lawyer and Lend-Lease coordinator chaired the Committee on Trade Agreements, taking over the helm of the State Department's Division of Commercial Policy from Harry Hawkins. Brown was smitten by free trade fervor. He also knew that the offers would provoke protectionists, for they called for tariff cuts on such sensitive import items as wool, butter, meat, shoes, and textiles. Brown believed that only political finesse would get the list to the GATT talks intact, safe from the clutches of protectionists.[1]

He had a strategy in mind. Secretary of State James Byrnes would approach the venerable GOP leader Arthur Vandenberg for approval of the list. In the meantime, Brown published the GATT list in layman's language, lumped the concessions under broad categories to give the impression that they were not so numerous, and tied them to other elements of Truman's economic program. Undersecretary of State Dean Acheson then pledged that no tariff cuts would occur without reciprocal action from other nations.[2]

The administration contended that multilateralism, or the liberalization of barriers by all countries, would boost exports and thus profit society at large. By 1947 U.S. sales abroad represented one-third of global exports. An economic behemoth, the United States produced 41 percent of the world's goods and services. In 1947, however, signs of recession appeared. Automobile and commodity prices fell, the stock market plummeted, and sales of consumer goods lagged. Export expansion could help the economy. And allies relied on U.S. trade, production, and capital as well as the American market for their goods. Tariff cuts at GATT, concluded the administration, would benefit all nations' economic interests.[3]

The Cold War was another rationale for freer trade. Crisis diplomacy, induced by Britain's intention to withdraw from influence in Greece and Turkey, led to the promulgation of the Truman Doctrine on March 12, 1947. Asking Congress to approve an aid package for these two nations, the president announced that American foreign policy would protect free nations from external aggression or internal subversion. In short, America would contain the expansion of Soviet-directed international communism.

Planning soon followed for the European Recovery Program, or the

Marshall Plan. Intended to serve strategic ends, this huge grant of assistance would repair and integrate the economies of Western Europe and build a solvent alliance against communism. Columnist James Reston observed that America's ability to engage the Russians in power politics would be "meaningless unless it was backed up with economic action." He meant, among other things, higher levels of U.S. imports. Thus, the containment policy and the defense of the American capitalist way of life spurred trade liberalization efforts.[4]

Many interests aided the cause. In a publicity stunt, the World Trade Foundation sent twenty planes to Latin America loaded with U.S. products and then returned full of imported goods. The Export Managers Club of New York had to turn away applicants for a course on trade while businesses and schools organized rallies, conferences, and prizes on behalf of multilateralism. The Junior Chamber of Commerce sent out material on the London Charter to 890 local chapters, followed by a meeting in Dallas. Even CBS television scheduled a program on the International Trade Organization (ITO). From New Orleans to New York, trade marts, foreign trade zones, and associations promoted imports and multilateralism.[5]

The goal was to guard the trade agenda from the Republicans. Senate Democrats, for instance, ridiculed the GOP as shortsighted. "Just let them try to write a tariff bill," challenged Senator Millard Tydings of Maryland, and then face a tidal wave of voter disapproval. The GOP was wrong to disparage the administration for its treatment of U.S. producers, for the Reciprocal Trade Agreements Act (RTAA) contained loopholes and exceptions to free trade. In reply to Minnesota Republican and House Ways and Means Committee chairman Harold Knutson's effort to postpone the General Agreement on Tariffs and Trade, the new secretary of state George Marshall warned that such action would undermine rehabilitation abroad, encourage regimentation, and exacerbate discrimination against the United States.[6]

Hearings held in seven cities in February and March 1947 to gauge support for the London Charter of the ITO were heartening for the planners. A striking 208 of the 245 witnesses backed the draft, 165 with little or no qualifications. Only a dozen or so die-hard protectionists, led by the American Tariff League, came out in opposition. The complexity of the document and apathy on trade matters caused a low turnout in Chicago. But Denver and San Francisco had robust attendance. Normally plaintive Rocky Mountain metal and cattle interests issued no objections to the draft's aims. California vegetable growers realized that imports had to rise. Free trade purists in the big business community expressed their concerns about regulatory provisions. Yet the hearings showed that the London Charter was salvageable.[7]

Advocates also played the Cold War card at hearings before Knutson's hostile Ways and Means Committee in Spring 1947. Without multilateralism, warned Will Clayton, "we are going to leave a vacuum into which, inevitably, will move an economic system based on principles alien to our ideas, injurious to our interests, and highly restrictive on the volume of world trade." Echoed Clair Wilcox, at issue was not only dollars and cents but "our leadership in international affairs, our foreign trade, our system of private enterprise, our national security."[8] The president concurred.

Harry Truman's crowning moment on trade issues came in an address at Baylor University in Waco, Texas, on March 6, 1947. He chided the notion that protectionism was a viable path. Because "foreign relations, political and economic, are indivisible," multilateralism was imperative. America's way of life hinged on the promotion of private enterprise. Without a code that limited discrimination and tariffs, regimentation and socialism would arise at home, too. The GATT negotiations would afford access to global markets for U.S. exporters, but the country would have to admit more imports. To be sure, the State Department would not sacrifice producers; escape clauses and item-by-item bargaining would protect beleaguered producers. But Truman concluded that there was no alternative to lowering barriers except poverty, instability, and world conflict.[9]

The liberal traders had obviously not folded up their tents. But Republican protectionists, charged by their new leverage on Capitol Hill, mobilized against the trade agenda, its internationalist principles, and multilateralism as a whole.

Lingering isolationism within the GOP disguised a consensus to sweep away the New Deal and its encumbrances, including the Truman presidency. The House was now full of rabid isolationists and partisan enemies of the New Deal. The Senate, under Robert Taft, was more moderate. But in the bitter politics of postwar America, the Republicans pledged to scale back liberal spending, big government, and pro-British foreign policies. They were determined to win back the White House in 1948 after a twenty-year hiatus. And along with a handful of Democrats, they relished the idea of destroying free trade dogma.

Enjoying a 51–45 edge in the Senate and a 245–178 advantage over Democrats in the House, the Republicans of the Eightieth Congress set off alarm bells in the State Department. Arthur Vandenberg, the chairman of the Senate Foreign Relations Committee, leaned toward internationalism but even his help on trade matters was suspect. Anti–New Dealers like Robert Taft, Senator Eugene Millikin of Colorado, and Speaker of the House Joseph Martin of Massachusetts aimed to slash taxes and spending and to slow down tariff cutting. Of special concern were the House Republicans, led by Harold Knutson, chairman of the Ways and Means Committee. Virulent right-wingers in their ranks sought to gut Democratic policies. Internationalists screeched that the GOP would return the country to the days of isolationism and trade wars.[10]

Multilateralism was more at risk than trade liberalization. The RTAA was safe until its renewal in June 1948. But the GATT talks, scheduled for April 1947, might be suspended. Resurgent protectionists might also provoke the nuclear club to retain discriminatory controls, thus bog down the revision of the London Charter. Indeed, declared the Associated Press, the tariff issue would be Secretary of State Marshall's "major homefront headache."[11]

The Republicans had no remorse. A week after the elections, Senator Kenneth Wherry, of Nebraska, a small businessman who had long sought tariff protection, demanded research into the effects of liberal trade before the GATT negotiations began. Days later, Congressman Knutson asked for a probe by "unbiased experts" to offset "propaganda" against protectionism. Taft renewed his call for a flexible tariff, based on Tariff Commission assessments of the cost of production of each item. Other legislators, moderate and extreme, simply championed constituent interests. Oregon's Wayne Morse, for example, disliked the extreme protectionists of his party, but he, too, demanded tariff aid for agriculture to promote self-sufficiency and thus national defense in the Cold War.[12] Free-traders were in an unfamiliarly defensive position that was eroding, fast.

A barrage of bills, many of which had failed over the years, exemplified the attack on free trade. House right-wingers, backed by many senators, called for quotas, high tariffs, taxes, curbs on executive authority, Senate ratification of agreements, and cost-of-production formulas. Ohio congressman Thomas Jenkins adopted Wherry's idea and introduced legislation to delay the GATT talks until the Tariff Commission completed a study of the trade agreements program. Worried about the effect of imports on Ohio pottery factories, Jenkins wondered if truly reciprocal accords had been negotiated in the past. Like other protectionists, he suspected that producers had been sacrificed to the god of free trade ideology. "Brother, I am for

America first, last and always," trumpeted GOP congressman Robert Rich from Pennsylvania.[13]

In January 1947 protectionists targeted the Committee for Reciprocity Information hearings, which enabled producers to protest tariff concession lists prepared for negotiations. The GATT offer sheet was "a direct affront to the popular will expressed" in the elections, charged Senator Hugh Butler of Nebraska. It would cap thirteen years of trade agreements under the RTAA that had already cut 1,200 tariff rates. Compromises with the Commonwealth in the London Charter hinted that GATT, too, would continue State Department giveaways to foreigners. Anyway, argued Butler, the whole complaint procedure was a hoax, for the committee was packed with pro-administration free-traders.[14]

But complain they did, pouring into the hearing room to revise the concession list and condemn foreign trade practices, as well as the Reciprocal Trade Agreements Act. The fish industry, for instance, pointed to competition from Canada, Scandinavia, Britain, Mexico, Russia, and Japan. Many of these nations would not attend the Geneva talks. But representatives of 150 fishermen, processors, boat owners, and packers from Pacific, Gulf, and Atlantic ports sought protection from nations that supposedly gained from low wages or shortcut sanitary practices and maintained efficient trawler fleets. Quotas, the type of discrimination despised by the U.S. planners in London, were a desired course for the industry.[15]

These protests added to Republican pressure for modification of policy, and this caused great alarm in the administration. Officials hoped to manage protectionism by counting on Senator Vandenberg. As an advocate of a bipartisan, internationalist foreign policy, Vandenberg despised extremism in his own party. The isolationist Right might taint the GOP in Congress, he worried, or smear a Republican presidential candidate in 1948. He did think, though, that free trade multilateralism was dangerous for producers and impractical in a world of discrimination. The planners should adjust their grand designs. Otherwise, they risked a suspension of the second Preparatory Commission meeting, which would consider the London Charter and engage in GATT negotiations.[16]

Joined by Eugene Millikin, chairman of the Senate Finance Committee, and Robert Taft, Vandenberg had a deal in mind. Millikin, a brilliant guardian of congressional prerogatives, had risen in the GOP command in just five years. This protectionist, a former Denver lawyer who had represented independent oil companies' efforts to curb imports, also embraced moderate internationalism. On February 8, 1947, led by Vandenberg, the three an-

The GOP foreign trade policy "Command": (left to right)
Senators Arthur Vandenberg, Eugene Millikin, and Robert Taft.
(Courtesy Archives, University of Colorado at Boulder)

nounced their willingness to defer action on tariffs for a year if the administration inserted an escape clause in each GATT agreement. That is, a concession could be withdrawn or modified if deemed harmful to industry by
the Tariff Commission. The escape clause was a major loophole in the
commitment to free trade. Truman accepted it, even though nations would
likely censure the United States for reneging on its promise to cut tariffs
drastically. The president supported the deal, however, to save his trade
program.[17]

The notion that trade agreements should not injure domestic producers
had been a founding principle of Cordell Hull's trade program and was upheld by the cautious, item-by-item tariff cut process. A U.S.-Mexican trade
accord of 1942 also contained an escape clause. Yet no procedure existed for
determining when it should be invoked. Vandenberg wanted the Tariff
Commission to have jurisdiction over complaints, rather than the Committee on Trade Agreements and the Committee for Reciprocity Informa-

tion, which he judged unsympathetic. That would prioritize the domestic economy over diplomacy. Edgar Brossard, a veteran tariff commissioner who Vandenberg called a "rational protectionist," also argued that industry needed to be heard. Will Clayton promised to ponder the powerful logic of the escape clause.[18]

Discussions yielded, on February 25, 1947, Executive Order 9832, which established the escape clause procedure. The Tariff Commission would hold hearings, after which producers could be exempted from tariff concessions. Agreements reached in GATT would require an escape clause. The senators would not touch the Reciprocal Trade Agreements Act until it expired in June 1948. After most of Congress went along, Truman was satisfied that he could now complete the GATT agreements and finish up (and possibly ratify) the ITO Charter.[19]

The pragmatic compromise of the executive order was lost on the Republican Right and free trade ideologists alike. Harold Knutson, backed by many of his colleagues, still planned hearings to gut the trade agreements program. That GATT would proceed showed that the deal merely took "power away from Mr. Clayton's right hand and place[d] it in his left," criticized Senator Butler. Even Taft soon jumped the Vandenberg-Millikin ship. From the free trade side, commentators in mainstream periodicals like the *Nation* and *Newsweek* referred to Vandenberg and Millikin as saboteurs of postwar recovery and peace.[20]

The appeasement of protectionists embodied in the executive order would backfire, claimed free-traders at home and abroad. That was the view of the *Economist*, in Britain, which argued that the escape clauses, coupled with the selective approach to tariff reduction, emasculated the drive for liberalization. The world required a revolution in U.S. tariff policy, not a mere revision. The GATT talks would begin under a cloud of protectionism. The Bank of England agreed but saw even more serious implications. Its trade delegate, Lucius P. Thompson-McCausland, complained that the Americans had "now abandoned the concept of a radical adjustment of their economy—which certainly could not be achieved without some industries suffering in the process." In light of America's "defection," he advised that Britain seek protection through escape clauses in the ITO.[21]

Yet without the deal, the entire planning agenda might have collapsed, thus impairing initiatives for European recovery and containment of the Soviet Union. Republicans like Harold Stassen now endorsed GATT, fortifying a consensus around liberal—though not free—trade principles. Many British officials also downplayed the executive order. The Foreign Office reasoned that if the Vandenberg-Millikin arrangement brought Congress in line, it "would be a great step forward" for U.S. trade policy.[22]

Executive Order 9832 cleared the way for the administration trade agenda. It shelved dogfights between Congress and the White House until the 1948 election. By then, Truman hoped that public opinion would have turned against the GOP. In any case, political reality had forced the compromise. The president had responded sensibly, managing protectionists in a way that preserved his freedom to lower tariffs. That objective would bolster the fight against the communist menace in Europe.

The revolt against free trade persisted, however. State Department polls showed that only eleven states could be counted on to support GATT and the ITO Charter. Ranging from dairy farmers to bicycle manufacturers to sardine canners, producers relished the fact that Knutson would hear their complaints. Despite longtime support for liberal trade, southern farm interests wanted imports limited to commodities not natural to the United States. Protests were also creative. Dressed in a toga, a leader of a watch union marched in front of the White House bearing a sign that read "Rome burns while Byrnes roams." This referred to the former secretary of state's liberal trade agreement with Switzerland in 1946.[23]

As the trade conference neared, the right wing–run Ways and Means Committee tried to embarrass the administration. Critics resented a policy that, they charged, did not include Congress and assumed that free trade was best for the world. Furthermore, the British still had not agreed to abolish imperial preferences. "We have to start all of these conferences confessing complete defeat," concluded California congressman Bertrand Gearhart, "before we even sit down to negotiate the first agreement." The GATT protocol in particular would be a field day of "superduper propaganda" by the "silk-hatted diplomatic brigade of the State Department" who engaged in an "orgy of tariff slashing" to the detriment of American producers.[24]

These words reflected an isolationist thrust and a hatred of the New Deal, combined with the invidious red-baiting propagated by the hard Right at the time. "Reds" posted throughout the government wanted tariffs cut, testified an aide to Senator James Eastland; like Karl Marx, they believed that free trade would bankrupt the capitalist system. Illinois Republican Noah Mason, a former member of the House Committee on Un-American Activities, determined to hunt out "subversives" among free trade lobbies and their "fellow travelers" in the State Department. Not that Clayton was suspect, but his negotiators seemed split "between Americanism and communism," claimed Congressman Daniel Reed.[25]

Although less shrilly, Senate Republicans still took to the offensive. Many held that having the Tariff Commission decide the level of imports was a sound idea. Also, Millikin's Finance Committee held hearings on the London Charter in March and April 1947. Millikin scrutinized the ITO, a supranational body that clashed with his narrow interpretation of the Constitution. The senator accused the State Department of being disrespectful of Congress's rights. At one point, he asked for a glass of milk to prevent the trade plans from giving him ulcers. Millikin exhibited such expertise on the charter, and posed such a threat to it, that Clayton tried to appoint him to the negotiating delegation. Fearful that Millikin would block the project, State Department superiors vetoed the plan.[26]

But they could not sweep away the protectionist aura that hung over the planning agenda. Since the inception of the RTAA, officials had treated Congress with care by making allowances for protectionism. The Republican domination of Congress now forced even more compromises. For instance, a protectionist bill to curb wool imports from the Commonwealth nearly shut down the GATT talks in 1947. And in 1948, the administration witnessed the most serious attack on the reciprocal trade program to date. The GOP actually changed the law, displaying the power of protectionism.

In March 1948, after GATT and the ITO Charter had been negotiated, Truman asked for a three-year extension of the Reciprocal Trade Agreements Act. He was not optimistic. The Ways and Means Committee confined hearings to sessions of a subcommittee run by GOP protectionists. By a majority vote in late May, a one-year extension was reported to the House, which passed it without amendment. After the Senate Committee on Finance held hearings in early June and attached new amendments, the full Senate passed the legislation.

Truman's signature on June 26, 1948, renewed the RTAA in its most vitiated form ever. The one-year limit lent an uncertainty to America's commitment to cut tariffs. And after years of effort, the protectionists had significantly enhanced the power of the Tariff Commission by approving a so-called scientific adjustment of tariffs. The president would submit a list of tariff offers to the nonpartisan experts of the commission, which would hold hearings and within four months report the maximum allowable concession for each product at negotiations. The president could only drop below these ceilings, or "peril points," with good reason. To prevent the RTAA from becoming an election issue and to avoid an even severer law, Truman grudgingly accepted the bill.[27]

He took the advice of worried planners. Facing hostile Republicans, Clayton and Wilcox accepted an arrangement offered by the GOP leadership, including Vandenberg. In return for the renewal of the trade law, the administration would refrain from lowering tariffs during 1948. Such action would allow Congress to focus on the Marshall Plan and the ratification of the ITO, and permit a newly elected administration to return the trade agreements law to its original form in 1949. Truman understood the politics of trade and decided to save the RTAA.[28]

To be sure, the liberal traders had fervently resisted the Republicans. Officials testified to the RTAA's importance to foreign policy, contending that stockpiles of critical materials and exports important to national security depended on the law. Warned the large Citizen's Committee for Reciprocal World Trade, a vitiated RTAA "would disorganize our good relations with the friendly nations of Western Europe as well as of the Western Hemisphere and the Far East, and would play directly into the hands of the Communists." Polls revealed that four-fifths of the fraction of people familiar with the law endorsed it. Truman also activated his election strategy of denouncing the "do-nothing" Eightieth Congress. In late April 1948 he lamented the "sabotage of the trade treaty agreement" program by Congress.[29]

Democrats despised the bill. Asking protectionist Bertrand Gearhart to sponsor the law in the House was "like an unbeliever trying to revise the Bible," claimed former Ways and Means chairman Robert Doughton. The minority Democrats were outraged that the House hearings were closed to the public. And they pointed out that Vandenberg and Taft disliked the bill's partisanship. Above all, the peril points were dangerous. Pressured by lobbyists, the Tariff Commission could delay trade negotiations as it tried, futilely, to set levels of protection. Congress could also turn away agreements if the president breached tariff ceilings. Senator Walter George, of Georgia, a leading Democrat, protested that the peril point provision fixed the parameters in which the president must operate, "much like going over the head of the umpire and asking all nine of the players on the team what they think of a given play." Commitments to global cooperation on the part of top Republicans, including presidential hopeful Thomas Dewey, would be undermined and the Marshall Plan repudiated.[30]

Undaunted, the Republicans stood their ground. Congressman Doughton's minority saw its motion to extend the RTAA for three years, as well as prevent a gag rule on the House floor, defeated along party lines. Illinois congressman Charles Halleck told the Democrats to "quit their cry-baby stuff," as the gag rule was not unusual. He also criticized the State Department's advice that Congress should vote for a three-year extension or nothing at all. And the peril point procedure was merely an assurance that the Tariff Commission would uphold "the idea of true reciprocity." But the House version also included an extreme measure for a congressional veto over all trade agreements.[31]

The peril point was a boon for protectionists, who delighted at reasserting congressional prerogatives over tariffs. Tariff levying was a constitutional power of the legislative branch, they announced. Congress would now check up on the president for the first time since the RTAA had become law, in 1934. Investigative power would be removed from the Committee for Reciprocity Information, a free trade body dominated by the White House. At long last, the "bipartisan, independent, public" Tariff Commission, an arm of Congress, was invested with proper authority.[32]

In addition to economic and political arguments, Republicans defended their Reciprocal Trade Agreements Act on the grounds of national defense. Glass producers, for instance, criticized Czechoslovakia's impending participation in GATT. Worse than the State Department's failure to invoke the escape clause against this cheap-labor nation was the fact that America aided a "communist racketeer government," declared Congressman George Bates. The administration had begun to cut ties with Soviet satellites by issuing export controls limiting trade between the communist bloc and the West, but Truman had activated the GATT agreement with Czechoslovakia in April. Republicans erupted in anger.[33]

The RTAA of 1948, claimed the GOP, represented a reasonable approach to trade that did not sacrifice the nation's economy and security. Party members had voted for the Marshall Plan in 1948 and were willing to increase imports and expand world trade. All they sought by a one-year extension was an opportunity for review after a short period, as they required for the European Recovery Program. And peril points would promote reciprocity, the basis, after all, of the trade program. The RTAA of 1948 represented a middle course, not a return to a fortress America mentality. The bill was a milder form of the escape clause executive order of 1947, added Millikin and Vandenberg. Trade agreements were a necessity, wrote Vandenberg, who had just issued his famous repudiation of isolationism. But the "orthodox" RTAA of the past "can no longer be a standard pattern." A blind adherence to free trade policy was simply out of the question.[34]

Republican moderates made a good case for protection, but the extreme Right tainted their stance with a conspiratorial brush. Congressman Daniel Reed added to his accusation that the trade agreements program had instigated Japan's attack on Pearl Harbor with the moralistic charge that free-traders allowed U.S. markets to be flooded with foreign liquor. The second Red Scare also entered the hearing room, as the Right lashed out at a subversive State Department influence that cut tariffs, thereby allowing communists to weaken the country. House Republicans and conservative commentators alluded to the dangers of Democratic Party rule and the years of big government reform. "New Deal totalitarianism" threatened the Constitution and thus required constraints on trade policy.[35]

Vandenberg, Millikin, and to a lesser extent Taft tempered this extremism. After the RTAA bill cleared the House by a 234–149 margin, they curbed its excesses. In return for a one-year extension, the Finance Committee inserted the peril point and junked the amendment for congressional veto power over trade agreements. When Colorado Democrat Edwin Johnson joined the Republicans to report out the bill by an 8–6 margin, the GOP beat back amendments from the Senate floor that aimed to extend the law for three years. Taft preferred the restrictive House bill but went along with his colleagues because of the peril point provision. The bill passed the Senate by a vote of 70–18.[36]

Truman swallowed the compromise as Republicans warned him not to play politics. Grasping for an issue to reverse his apparently losing election bid, the president would portray the legislation as a return to isolationism, charged the Republicans. Indeed, Truman called the RTAA an "unwise" law that "cast some doubt upon our intentions for the future," but he signed it to prevent the program from lapsing. He promised to restore the full powers of the law once elected in 1949, however. Commentators applauded his action, for a veto would have destroyed the trade program.[37] But the president then used the GOP law in his attack on the Eightieth Congress during the election campaign of 1948.

From the Democratic convention in mid-July to election day in early November, Truman derided Republican protectionism as a detriment to prosperity and peace. The GOP trade agreements law mimicked Smoot-Hawley protectionism, he claimed, whereas the Democrats had boosted exports and stimulated peaceful commercial relations. Farmers in particular had been ruined by the Republican tariffs of the 1920s that had cut crop prices and raised the cost of manufactured goods. In North Dakota, he mentioned the ITO to attract wheat growers interested in export expansion, even though the audience had no inkling of this esoteric issue. But above all, the RTAA of 1948 was "the first step back to isolationism," Truman warned, and the Republicans would "finish the job" by ending the trade program if their nominee, Thomas Dewey, assumed the presidency.[38]

Although an exaggeration, the charge rang true. While the Democratic platform endorsed the old Reciprocal Trade Agreements Act, the GOP leaned toward protectionism. Dewey and his running mate, Earl Warren, were confirmed liberal traders. As governor of California, Warren had resisted pressure from fruit growers for protection. Both had favored a three-year extension of the RTAA and had kept the ITO Charter out of the platform for fear that protectionists would denounce it. Although the Republicans accepted the trade program, their support was distinctly qualified when compared to vigorous Democratic backing. Besides, the Right had opposed the Marshall Plan and grudgingly backed foreign aid programs.[39] Economic nationalism still appeared to drive the Republican Party and thus endanger Cold War security.

That stance was soon irrelevant. Truman's stunning election win in November 1948 and the return of a Democratic majority to Congress in 1949 halted extreme protectionism. Truman rushed to Capitol Hill to restore the RTAA to its original form. But there was little doubt that the Republicans had left their mark on trade policy. For instance, although the Democrats promptly removed the peril point procedure, this measure floated around in policy circles until reinstated in the RTAA of 1951. It remained an element of trade law for over a decade.

In the immediate term, protectionism had threatened trade liberalization and planning that were entering a critical phase as nations gathered in Geneva, Switzerland, for the GATT and ITO talks. Republican control of Congress had compelled the president to employ all of his skills of persuasion to manage protectionism. Truman had done so to protect an agenda considered a pivotal part of U.S. foreign policy and security. The administration hinged the recovery of anticommunist allies in part on raising imports, but GOP protectionists had impeded that effort. Thus, the president accepted some protectionism in order to open America's markets. That was his goal at the second Preparatory Commission meeting in 1947, in Geneva, that, like Republican rule in Congress, also tested his skills at managing protectionism to the limit.

CHAPTER 6

Managing Protectionism
1947

Albert Gallatin, America's fourth secretary of the Treasury, believed that tariffs violated "the liberty of the citizen."[1] Free-traders hoped to honor this native of Geneva, Switzerland, by reducing tariffs at the first round of the General Agreement on Tariffs and Trade. The GATT negotiations convened at the Palais des Nations in April 1947, in conjunction with the Second Preparatory Committee meeting that revised the London ITO Charter. Unfortunately for the hopeful planners, obstacles at home and overseas barred the path to their goal.

Republican protectionism impeded the administration's trade policy, but so did the resistance of the British Commonwealth. The Commonwealth determined to open the U.S. market but hold on to its discriminatory imperial preferential tariffs. It interpreted "mutually advantageous" terms of trade, as Article VII had prescribed a half decade before, as protectionism for the Commonwealth but trade liberalism and openness for the United States. Britain's bankruptcy entrenched this view. Once again, Truman was compelled to manage protectionism, this time abroad as well as at home.

During the initial weeks of the GATT negotiations, it was apparent that the British were not entirely willing partners in the pursuit of lower trade barriers. Will Clayton's delegation strode on to the stage with concessions designed to push the Commonwealth toward abolishing the Ottawa Agreement. Rather than applause, however, it met criticism from nations concerned about Britain's financial health. Free trade idealists thus confronted shrewd and self-interested Commonwealth bargainers.

The Americans exhibited what they claimed was generosity on their part. Clayton gave in to Britain's demand to start GATT before revising the London Charter. The British wanted to see U.S. offers before agreeing to revised trade rules. At his first press conference, Clayton not only asked for special consideration for recovering and developing nations but also tossed aside Article 9 of the loan agreement, which called for an end to discrimination. Not "especially interested [in the] complete elimination [of] all preferences," he would settle for their termination in selected commodities. Yet Truman had just signed the Philippine Trade Act—over Clayton's objections—which extended preferences with this new nation for twenty-eight years. Clayton now refused a similar lease for the Ottawa Agreement, to the chagrin of the Commonwealth.[2]

The United States was the only nation to present a complete tariff schedule when the nuclear club convened in Geneva. Truman had approved a list of maximum offers designed by the Committee on Trade Agreements, agreeing with free-traders in that body to ease protection whenever possible. For instance, the Texas City smelter would get a subsidy instead of tariffs against the tin imports of the British colonies. He also refused to see a group of zinc producers from his home state of Missouri who protested defense stockpiles built from foreign sources. Truman brushed aside complaints about cotton textile imports, noting high industry profits. And he invited in British woolens. Aware of the potential for a protectionist backlash, the president not only told his advisers that "I am ready for it" but also pledged "further action" to ensure the success of GATT. He figured that the executive order of February, establishing the escape clause procedure, covered him in Congress.[3]

The schedule was impressive in terms of the constraints on the administration. America asked for foreign concessions on $1.433 billion on the value of imports in 1939. This was split between tariff cuts and bindings of present rates, and requests to abolish or narrow preference margins. In return, the United States offered concessions on $1.407 billion of its imports, of which tariff cuts would account for $416 million and bindings (freezing rates at their current level) for $991 million. Most of the bindings were on items that already entered duty-free. Of the 3,500 recommendations for reductions, all but 17 had been unanimous within the Committee on Trade Agreements.[4]

The offer list, which Clayton proudly presented in a fat document, was an effort to make the maximum number and percentage of concessions possible without provoking riots on Capitol Hill. It even included offers on items in which no nation had requested concessions. The offers covered 93.2 percent of the imports of the nuclear nations, and 60 percent of the duty reductions would be in the maximum range of 36–50 percent. The list would drop the average U.S. duty under 20 percent, below pre–World War I levels. And the British were given an even better deal by the binding of 86 percent of their duty-free products and the granting of large tariff cuts on two-thirds of their dutiable imports. The Americans would also terminate most Cuban preferences. The offers of the seventeen other nuclear club members that trickled in were feeble in comparison to the U.S. schedule. Clayton proceeded anyway in the hope that his offers would move the Commonwealth.[5]

They did not. The British nations wanted the United States to act like a creditor, that is, make an inordinate number of concessions. The list, argued the British, suffered from a basic fallacy. Lowering the average height of U.S. tariffs was not generous. Offers should be appraised by their effect on reducing individual rates and by their impact on U.S. trade surpluses with each nuclear nation. Each country, in fact, suffered from a trade deficit with the United States. Thus, the objective of rectifying this imbalance relied on one-sided American concessions; equilibrium in the world economy was the responsibility of the United States.

Britain accounted for one-fifth of the Western European payments deficit —or dollar gap—of $5 billion in 1946. A large import surplus and lagging production in the key coal, steel, and textiles sectors, coupled with the breakdown of intra-European trade, had dimmed the nation's economic prospects. And the American loan was draining away. A resurgence in Western Europe in late 1946 masked a dysfunctional production system, worsened by a particularly cruel winter, a lack of relief funds, and the stalled international monetary apparatus. By 1947 Britain's payments deficit blossomed by 50 percent over the previous year. French and Italian shortfalls raised the region's payments deficit to $7 billion.[6] Britain desperately demanded help from the United States.

Before embarking for Geneva, Richard Stafford Cripps, Britain's delegation chief and president of the Board of Trade, downplayed the GATT talks to the House of Commons. As the Americans would allow only selective cuts in tariffs, Britain would not gain enough in Geneva. Indeed, British commentators across the political spectrum urged resistance to free trade, and even a repudiation of the Article 9 pledge to end discrimination. Truman's executive order had revealed that the United States would try to weasel out of onerous concessions, critics argued, thereby vitiating the effort to correct the European payments problems. Britain's debtor status signaled that a premature return to unrestricted trade would bring ruin. All politicians, to some degree, agreed that the Ottawa system protected British interests.[7]

The Commonwealth, in short, was not impressed with Clayton's offers. That the United States could escape from commitments in GATT revealed a policy full of "inconsistencies, half-baked theories, hypocrisy and downright ignorance," wrote Britain's *Spectator*. America refused to act out its destiny as a leader, claimed the South Africans and the Australians, seemingly unaware of its obligations to help out weak trade partners. To be sure, Americans did not seek to profit from British distress, welcoming imports and tolerating regulated expansion to rehabilitate Britain. But the Commonwealth would await offers that fully accounted for U.S. power and British decline.[8]

Cripps would only consider reducing preferences if the Americans sweetened their offers on behalf of Britain's export drive. Preferences would not be ended, for domestic political pressures and the Ottawa contract with the dominions necessitated their retention. GATT would be treated as an extension of the 1938 Anglo-American agreement, in which some margins had been narrowed, not abolished. The Ottawa system was simply a lever against U.S. protectionism, Cripps's bargaining chip in Geneva.[9]

The Commonwealth, except for Canada, had developed this strategy prior to Geneva. Having failed to coax the dominions into drastic reductions of preferences, Canada won release from the Ottawa commitment to guarantee fixed margins. Delegation head Dana Wilgress judged U.S. offers as satisfactory. Eager for large tariff cuts to reverse Canada's half-billion-dollar deficit with the United States, this respected economic planner would mediate between America and the Commonwealth. So would Prime Minister MacKenzie King, who urged Truman to admit more imports to push the Commonwealth on preferences.[10] But Canada was a lone voice for free trade in the empire.

The Canadians were too pro–American, believed the British, but Australia was a wholly different worry. Canberra believed that it had every right to impose high tariffs against British exports now that the Ottawa accord was being shredded. The nation also gave the Americans fits. The other southern dominions and India viewed U.S. offers as a good start, but Australia insisted on a drastic revision. Minister of Commerce and Agriculture Edwin Macarthy had told Clayton that he expected a halving of wool, meat, and dairy duties. Clayton laughed, "these three items are just about the toughest on the whole list" of offers. Australia saw nothing funny. The opposition Conservatives and the rural-based Country Party, both led by former prime ministers, sought to maintain preferences for fruit, a major target of America's drive against the Ottawa system. Prime Minister Benjamin Chifley was cautious. He appointed nine advisers to his delegation in Geneva and, pointedly, two from the fruit industry to show that he meant business on requiring U.S. tariff cuts.[11]

The southern dominions fully grasped that preferences gave the Commonwealth a tactical advantage in opening the U.S. market. To bolster its bargaining power, the Commonwealth also refused to accept an American amendment to the London Charter for automatic cuts on preferences. That demand, protested the British to the Americans, "will seriously diminish our bargaining power" and force the Commonwealth to cut back its offers, thereby "hampering the negotiations." Selectively reducing margins, these stingy nations thus hampered the U.S. trade bureaucrats' free trade aims.[12]

Given the Commonwealth's attitude on preferences, Clayton found its offers to the United States unsatisfactory. British tariff rates, lower than America's, partly justified the meager concessions on just half of the U.S. requests. Following a U.S. request for a cut in the duty, Britain's recent tariff hike on tobacco to protect the payments balance was another irritant. Worse was the fact that Britain had marked only two margins for elimination. London had made no offers at all on over three-quarters of the preferences it granted and had conceded little on the remainder. Meanwhile, the southern dominions had also submitted weak schedules, with no concessions on 40 percent of their trade covered by preferences. Even Canada's offers were shallow. As a U.S. delegate concluded, the Commonwealth had thrust "protective considerations very much to the fore."[13]

Commonwealth parsimony set the tone in GATT. An impressive 96 of 120 bilateral negotiations had been scheduled by late April, but the Americans were unhappy. France met a mere 1 percent of U.S. requests, seeking to raise its duties in order to convert to the ad valorem system. Benelux and Czechoslovakia had similar problems. Cuba protested plans to end its preferential treatment, and Chile wanted preferences with its South American neighbors. China and Norway made thin offers. Only Brazil and Syria-Lebanon offered adequate lists. Clair Wilcox, Clayton's deputy in Geneva, warned that without improvements, America would retract some offers, thus minimizing the impact of GATT. This would play well in Congress but not in foreign capitals.[14]

By mid-May 1947, five weeks of Anglo-American dickering over the meaning of "mutually advantageous" concessions had brought little progress. Clayton's assistants conceded that the goal of abolishing preferences was unrealizable, but their boss held out hope. Yet only South Africa had scheduled bilateral negotiations to discuss preferences. The British were dragging their feet, shirking, claimed Clayton, six years of commitments.[15] The Ottawa Agreement—Clayton's phobia—had indeed become a bargaining lever for the Commonwealth.

The British put the onus on America. Their offers did not signal a departure from prior pledges but rather a fulfillment of the understanding that both nations would reap advantages from trade liberalization. Because Britain had promised not to impose new or increase existing margins, its offers honored the spirit of Article VII, officials argued. Until America ran an import surplus to ease the dollar gap, GATT would bring nothing but "mutually *dis*advantageous results" for nuclear nations. Trade negotiator James Helmore spelled out Britain's basic philosophy. Trade expansion would end the payments crisis only if the United States, as a creditor, granted concessions that actually hurt Americans. Perhaps, he suggested, GATT should award a medal to the U.S. negotiators who made the worst bargains and thus facilitated a solution to the dollar gap![16]

Unmoved by American pressure, the Commonwealth assumed a familiar posture. Willing partners in the multilateral project, the British nations insisted on sacrifice by the United States before acting on Ottawa preferences. In light of Britain's economic difficulties, this stance was justifiable. A major controversy over wool tariffs drove the point home. Conflict over wool trade exemplified the push for America to open its markets but accept moderate protectionism abroad.

Wool, said a member of the U.S. delegation, was "the key problem on which successful outcome of the tariff negotiations with British countries depends." Southern dominion producers, not surprisingly, were incensed when the United States offered to freeze, not cut, its raw wool tariff. The Americans claimed that the binding represented an important concession, particularly as Congress contemplated legislation to raise wool tariff rates. But both the tariff offer and the possible duty increase threatened to destroy the GATT negotiations.[17]

Commonwealth wool exporters targeted the U.S. market, the world's largest. During the war Britain had bought the entire wool clip of Australia, the top global supplier. But that nation could no longer count on the frail British. Australia looked to such primary goods as wool and meat to fund development and full employment programs. Wool accounted for over 40 percent of its merchandise exports. Americans simply had to expand their purchases by cutting the U.S. wool duty of 34 cents per pound, a duty greater than Australia's cost of production.[18]

But American wool interests were on guard. During the Second World War, they had seen imports skyrocket to two-thirds of domestic consumption and then even higher by 1947. Britain had priced dominion wool so that the Commonwealth undersold U.S. producers in the wool-starved wartime American market. The U.S. military and Commodity Credit Corporation (CCC) had stockpiled this wool, which created a huge surplus after the war that suppressed prices at home. Since 1943, the CCC had purchased the domestic clip to maintain uncompetitive sheep farmers. Allied with protectionist New England woolen manufacturers, Rocky Mountain producers in the National Wool Growers Association reminded Congress how herds had clothed and fed soldiers after Japan had cut off supplies from the South Pacific. Senator Joseph O'Mahoney, a Wyoming Democrat and erstwhile critic of the Reciprocal Trade Agreements Act, had used his Special Committee on Wool to unite growers, manufacturers, and unions in an inquiry into U.S. policy in 1945. They wanted the subsidy maintained and wool and woolen imports curbed.[19]

Wool interests warned that lower tariffs would ruin them. Having flown over her vast state, a woman from Idaho noted that without sheep, the land would be barren. The farm economy would collapse, for vegetables fed livestock, which, in turn, produced wool, food, fats, and oils and provided taxes. Yet the State Department, wool interests charged, dreamily permitted imports to rise in hopes of peace. The National Wool Growers Association called for a protective tariff and denounced foreign dumping of surplus wool. In 1946 Congressman Frank Barrett, a Wyoming Republican, asked Secretary of State James Byrnes to negotiate an agreement to limit wool imports as he had done with Switzerland regarding watches.[20]

Senator O'Mahoney heard a myriad of options to deal with imports, including equalizing domestic and foreign prices by excise taxes or quotas. He would also consider subsidies as a nonprotectionist way to help producers at home. He asked the president in January 1946 to frame a long-term policy in response to the Empire Joint Wool Organization, a Commonwealth cartel that priced, marketed, and disposed of dominion wool. He sought continued CCC purchases, low grazing fees on government land, and an end to price controls. And O'Mahoney opposed tariff cuts for British wool and woolens. Truman issued a wool program on March 11, 1946. It approved of

Senator Joseph O'Mahoney (right) with Senator Tom Connally in April 1947.
(Courtesy American Heritage Center, University of Wyoming)

a more permanent CCC program of parity price payments and research, development, and marketing aid for growers. The plan also proposed a global agreement to coordinate policies. This "program will tend to encourage wool consumption in the United States and will be consistent with our general foreign economic policy," the president informed O'Mahoney.[21]

Cognizant that wool was the single most important commodity in the upcoming GATT negotiations, the administration persuaded Britain to set up an international meeting on wool. Thirteen nations formed a Wool Study Group that met in April 1947, just as GATT convened. To head off quotas, the Americans asked the empire nations to liquidate their wool stocks. But the other countries leaned instead toward a producer cartel. Meanwhile, on the domestic front, the Senate Committee on Agriculture and Forestry had introduced a bill that embodied Truman's program. An agreement with foreign wool suppliers on prices and import levels would deter quota or tariff riders to the bill.[22] American growers wanted more, and they counted on the new Republican Congress to protect them.

Wool interests sprang into action as the administration prepared for the Geneva negotiations. On January 11, 1947, Wyoming's governor, Lester Hunt, called every sector of the state's economy to Cheyenne to illustrate the seriousness of the decline in wool production. Participants demanded CCC parity payments past the April deadline and import restraints on foreign wool. At the Committee for Reciprocity Information hearings in February, growers and woolens producers lobbied against planned tariff cuts on imported raw wool and wool textiles.[23]

Congress then stepped in with legislation. A bill sponsored by Senator Edward Robertson of Wyoming cleared the Agriculture and Forestry Committee in April, just days before the Geneva meeting. It renewed the CCC program and replaced parity prices with a "comparable price" related to the cost of major commodities during the period 1935–39. The result would be an increase in parity prices by one-quarter. In 1947 the parity price was 40.26 cents; the comparable price would be 50.16 cents. Only dried field peas, soybeans, and peanuts for oil enjoyed a comparable price. New England senators blocked the measure, for wool consumers would foot the higher cost, agreeing instead to a floor of 90 percent parity. After Senate passage, disappointed growers counted on the House of Representatives to return Robertson's measure. House Republicans did more than that, however.[24]

Chairman Clifford Hope of Kansas reported out the Senate bill from his House Agriculture Committee in mid-April, with one major addition. The secretary of agriculture would levy an import fee of 50 percent on foreign wool if imports threatened the price supports program. Norris Dodd had thought of the import fee idea. A former head of the nationalistic Agriculture Adjustment Administration now occupied with foreign policy in the Department of Agriculture, Dodd detested the State Department free-traders and sought to protect farmers from foreign competition. House Republican leaders modified the Senate bill, giving the president authority to impose the fee after investigations by the Tariff Commission. The bill then went to the House floor in mid-May 1947, acclaimed by protectionists but vilified by consumers, free-traders, and the shocked British Commonwealth.[25]

Even O'Mahoney agreed with the State Department that the import fee was bad news. He held that adjusting the wool tariff would be too time-consuming. The State Department was mortified. The fee would set off a chain reaction of retaliation in Geneva that would doom GATT and the ITO Charter. Undersecretary of State Dean Acheson wrote Truman that the

wool tariff binding was the least America could offer to get action on imperial preferences. The wool bill would kill the talks; it "would raise doubts"
about "the dependability of the foreign economic policy of the United
States" so eloquently expressed by the president in Waco a month before.
The fee must be excised or the bill vetoed, urged Acheson. He readied an
appeal to Senator Vandenberg and Congressman Charles Eaton, of New
Jersey, chairman of the House Foreign Affairs Committee.[26]

Acheson's fears were justified. The Republican attempt to impose an import
fee on such an important product for the British Commonwealth was bad
enough. But the administration was trying to sell the multilateral idea to its
trade partners. At stake, in short, was nothing less than the success of American foreign economic policy and the pursuit of a solvent and stable Cold
War alliance against communism. Thus, Truman confronted the wool protectionists.

The foreign response to the wool bill was overwhelmingly negative. Demanding free trade, dominion growers warned that the import fee would
doom planning and lead to greater obstructionism on preferences. Australia
in particular recoiled. Considering that Australia and America had discussed
halving the U.S. wool duty prior to Geneva, the offer to freeze the tariff,
combined with inadequate concessions on butter and beef, was grounds for
halting the GATT meetings. An import fee would simply provoke a walkout by Australia that the entire Commonwealth would second. As a member of the British Foreign Office warned, wool had become the "Achilles
heel of the ITO discussions."[27]

Trade, moreover, affected overall U.S.-Australian relations. The two
countries had recently swapped ambassadors, and Canberra pursued a regional security organization that dovetailed with Anglo-American arrangements. The dominion had ambitions in the South Pacific, however, and had
protested America's plans to build a base on Manus Island, which Australia
viewed as its turf. Contentious economic issues might give the bombastic
minister of external affairs, Herbert Evatt, more reason to assert Australian
rights. The nation's $4.2 million trade surplus, built by wool exports, was
falling. Thus, binding the 34-cent U.S. duty or, worse, raising it with the
import fee were unacceptable. Either measure would sour Australia on U.S.
policies, especially multilateralism.[28]

Australian officials hammered away at that point in Geneva. Delegation
chief Herbert Coombs informed Clayton that Australia's reason for coming

Herbert C. Coombs, Australia's delegation chief in Geneva.
(Courtesy National Library of Australia)

to Geneva had been "radically altered" by the binding and the wool bill. Prime Minister Chifley banked on the political support of wool districts to offset the expected wrath of fruit growers, who would lose their reserved empire markets once preferences were curbed. Livestock industries also awaited a decent GATT deal. Without better concessions on wool, meat, and dairy products, preferences would remain. Minister of Commerce and Agriculture Edwin Macarthy considered resigning his post when he heard about the feeble U.S. offer on wool. The situation forced Canberra "to choose between defeat or withdrawal from Geneva," he cautioned.[29]

In talks with Macarthy and Coombs on April 24, Will Clayton explained that his hands were tied. Considering the wool bill pending in Congress, the binding was "pretty good," he believed. Australia would retain its share of the U.S. market, for American sheep numbers were low and demand was high. The State Department warned that a pushy Australia might arouse such sympathy for U.S. growers that Congress would refuse even to bind the current duty. Macarthy was flabbergasted. He could not tell Australians that "what they got at Geneva, a conference for the reduction of trade barriers, was a promise not to increase barriers to their exports and that, otherwise, things would be much worse!" Coombs added that the wool issue tested U.S. sincerity regarding multilateral principles. Clayton should ponder the "political consequences resulting from a failure of the Geneva negotiations." Put off by this threat, Clayton told the Australians that their withdrawal from the Geneva conference would be calamitous.[30]

Undeterred, Australia decided to suspend negotiations with the United States until the wool question was settled. In early May 1947 Canberra withdrew permission for its empire partners to waive preferences; they now could not bargain away margins. Worried about the domestic and international repercussions of the decision, Chifley ordered his minister of postwar reconstruction, John Dedman, to pack his bags for Geneva. The other southern dominions applauded Australia. South Africa had found the U.S. wool offer unappealing. New Zealand confessed that it was not so bad, but as the world's third largest wool producer, Wellington had nothing to gain from the Geneva talks except lower duties on the commodity. If negotiations broke down, held the dominions, the onus would be clearly on America's shoulders.[31]

When the Canadians and the British also took that position, the Americans knew they had to remedy the situation. Canada's Dana Wilgress, the mediator between America and the Commonwealth, welcomed Australia's decision to at least remain in Geneva until Clayton made the necessary concessions. The British also worried that an Australian walkout would not only take pressure off Truman to act but also undercut the export drive by destroying GATT and the ITO Charter. A public protest in Australia might move the president, but Britain preferred to work quietly, uttering a "serious warning to the Americans" that the binding offer and the wool bill were about to jeopardize years of international commercial planning.[32]

☙

America faced two tasks. One was blocking the import fee, the other was improving the wool offer. Paul Nitze, who headed the State Department's Office of International Trade, which advised the Executive Committee on Economic Foreign Policy, suggested that Clayton return home to fight the wool bill. Clayton could then hear out Winthrop Brown, of the Committee on Trade Agreements, who had proposed a maximum 50 percent tariff cut on fine wool to replace the binding. Halving the duty could be deferred to 1948, until a disposal plan for surplus wool had been devised. The Department of Agriculture dissented but Brown persisted. Without the offer, he warned, the GATT talks would pass the deadline of August 15, 1947, and Australia would stir up developing nations against the ITO. Clayton flew the thirty hours home and Australia's Coombs returned to Canberra for consultations. All eyes turned to Capitol Hill.[33]

Clayton arrived too late. On May 23 the House passed the wool bill, 151–65. Protectionists and farm-state legislators overran the liberal traders. Clayton was livid. Until the United States understood that its wool tariffs were excessive, he scolded, "it would be wise to view the proceedings at Geneva as a performance of somewhat academic interest." The British readied a formal protest in the event that the bill became law.[34] That response paled in comparison to the explosion in Australia.

There, politicians, the press, and interest groups lashed out that the U.S. Congress had shown a lack of respect for their nation. Parliament demanded that the prime minister send a delegation to Washington, D.C., to complain. Chifley refused. Yet he did send John Dedman, his top minister, to Geneva to let the Americans know that if Truman signed the bill, Australia would seek to adjourn the GATT meeting. Indeed, the stunned Chifley regarded the House approval of the bill as tantamount "almost to an act of international provocation." He would delay the GATT talks until the bill reached President Truman's desk.[35]

Both sides of the wool bill flooded Congress with arguments. The import fee, claimed the National Wool Growers Association and the American Farm Bureau Federation, jibed with Truman's escape clause order of February 1947 because it could be imposed with discretion. And the fee gave growers protection comparable to the quotas placed on other commodities. But the public opposed the fee, countered the free-traders. Secretary of State George Marshall sent pleas from the sick Cordell Hull and from former secretary of war Henry Stimson. They reminded senators of the "serious issues involved from the point of view of our foreign policy" regarding wool, a commodity that constituted just 1 percent of total U.S. farm income.[36]

Congress paid no heed. A conference committee considered the Senate subsidy bill alongside the severe House legislation. The committee included quotas as well as tariffs in the import fee provision, though it prohibited these protectionist measures from contravening a trade agreement. The Senate approved 48–36, ominously even with twelve Democrats in favor. Rejecting a motion by minority leader Sam Rayburn to recommit the bill, the House passed the conference committee report.[37] Only Truman's signature was left before the import fee bill became law. Only a presidential veto could save GATT from likely destruction.

While most Democrats, internationalists, and the State Department fumed, Truman readied his veto. Secretary of Agriculture Clinton Anderson had warned him that his 1948 electoral chances in eight western states hung in the balance. But Cold War diplomacy, and the fact that Vandenberg, O'Mahoney, and other legislators from wool states would accept domestic subsidies over protectionism, dictated his decision. The Senate vote also fell short of the two-thirds needed to override a veto. Thus, on June 26, 1947, the president announced that the bill "contains features which would have an adverse effect on our international relations and which are not necessary for the support of our domestic wool growers." Truman vetoed the protectionist wool bill, preferring subsidies to help growers. The American delegation in Geneva was ecstatic. Will Clayton called the veto "the greatest act of political courage that I have ever witnessed."[38]

Such hyperbole reflected his relief that the tariff talks had gotten new life. On the same day as the veto the Senate passed a subsidy bill, which the president signed on August 5 to the disgust of the Republican Right and wool growers. Clayton had already returned to Geneva to meet with John Dedman. On behalf of Prime Minister Chifley, Dedman now demanded a reduction in the U.S. wool duty. Clayton was willing, for a halving of the tariff would give him reason to insist on the elimination of important imperial trade preferences. Even a lesser offer would move the Commonwealth, he claimed. Dedman awaited American action.[39]

George Marshall refused to improve the U.S. wool offer until the wool bill controversy was over. Once it was out of the way, he informed Truman, a better offer was in order to win Commonwealth concessions on preferences and save the ITO Charter. But the secretary of state, wary of pressing his luck with Congress, would not halve the wool duty. He granted instead a 25 percent reduction, or 8½ cents on the 34 cents tariff, to be delayed to the following year so that the CCC and producers would have time to liquidate stocks at good prices. Attending to the death of his mother in Missouri, the president finally gave the go-ahead to Clayton on August 2. "The Boss and I know what Will is up against and hope he has luck," wired White House aide John Steelman to Geneva.[40]

The Australians were disappointed. Dedman and Coombs were instructed by Canberra to proceed with the negotiations, but both were angry at the skimpiness of the offer. Australia had secretly hoped for at least a 33 percent cut of just over 11 cents. South Africa wanted to hold out for more. Yet Coombs recognized that Clayton had run out of authority. Still, Chifley made clear that the 25 percent offer was inadequate.[41]

Dedman met with Clayton in Paris in mid-August during talks on the European Recovery Program. The minister insisted on a better wool offer, conjuring up fears that Australia's Parliament would not ratify GATT or the ITO Charter. Besides, U.S. growers would surely enjoy enough protection from a 17-cent tariff, along with subsidies. But he had reached his "absolute limit," said Clayton. The Department of Agriculture had resisted the 25 percent cut and Republicans could use that dissent to protest GATT, the ITO, and the Marshall Plan. Dedman reported back to the prime minister that Clayton would budge no more. The South Africans also tried but failed to move him. The Australians pledged to maintain pressure by withdrawing some concessions and asking Canada, New Zealand, and Britain to pull back offers on preferences for canned and dried fruit.[42]

The American offer stood, and it actually turned out to be a good deal for the dominions. The U.S. Tariff Commission found that the concessions established the lowest American wool tariff in decades. The positive response from Australian wool producers, and the outcry from American growers and O'Mahoney, proved that point.[43] In any case, Truman's veto of the wool bill and the new American wool offer jump-started the GATT negotiations.

The outcome of the wool conflict and the first months of the GATT negotiations had benefited the Commonwealth. Southern dominion wool growers would enjoy more access to the important U.S. market. Thanks to Truman's courage and skill in managing protectionist excesses at home, the GATT discussions had not been derailed. To be sure, America's tariff offers had not catalyzed Commonwealth partners to abolish imperial preferences. But because of the president's veto, by July American protectionists had ceased to be the primary concern of GATT negotiators.

Unfortunately for all nations in Geneva, the simultaneous collapse in British finances cast a darkening shadow over the GATT and ITO talks. The pall was felt most of all by Clayton and other free-traders. New, and ultimately insurmountable, financial and political obstacles blocked their drive to abolish Ottawa preferences. Of course, the Commonwealth was an impediment. But officials in the Truman administration itself, concerned about British economic health that related directly to their agenda of communist containment, also soon stood squarely in the way of free trade multilateralism.

CHAPTER 7

Concessions for the Commonwealth
1947

America went into the GATT talks in April 1947 to wrangle concessions on preferences from the British Commonwealth. That aim, the Americans had known from the start, would be difficult to attain. Yet they had no idea of the impact that the British financial calamity would have in Geneva. The collapse of the pound, and with it the hope that Britain could end its trade and exchange discrimination, worried U.S. policymakers and caused them to scale back their initial ambitions.

The Americans would cut tariffs to aid their allies, but they got back much less than they had hoped in return. The Commonwealth doggedly protected the fragile British economy, defending the Ottawa Agreement on imperial preferences. The result was that the General Agreement on Tariffs and Trade, shaped by politics, pragmatism, and national security imperatives, replaced free trade ideals.

Despite the solution to the wool crisis, Britain's financial situation bogged down the GATT negotiations. On June 5, 1947, America had announced the Marshall Plan to address the European dollar shortage and stabilize production in the region. Just over a month later, Britain honored the Anglo-American loan agreement and converted the pound into dollars. The new age of multilateralism lasted a scant few weeks, however, when disaster struck the British economy.

Even before this crisis, Board of Trade president Cripps disparaged the GATT talks. He resolved that offers in Geneva "should not lead to any comparable increase in imports into the U.K." Of the sixty-five U.S. requests pertaining to the preferences that Britain enjoyed in dominion markets, Cripps conceded only on margins of frozen salmon and motor bikes. No colonial preference was submitted that was important to America. The offers were "pitiable," Clayton told Cripps on July 12.[1]

Cripps relied on his wartime arguments, however. Britain had agreed not to raise or create new preferential margins and would work toward closing margins permanently. But U.S. concessions could be withdrawn and tariffs hiked whenever the Reciprocal Trade Agreements Act (RTAA) was renewed. Thus, preferences were a "matter for bargaining." In addition, until the dominions consented, Britain would concede nothing. Cripps recommended that if Clayton was unhappy, he should withdraw some offers to seek a better balance.[2]

According to Clayton, Cripps had repudiated every pledge since the Atlantic Charter of 1941. Britain was supposed to consult the dominions only in rare cases, not as a matter of course. Besides, Congress had never canceled a trade accord; tariff cuts had been permanent. In any event, it had been assumed that the British would phase out the Ottawa system. Congress would simply rebel at Cripps's offers. And Clayton would certainly not worsen a final deal by withdrawing concessions. He thus proposed that Britain gradually reduce preferences by 20 percent each year to clinch an Anglo-American bilateral agreement.[3]

When Cripps reported this plan to London, he knew it was unacceptable. For one thing, the dominions would balk. And, he noted, not all preferences could be eliminated. Summing up British feelings, C. T. Crowe of the Foreign Office wrote that "I am afraid we have still a long way to go in educating Mr. Clayton to the realities and needs of the U.K. position."[4] When Britain's finances came crashing down in early August 1947, that mission became the basis of British policy in GATT.

Chancellor of the Exchequer Hugh Dalton called 1947 "a pig of a year." Throughout Western Europe fluctuating currencies, huge trade deficits, scarce goods, and starvation supplanted forecasts of recovery. The region's dollar gap shot to $11.6 billion, up from $7.8 billion in 1946. In Britain, the crisis was debilitating. The payments shortfall reached $2 billion. As financial reserves dried up, inflation ruined Labour's expansionist money policy. Revenue from exports, shipping, and investments did not reverse the trade deficit. Coal shortages braked transport, reconversion plans, and construction. The cashing in of sterling for dollars under the terms of the Anglo-American Financial Agreement further strained Britain's payments.

In August Prime Minister Attlee changed course, suspending convertibility and returning to trade and exchange controls. Cripps imposed an austerity program in September, postponing the export drive and curbing

Clayton and Cripps square off in Geneva. (Courtesy Department of
Public Information, United Nations Photo Archives)

consumption of imports and nonessential luxury goods. Labour spenders
were vilified; Hugh Dalton resigned in November.[5] Britain could sacrifice
no more.

Hopes for free trade multilateralism vanished along with British reserves.
Britain would not expose its economy to the open market. On July 29 Foreign Secretary Ernest Bevin informed the Americans that Britain sought release from its obligation of nondiscrimination under the loan agreement
and London Charter. The country would still negotiate in Geneva, but
Cripps warned that the economic crisis portended that "Geneva would
produce no substantial tariff reductions." He suggested delaying GATT concessions until recovery began. Truman acceded to Britain's wish to embrace

discrimination once again, counting on the Marshall Plan to solve regional problems instead.[6] By doing so, however, he dealt a fatal blow to free trade dogma and dreams.

A pattern, developing since the first Anglo-American talks a half decade before, became entrenched in Geneva. Every time the Americans offered a way to reduce the Ottawa system, the British promised to consider the plan and then rejected it. For Clayton in particular, such resistance was irksome. The flag bearer of free trade in the Truman administration, he had set out to defend the principles of Cordell Hull. At this time, Clayton was also involved in formulating the Marshall Plan. But he was not to be distracted from his primary nemesis in trade: imperial preferences.

Standing in for Clayton in Geneva, Clair Wilcox wrote that the GATT talks were not going well. The Americans could obtain good deals with some nations but others were unpromising. France sought to convert its tariffs from specific to ad valorem duties by raising, not lowering, rates. But Britain was the biggest worry. London "had no intention of making concessions that involve any real progress toward the elimination of preferences," feared Wilcox. The British insisted that their original offers were fair. Attlee refused to take political risks and would, he complained, "extract every concession that we will make toward easing their short-run situation without making any appreciable concessions with respect to long-run trade policy."[7]

To convince Britain of his good intentions, Clayton thus improved his first phase-out offer. The Americans now reduced their requests to end preferences to just a handful of cases and insisted on gradual, progressive cuts in the large number of margins that would be left over. This proposal was bait for Britain, and it would show Congress that the State Department hoped to crack the Ottawa system. So far, tariff offers, aid, and consent to renewed currency discrimination had not moved the British. Without a deal on preferences, warned Wilcox, the entire trade program, and possibly the Marshall Plan, might be rejected by the Republican conservative Congress. That would also raise American resentment toward a seemingly ungrateful Britain, a close Cold War ally.

With these concerns in mind, Clayton headed a delegation to London in mid-August comprised of Wilcox and the U.S. ambassador to Britain, Lewis Douglas. They presented Cripps with new requests on preferences, approved by the Committee on Trade Agreements, under a revised phase-out plan. But Clayton hit a wall. Cripps replied that the dollar crisis limited his actions. Not only was he skeptical of America's willingness to import at adequate levels, but also the dollar gap made "multilateral trade almost an impossibility." In any case, he boldly concluded, Britain had lived up to its prior obligations by merely taking part in the tariff negotiations.[8]

This was all part of a shrewd bargaining strategy. As far as Cripps was concerned, GATT favored the Americans. High U.S. tariffs against British manufactures remained. He would not "reduce or eliminate preferences for nothing." But actually he had few options. The Labour and Conservative Parties, and unions as well, preferred protectionism in this time of distress. There was also the challenge of the "super preferential system"—the Western European customs union—supervised by the Marshall Plan. Clayton jumped at this reference. Such integration was not discriminatory. And Britain was more than welcome to join in a Western European free trade area in which preferences would gradually diminish, consistent with his phase-out offer. But Cripps agreed only to present the new list of American requests to the cabinet and respond by September 9. He held out little hope.

The frustrated Clayton immediately announced that a rejection of his list would be ruinous. He would either sign a feeble bilateral deal by withdrawing offers or he would adjourn the negotiations. He preferred the latter course. It might cast a pall over the International Trade Organization (ITO) and the campaign for the Marshall Plan, but Clayton was convinced that Americans would revolt against tariff cuts unless the Ottawa system was modified. After the Committee on Trade Agreements concurred, he suggested that Undersecretary of State Robert Lovett send a letter to Cripps reminding him of British commitments, American generosity, and the peril to the Marshall Plan without action on preferences.[9] Clayton had tired of British intransigence.

Yet the administration reined him in. Wilcox drafted the letter to Cripps in the event that America terminated the talks with Britain. Dana Wilgress of Canada pleaded with the British to concede. Paul Nitze's Office of International Trade Policy also prepared a message for the president to send to Attlee. Nitze frowned on Clayton's tough response, however. He expressed concern about a rupture between two nations allied against communism. That was also Lovett's concern.[10] The Cold War took precedence over free trade doctrine.

Preserving relations with a key ally led the administration to withdraw concessions rather than postpone the GATT talks, as Clayton desired. Lovett, Nitze, and even Harry Hawkins, one of the original free trade planners, agreed that reducing offers was the lesser of two evils. President Truman agreed. He refused to send the letter to Attlee. Clayton could send the Wilcox letter to Cripps only after Lovett had made sure it was consistent with the recent financial talks, in which the Americans had consented to British discrimination. The British economic crisis forced an end to Clayton's quest against the Ottawa system of preferences.

Officials feared that Clayton's idea to end the talks with Britain would thwart Cold War policy. Moscow would "exploit fully any such differences between [the] US and U.K. just as they are now trying to capitalize on British weakness by increasing pressure throughout Eastern Europe and [the] Near East," warned Lovett. Therefore, Clayton should obtain the best agreement possible by trimming offers. First, he could coax Britain to close margins of importance to the dominions. Then, he could withhold a number of offers until the current crisis had subsided and the United Kingdom was ready to negotiate. Surely, concluded Lovett, a "thin agreement" was "better than none."[11]

Lovett's view and Truman's decision were well advised, for the British were prepared to resist Clayton to the end. Although anxious about a breakdown, Cripps was alarmed by the request for "spectacular eliminations" of preferences.[12] He was determined not to narrow any margin that might damage British exports, even if that stance undermined GATT. He did not want that, but neither would he commit to U.S. demands. Perhaps concessions on a few more preferences might appease Clayton. Cripps began to develop this line of action.

On August 27 he suggested that the prime minister meet some American requests in return for more concessions. Cripps's plan involved subjecting less than 10 percent of British exports to the Commonwealth to competition by eliminating a few preferences. Once the dominions consented, the moderate concessions would give Clayton a face-saving agreement to take home. In return, Britain would demand that America open its market to two of the colonies' largest dollar earners, rubber and vegetable oils. Clayton had no authority to negotiate on these items; Congress regulated rubber production, and quotas regulated imports of vegetable seed oil. But Britain could end the impasse in Geneva, wrote Cripps, "by offering something of value and answering the criticism that London refused to carry out its commitments."[13]

The dominions were not impressed. They liked the linkage of Clayton's new list to rubber and vegetable oil concessions. In principle, they would narrow margins. But they countered that the Ottawa system should be used to lever open the U.S. market. The southern dominions wanted the United States to drop barriers on meat and butter imports. Claiming that the United States had made more appreciable offers on manufactured goods than on their primary products, they defended preferences to offset the access that America would enjoy in the empire. The United States must pay for this privilege. The dominions thus balked at Cripps's request to eliminate margins, and consultations on Clayton's list also got nowhere.[14]

Dominion stonewalling helped Attlee head off Cripps. The cabinet rejected Cripps's idea to abolish some preferences in return for U.S. rubber and vegetable oil offers. The Foreign Office had endorsed the compromise, seeking to prevent GATT from embittering Anglo-American relations and the Marshall Plan campaign. But the cabinet held that the plan would break up the empire. Attlee echoed these worries. Britain was being squeezed between the Americans on one side and the Commonwealth on the other. He just could not "see where we are getting to in these Geneva negotiations." Thus, he also spurned Clayton's phase-out offer. On September 10, 1947, a day after receiving the verdict, an angry Clayton broadcast from the Paris discussions on the Marshall Plan that the aid program would fail without adequate concessions from the Commonwealth.[15]

Five days later Clair Wilcox tried his hand at moving the British. If Attlee got his way, he noted, Britain would retain 80 percent of the preferences that favored its exports over those of the United States. The percentage for South Africa would be 76 percent, that for Australia 69 percent, for Canada 61 percent, and for New Zealand 35 percent. The colonies and Southern Rhodesia would keep 100 percent, India almost that much, and Ceylon and Burma 82 percent and 62 percent respectively. Also, a mere 7 percent of all preference margins would be abolished while 71 percent would be left untouched. Moreover, the colonies had not responded to America's $118 million in offers. America was obviously not "seeking scalps for our belts," Wilcox told an assemblage of Commonwealth delegates on September 15. Congressmen would not permit drastic tariff cuts, the regulatory provisions of the ITO Charter, and billions of dollars in aid "when they can see no immediate gains for the US," he admonished. Clayton required something to show back home for his efforts.[16]

Wilcox had a last offer. He would accept Cripps's original offers from April and postpone further requests on preferences for three years. After that, margins would be phased out over ten years on the condition that U.S.

tariffs continued to fall. Such gradual action would cost Britain very little for years. And the plan would dispose of the argument that U.S. concessions under the RTAA were temporary but British offers were forever.[17]

Clayton sent Cripps the Wilcox plan, a third offer that was a great gamble for the assistant secretary. He risked censure and ridicule in Congress. And Clayton had now retreated substantially from his cherished free trade beliefs.[18]

The Commonwealth worried about a breakdown in Geneva. Its representatives met the morning after Wilcox spoke, on September 16. The dominions wanted to clarify their position. They now hoped for an agreement on the basis of the phase-out plan, which they would gladly use as a basis for granting concessions. But they also would not revise the Ottawa Agreements if Clayton walked out.[19]

Meanwhile, the British assessed the larger implications of a collapse of the talks. The Russians had recently attacked the West at the United Nations and refused to participate in the Marshall Plan. The Foreign Office predicted that the GATT conflict would give Stalin an opening at the upcoming Council on Foreign Ministers' meeting in London to split Britain from the United States. The diplomats thus backed the U.S. plan. They explained that America would maintain its concessions for thirteen years but Britain would not have to take action for three years, until its economic problems had passed. In the meantime, the Americans would guard Western Europe's security.[20]

Cripps preferred to focus on the economics of the situation. He found Wilcox's analysis to be biased. Rather than look at the percentage of margins covering trade, the Board of Trade considered the volume and value of exports. Concessions in the dominions would amount to $108.9 million; reductions of British margins alone would be $83.3 million. Compare that to the American offer to Britain of $81.6 million in tariff cuts and bindings and then add in British offers. The United States came out the winner. Also, British offers affected more important items than America's. Cripps concluded that the United Kingdom had gone far enough. Circumstances had not changed; Britain still suffered a huge dollar gap. He hoped "that our American friends will not press us to go further by way of the elimination or reduction of preferences than facts and psychology make possible for us at this time."[21]

Meeting with the Americans on September 19, Cripps promised to hand Wilcox's proposal to the cabinet. But he warned Clayton not only to curb his ambitions against the Ottawa system but also to improve offers to the empire. Australia sought a better deal on wool and the colonies wanted more access to the U.S. market for rubber, their largest dollar earner. A cabinet study group had blamed declining rubber prices in Malaya on America's synthetic rubber industry. Rising colonial output, in tandem with U.S. production, had led to a world glut and thus falling prices. America, the world's top consumer of rubber, could remedy the surplus by buying more natural rubber from the colonies. The Americans would have to concede much more in GATT.

Clayton was at wits end. Wool was a done deal, he replied. And the United States had already scrapped most of its rubber industry and had bound rubber duties. To safeguard supplies in the event of an emergency, "mixing regulations" required that one-third of U.S. consumption be derived from domestic synthetics. But the colonies determined to reduce this ratio to one-fifth for artificial rubber. If America did not come through, said Cripps, most of the cabinet "would not shed tears if the negotiations broke down altogether."[22]

Such defiance led to a further erosion of Clayton's stance. Winthrop Brown, chief of the Committee on Trade Agreements, noted that the Clayton-Cripps talks had evidently revealed an unmovable impasse regarding the commitment on preferences. Clayton was the problem. If he ended his fanatical pursuit of the Ottawa system, a mutually advantageous deal could be reached. The Commonwealth counted on senior State Department officials to step in and put an end to free trade dogmatism. George Marshall, Dean Acheson, Robert Lovett, and Harry Truman looked beyond the trees of preferences to the forest of foreign policy concerns. They would promote Britain's solvency rather than lofty principles. Even Clayton's assistants boiled down the issue to the restraints of the dollar crisis, which weakened Cold War allies.[23]

Clayton pressed on, but the floor was being cut out from under him. Meeting on September 21 with Foreign Secretary Bevin and Cripps, he pointed out the negative domestic and global effects of Britain's trade policy. But Bevin confessed "that the British have not had much luck in living up to commitments which they have taken up in the recent past and do not want to take up commitments which they cannot live up to in the future." Empire isolationists had also rallied against the GATT "economic Disarmament Conference" and urged Conservatives to prevent the Labour government from trading away national interests. The cabinet would convene in two days to discuss the Wilcox plan, but the Americans predicted no good from the meeting.[24]

The discord raised anxiety levels in Geneva. GATT was in jeopardy; dozens of bilateral accords would unravel without an Anglo-American deal. The round might not just extend past its October 15, 1947, termination date, but it could break down entirely.

The dominions were particularly worried. Their bilateral agreements hinged on Britain's willingness to narrow margins in their markets. Canada's Dana Wilgress suggested a meeting of key nations to get the Americans and British back on track. Canada and Australia offered to put preferences on the table and sign accords with the United States. Having been released from the Ottawa Agreements in August, Canada was now irritated when Attlee reneged.[25] Clayton was not the only problem in Geneva.

Frustrated by British policy, the mediating Canadians nevertheless saw an American retreat as the only way out of the stalemate. Wrote Wilgress, Cripps had "been more catholic than the Pope." Along with the Colonial Office, Cripps's inward-looking Board of Trade had dominated the British delegation while its bureaucratic rival, the Foreign Office, was preoccupied with the Marshall Plan and peace treaties. Thus, in Geneva, Britain had lacked an appreciation of the wider issues involved in trade and had taken a decidedly anti-American line. The ploy of tying Britain's destiny to the Ottawa system had placed Attlee in a difficult political position. But the economic crisis rendered Britain "incapable of rational consideration of the Preference problem," noted Norman Robertson, Canada's high commissioner in the United Kingdom. America should turn down the heat.[26]

That had become the State Department's position. Good deals with other nations and agreement on GATT procedures were in sight. Winthrop Brown claimed that in "the overall picture of success, the comparative failure on preference negotiations will not loom large."[27] Goodwill would prevail, America would appear as a constructive leader, and the ITO Charter would be launched, ready to replace the Marshall Plan once conditions improved. Clayton's desire to walk out of the negotiations would provoke retaliation by the Commonwealth, kill the charter, and provide the Russians with the sort of negative propaganda concerning Western disunity that they savored.

Thus, assisted by Harry Hawkins, Brown devised a strategy to end the talks and guard Truman's flank in Congress. Australia must waive fruit preferences it enjoyed in empire markets for a halving of U.S. beef duties and an increase in butter quotas. A lowering of preferences in the colonies might also prompt a deal on rubber. Perhaps America could revise its offers on whiskey and a few other items to sweeten the pot for Britain.[28] When

Dana Wilgress of Canada, chairman of the GATT Contracting Parties and ITO Preparatory Committee in Geneva. (Courtesy Department of Public Information, United Nations Photo Archives)

the expected British rejection of the Wilcox plan came on September 27, these recommendations became the basis of U.S. policy.

In refusing the Wilcox plan, Cripps warned that if the Americans turned around and denied Marshall Plan aid to Britain, the likely collapse of their entire foreign economic agenda would hand a major victory to Stalin and the European communists. Cripps doubted that President Truman sought such an outcome. The cabinet banked on Secretary of State Marshall to control Clayton and elevate Cold War diplomacy over tariff dogmatism.[29]

Winthrop Brown.
(Courtesy Harry S. Truman
Library)

Diplomats now scrambled to avert a breakdown. U.S. ambassador Lewis Douglas softened Cripps's rather austere message by coaxing the British away from such a flat repudiation of Article VII. Cripps was miffed, but tariff negotiator James Helmore and Edmond Hall-Patch of the Foreign Office revised the message. Lord Inverchapel, the British ambassador to the United States, then approached Marshall—before Clayton got to him—and arranged for an interview. Bevin reminded Marshall that "it is surely a singularly inappropriate moment" for America "to be pressing us to take a considerable further step in the dark, merely, it would seem, to satisfy a doctrinal objection to a preferential system as such."[30]

Meanwhile, Winthrop Brown, who devised U.S. offers as head of the Committee on Trade Agreements, bypassed Clayton and worked in Geneva toward an accord with the Commonwealth. When he met with Herbert Coombs of Australia and Dana Wilgress of Canada, Brown learned that both would improve their preference offers in return for U.S. concessions. Coombs admitted that abolishing canned and dried fruit margins would be difficult, for they had nurtured infant Australian industries. Yet he would consider the proposal. Also, the Indian delegate, Sir Rahaven Pillai, agreed to apply pressure to Britain for a waiver on auto preferences. Brown, Wilgress, and Coombs set out, above all, to bring James Helmore back to Geneva to restart the bilateral bargaining. The British negotiator eventually agreed. Just two weeks before GATT's October 15 deadline, the talks became frenzied.[31]

On September 30, while he awaited Helmore's return, Brown described Geneva's beautiful scenery to Wilcox, concluding that the "only blots on the landscape are British preferences about which I spend most of the night dreaming." The night before, Coombs had tossed in another preference, on prunes, and held out hope on other fruits contingent on a halving of U.S. wool, beef, and butter tariffs. Although Brown sought a larger cut in auto preferences, an Australian-American deal was imminent. Cuts in apple margins enjoyed by Canada in the Commonwealth, as well an end to British preferences on cotton textiles in Canada, would also seal a U.S.-Canadian accord. The Committee on Trade Agreements now pondered withdrawing offers on valuable bone china and woolen textiles in anticipation of British resistance. But Brown determined to head off this retaliation. Asking for patience, he readied for Helmore's arrival.[32]

As dominion representatives hovered nearby, Brown and Helmore reached a compromise on October 2 that pushed forward the Anglo-American talks. Canada helped the British by postponing its release from the Ottawa Agreement. Helmore realized that Brown sought "some comparatively innocuous improvements on our offers as regards preferences, which will enable him so to dress up his statistics as to have what appears to him to be a chance of getting away with it with Congress." For his part, Brown expected opposition from his Committee on Trade Agreements for not getting more from the British. But he planned to ask the president, in person, to accept the deal. In the meantime, Helmore prepared additional offers on preferences in the event that they were needed.[33]

The Brown-Helmore plan hinged on American compliance. The United States would abandon the idea of gradual elimination of preferences, accept Britain's original offers, and shift its demands on margins from Britain to the dominions. The United States would also confine its withdrawals to items (for example, whiskey) that would not risk unwinding other agreements. Helmore then threw in a 20 percent reduction on British preferences in the colonies, subject to an adequate increase in U.S. rubber imports, and lowered auto preferences in India and the tobacco margin for Southern Rhodesia. The negotiators set a three-year grace period for narrowing margins and required future concessions. Brown then polished off the accords with Australia and Canada.[34]

Clayton reappeared, however. By this time, his only ally was his deputy, Clair Wilcox. Both worried about a backlash once Congress realized that it had been sold a bill of goods regarding preferences the year before to ratify the British loan. Panicked about reneging on his promise to eliminate the Ottawa system, Clayton lobbied Secretary of State Marshall to reject the Brown-Helmore deal. Marshall preferred to await Britain's response to the bargain before answering Clayton. He did send chills through Geneva by complaining to Canadian ambassador Hume Wrong about British policy. But faced with an appeal by Prime Minister Mackenzie King on October 8, Marshall promised to calm down Clayton.[35]

Meanwhile, the British looked favorably on the deal. With Clayton's previous demand deleted, the Ottawa system was secure. The auto, tobacco, and colonial offers might inflict some pain, but they were limited and would boost trade and development. More to the point, the Brown-Helmore proposals "do not represent the end of imperial preferences nor even a damaging inroad into them," concluded Edmond Hall-Patch of the Foreign Office, for only 3 percent of the total number of margins would be abolished, and a mere 17 percent would be reduced. Furthermore, Britain would benefit instantly from concessions but the United States would not profit from British reductions until 1951, when the dollar crisis was over and the Commonwealth ended import controls.[36]

Significantly, Cripps found no losses for Britain when he discussed the plan with Prime Minister Attlee. He agreed with Helmore that the concessions were on "window dressing items" of little concern. Phasing out the small 9 percent ad valorem motorcar and parts preference in India over six years was like selling a dying horse, as no nation cared much about the margin. The colonial preference offer could be withdrawn if the U.S. mixing regulations required more than 25 percent synthetic rubber. On the other hand, the deal could raise American imports by 4.7 million pounds a year, depending on consumption. And in light of America's fixation on tobacco, the cut in the preference enjoyed by Southern Rhodesia was moderate. In return, Southern Rhodesia, which had initially refused the concession, would be admitted into GATT. In sum, Brown's offers were advantageous to the Commonwealth.[37]

Cripps and John Dedman, Australian minister for postwar reconstruction,
enjoy the last laugh over Imperial Preferences. (Courtesy Department of Public
Information, United Nations Photo Archives)

On October 9 the cabinet approved the Brown–Helmore plan, minus
the offer to cut colonial margins by 20 percent. This exclusion provided the
last bit of drama in Geneva. British ambassador Lord Inverchapel informed
Marshall of the decision and had the gall to ask that the U.S. rubber offer remain in return for a reduction in Britain's canned fruit tariff. Wilcox ridiculed
that idea, as Congress surely would. Venting his frustration, Wilcox exposed
his free trade stripes. He called Cripps a "self-righteous man" who, like the
rest of the Labour Party, lacked "the courage necessary to compete in an
open market." Brown, too, was angry. He had gone out on a limb to help

the British and now learned that they had appealed behind his back to Marshall. Fears of a breakdown in Geneva were rekindled.[38]

Australia added to the tension. America sought concessions on preferences of fresh and dried fruit and, if possible, lower auto tariffs. Herbert Coombs refused to close the fruit margins enjoyed in Canada and Britain until he received compensation from them and the United States. Furthermore, the infant Australian auto industry needed protection. But he had a deal in mind. An improvement in U.S. wool and beef offers, the butter quota, and a ten-cents-a-bushel tariff cut on fresh apples—to go into effect only from May to July—would prompt cuts in Australian margins. When Brown agreed with all the terms except on wool, Coombs cabled home for concessions on raisins and canned fruit. He noted that without approval, Truman might withdraw the wool offer. Prime Minister Chifley made the deal. When the U.S. Department of Agriculture would not reduce the butter tariff below ten cents (Australia had sought a seven-cents duty) without a lower quota, Canberra countered by not halving the raisin preference in Canada. But the 50 percent cut of U.S. beef tariffs, when combined with the butter, wool, and apple offers, clinched the bilateral agreement.[39]

On October 11 the Committee on Trade Agreements approved the Brown-Helmore deal but withdrew offers to the colonies. Concessions to the latter, including the rubber-mixing arrangement, would not be approved until Britain restored offers on colonial preferences or granted other compensation. Truman drove home the matter in an aide-mémoire that recalled British pledges on preferences. Helmore understood that giving way would be of great propaganda value for the administration in Congress and "of little economic cost to us."[40]

With so much to lose, the cabinet relented. As Roger Makins of the Foreign Office told Bevin, reinserting the innocuous colonial offer would help the British economy, facilitate accords between the United States and the dominions, and promote Anglo-American relations. The Colonial Office, Board of Trade, and Foreign Office agreed. Although British exports of manufactures would suffer, earnings from the rubber concession would go into the sterling pool and protect dollar reserves. The cabinet restored the colonial preference offer on October 14, ensuring the U.S.-U.K. agreement.[41]

The British decision cleared the way for the conclusion of GATT. A relieved Winthrop Brown reported that crises had been resolved. He predicted that the General Agreement would be signed by the end of the month. Asking for plane reservations home, Brown assured Wilcox that international cooperation had prevailed. Wilcox should "think of the road over which we have traveled, the obstacles we have overcome, the things we have done which not only the world but many of our own advisers said were impossible—and be of good cheer."[42]

On October 17, 1947, the Anglo-American trade agreement was reached, accords with the dominions and colonies followed a few days later, and the first round of the General Agreement on Tariffs and Trade ended. The United States earned many benefits, but not like the British Commonwealth. Although few inroads had been made on imperial preferences, however, foreign policymakers were content with GATT. They willingly allowed trade partners to protect their markets as part of a national security agenda to prosecute the Cold War.

The results of GATT were impressive. America forged accords with twenty-two nations. These included supplementary deals with new members Burma, Ceylon, and Southern Rhodesia—for whom Britain initially negotiated—and Pakistan, born during the talks. A total of 106 bilateral accords, applied to all members in one multilateral agreement of 16 tariff schedules, covered 70 percent of world trade and half of global imports. Concessions would go into effect on June 30, 1948. The GATT protocol embraced rules of non-discrimination, equal treatment, and limits on preferences. Escape clauses and exemptions from trade agreements tempered these measures. The General Agreement thus incorporated protectionism under the banner of trade liberalism.[43]

Winthrop Brown heralded GATT in a note to President Truman. Representing "the most extensive action ever taken with respect to trade barriers," GATT not only culminated years of planning but also was "the first major step to be taken by important nations to reverse the trend toward trade restriction and economic isolation which has persisted throughout the world since the first world war." It aided the reconstruction of Western Europe under the Marshall Plan by laying a foundation for commercial cooperation. Truman called GATT a "landmark in the history of international economic relations."[44] Indeed, the Geneva round was unrivaled over the next two decades in the scope of tariff reductions and volume of trade covered by GATT.

American concessions were substantial, roughly two for each one received. This dropped U.S. average rates on total dutiable imports, weighted by 1939 data, to the mid-nineteenth century levels of 25.4 percent. Concessions affected three-quarters of imports, mostly from the Commonwealth and Western Europe. The State Department's claim that reciprocity had been the rule was, therefore, a cover to head off domestic critics. The United States granted concessions on $1.776 million worth of goods, much with the maximum 50 percent reduction. The improvements of offers to conclude deals with the Commonwealth were significant, regardless of how much Brown downplayed them.[45]

Dissent in the Committee on Trade Agreements, which approved the accords, indicated U.S. generosity. A vocal minority urged the president to reject the GATT deal. The Departments of War and Navy also opposed cuts on strategic items. Abstaining on the Anglo-American accord, Tariff Commissioner John Gregg believed that the State Department had signed a lopsided bargain. Indeed, the Americans had given Britain $584 million in concessions, 30 percent more than it won in return. The committee's mostly unanimous recommendations for improvements in U.S. offers disguised discomfort. They arose because officials thought it better to have an unbalanced multilateral agreement than none at all.[46]

Brown also put a positive spin on the concessions that the United States received. America won a total of $1.192 million in concessions, yet two-thirds merely froze tariffs at existing levels. The country would get indirect benefits from the multilateralization of other bilateral accords, estimated to exceed $150 million. Just under 80 percent of foreign tariffs against U.S. exports were reduced by one-quarter or more. Yet the U.S. delegation accepted less than its original demands, and in many cases concessions were granted on products of little importance to the Americans. In protest, dissenters in the Committee on Trade Agreements resisted five bilateral agreements.[47]

In addition, the way that the State Department handled the negotiations and set up GATT showed it to be a forum to benefit foreigners. Argued John Leddy of the State Department Office of International Trade Policy, if the accord had gone before Congress, "the whole thing would have been torpedoed" and not just by the protectionists but by moderate liberal traders. Thus, participants were called "contracting parties," which assumed that they had no commitment to future trade talks. The term "General Agreement" itself implied that no formal organization or budgets had to be ratified by legislatures. A secretariat would run negotiating rounds but GATT was provisional. Nations could withdraw at any time or inject safeguards into the forum without violating the rules.[48] The procedural norms allowed American trade partners, as well as the United States, to protect their economies.

The foreign response to GATT gave the clearest reflection of American goodwill. Britain had gotten its way. The Foreign Office exalted that Cripps had restored "equilibrium in our economic relations with the Western Hemisphere, and particularly the United States." Meanwhile, the dominions and colonies were assured of greater access to nonempire markets. That meant increased dollar earnings for the sterling area. Officials stressed that GATT clearly defined the objective of raising dollar exports without forcing sacrifices to the Ottawa system or the imposition of import controls. Except for socialists and empire isolationists, the British Parliament agreed with that assessment and ratified GATT on January 29, 1948.[49]

The British press generally applauded GATT. The accord was an achievement in a period of economic gloom. America had behaved as a proper creditor, and GATT had strengthened the Marshall Plan. The most serious criticism was issued by the *Economist*, but not as an indictment of GATT itself. Instead, it reflected the notion that aid policy, rather than the "mouselike" results of the Geneva round, was the only route to British salvation. Trade was simply insufficient at the moment for Western Europe. But the journal did proclaim, correctly, that the Commonwealth had loosened the "theological straitness of American [trade] doctrine."[50]

By and large, the Australians endorsed GATT. Confronted by Conservative Party critics, Herbert Coombs claimed that no cut in preferences had occurred without equivalent reductions abroad. Besides, until the dollar gap ended, the United States could not benefit from concessions it had won. Meanwhile, U.S. tariff cuts were a boon. Perhaps "easy to exaggerate the effects," noted the Australian cabinet, "it is clear that a serious endeavour has been made to open the United States' market to imports" for the first time in decades. Despite being denied a 50 percent cut in wool tariffs, Australia got almost everything it had asked for. The *Sydney Morning Herald* extolled the Geneva talks as a victory over U.S. protectionism.[51]

New Zealand's minister of finance and GATT delegation chief Walter Nash declared that his country had made a good bargain. The results maintained New Zealand's access to Britain but also opened up the new U.S. market. Despite the protests of empire protectionists and Conservative opponents, the New Zealand Labour government had done well in backing the Commonwealth's resistance to U.S. demands. The full slate of American requests to eliminate preferences had been denied.[52]

Except for the Conservative opposition, Canada also lauded GATT. Prime Minister Mackenzie King announced that Canada gained because the United States had cut tariffs affecting over 80 percent of Canadian exports. He was more effusive in his diary. Because the General Agreement was "much more far reaching than any reciprocity agreements in the past," Parliament would end its session "in a blaze of glory" by ratifying the agreement. Canadian prestige also ran high. Dana Wilgress had taken a large role in mediating the two major disputes: the Anglo-American conflict and the wool issue. Minister of Finance Douglas Abbott focused on GATT's contribution to solving the dollar gap and placing Canada's relations with its neighbor on a more intimate basis.[53]

The reaction of foreign governments might be interpreted as an effort to sell a bad agreement to skeptical legislatures. But in reality, the Commonwealth had succeeded in its objectives. It had opened up U.S. markets and had protected its own producers from unfettered import competition. A gentleman's agreement within the Commonwealth also allowed for tariff increases once preference margins could not be widened, thereby permitting Britain to hike its duties without violating GATT rules.[54] Idealistic American free-traders had met defeat in Geneva.

For instance, the resignation of Will Clayton tempered their enthusiasm. Exhaustion at the age of sixty-seven and the demands of his petulant wife were the explanations given for his retirement. Canadian Prime Minister Mackenzie King, however, believed that Clayton wished to dodge congressional charges of appeasement on the preference issue. His failure at GATT was a likely stimulus to his leaving. Clayton remained a special assistant to the secretary of state and oversaw U.S. policy on the ITO Charter and the Marshall Plan. A confirmed free-trader for the rest of his life, Clayton now tended to focus attention on aid, not trade, as a solution to immediate global economic problems.[55] He was content that America had liberalized tariffs. But he had not seriously damaged foreign protectionism. The British had gotten the best of him.

American metropolitan newspapers had first frowned on the talks but then bought the administration's line that GATT represented a light in a dark world. Erroneous claims were made, however, that the empire network had been broken. Yet many commentators were guarded. They saw GATT as a piece in the puzzle of European recovery but recognized that it was no answer to world ills. The benefits of trade liberalism would come in a distant future. In addition, *Time* magazine perceptively claimed that the "British led a successful attack on the U.S. freer trade program." In response, Wilcox defended State Department policy in Geneva. Yet even he admitted that

Britain had not granted all American requests.[56] U.S. sacrifices, however necessary, were sacrifices all the same.

In fact, American protectionists had every reason to grieve. They claimed that the administration had sold out U.S. interests and vowed revenge by defeating or emasculating the Reciprocal Trade Agreements Act in 1948, which they did. Butter, wool, and beef producers were livid at the concessions. Matthew Woll of the American Wage Earners Protective Conference complained to Truman that the concessions "exceeded all reasonable expectations in the number and depth of the tariff cuts agreed to." Never during hearings earlier in the year had the State Department indicated the magnitude of their planned concessions. Woll predicted, accurately, that GATT would cause a backlash against the RTAA and embarrass the administration.[57] And protectionists were largely correct about the American giveaway in Geneva.

Congress echoed these views. Senator Hugh Butler declared that GATT had proven that the State Department had "lost all touch with the realities of foreign trade." Other legislators hyperbolically warned that imports would ruin U.S. farmers; wool state senators dramatically lamented the passing of the sheep industry. But from his perch on the Finance Committee, the reasonable Senator Eugene Millikin claimed that GATT had cut tariffs to the point that "in anything resembling normal times would be catastrophic." He questioned whether the administration had lawful authority to negotiate beyond specific tariff schedules. And House Ways and Means chairman Harold Knutson predicted that when the extent of the concessions were revealed, State Department global do-gooders would pay dearly. Most moderates noted that the Geneva talks had been badly timed; economic crisis had prevented rational bargaining.[58] GATT, they declared, should have been postponed.

The Republicans, of course, were playing partisan politics by denouncing GATT. But it could not be denied that American import policy had been good to foreigners. And certainly Clayton's mission against the Ottawa Agreement had failed miserably. Thus, the protectionists stood on solid ground in denouncing the State Department.

The administration rebuffed these claims by lifting the debate out of the realm of trade and placing it squarely in its foreign policy and Cold War agendas. Truman absorbed the sacrifices at GATT and approved the results as a building block of his national security policy. GATT was a stepping-stone to the ITO Charter, which was instrumental to the recovery of Western Europe. Such recuperation was, in turn, essential to the containment policy.

The deal in Geneva was important because it strengthened Britain and other anticommunist allies.

American concessions at GATT were welcomed by the State Department. According to Robert Lovett, opening U.S. markets was the "greatest assistance which we can render to world economic recovery." Officials had "no need to apologize for the bargain we have struck," for the Cold War front against Soviet expansion had been fortified by GATT. Democrats in Congress rallied to this reasoning. They stressed that European recovery and containment depended on building trade relations through a liberal commercial agenda.[59] They looked beyond the giveaways in Geneva. GATT fueled American diplomacy in the Cold War.

It also paved the way for the ITO Charter. This document emerged from concurrent discussions of the Second Preparatory Committee in Geneva and then a larger meeting in Havana, Cuba. Like the GATT talks, debate over the charter posed American free-traders against countries seeking regulated trade. That conflict would be fought out in various provisions of the charter in 1947 and 1948. Negotiators pursued a new era of trade relations in which a universal code governed commercial practices. Little did they know that the era of GATT would outlast their efforts.

CHAPTER 8

The Compromise Charter
1947–1948

The charter of the International Trade Organization (ITO) was a product of the shifting fortunes of its chief authors. In 1947 the contrast between Western European power and that of the United States and the Soviet Union was striking. In production, defense expenditures, and military strength, Europe fell behind the budding superpowers. And a world divided into two blocs—communist and capitalist—placed Europeans in a dependent role for the first time in centuries.

For no other country was this more evident than Great Britain. The empire had shriveled; the British had withdrawn from India, Palestine, Greece, and Turkey; the dominions were forging their own security networks; and expansion at home had screeched to a halt. No longer master of its own house, Britain occupied, claimed a business executive, a "precarious" position in the "economic tussle between two of the greatest and wealthiest land-powers the world has ever seen." The long era of British power was over, supplanted by the American century.[1]

Britain looked to the United States for salvation, in aid and trade. The formalization of the Marshall Plan for European recovery in late 1947, as the trade conference in Geneva came to a close, was welcome news. While Congress considered the aid program, the British retreated to protectionism in defense of their economy. Thus, Britain and every other U.S. trade partner in Geneva based their considerations of the London Charter of the ITO on their own needs. They expected America to reconceptualize the code of rules and principles away from free trade ideals. This became the core struggle during the final drafting stages of the ITO Charter.

The eighteen nuclear nations began work on the London Charter in Geneva on May 16, 1947, a month after the GATT talks had started. Seventeen of them confronted American free trade doctrine. Developing nations, the British Commonwealth, and the Europeans set out to ensure that the universal code bore their imprint of trade regulation.

The plethora of proposed amendments to the London Charter indicated that the Americans were under fire. These allowances for trade discrimination threatened the integrity of the document. Claimed the worried Belgium-Luxembourg delegation, they pointed to "a trend in the direction of confirming each and every special privilege simply because it exists, and of condoning every form of restriction merely because it has become a habit." Clair Wilcox, the leader of the U.S. delegation, urged a return to the spirit of free trade multilateralism.[2]

The London Charter's chapter regarding investments showed why he issued this appeal. American business had demanded that the chapter protect its capital. Developing nations were alarmed. They believed that the London conference had written a "bankers' Charter," as India labeled it, to intrude in their economies. Czechoslovakia reminded the delegates how German investments had helped the Nazis infiltrate Czech politics. Britain feared that an investment code might backfire, for the developing nations might coalesce to restrict foreign activity.

The United States retreated by shifting the chapter to an article in the economic development section of the draft charter. The article now pushed investments to boost industrialization. By August, most developing nations endorsed the provision, but India demanded it be withdrawn and New Zealand never backed it. Wilcox was satisfied, happy to have gotten some protection for investors. Yet the weakened safeguards angered free-traders in the business sector at home as another compromise of market principles.[3]

The developing nations also protested Article 13 of the London draft. That article required them to petition the International Trade Organization to raise or impose tariffs and quantitative barriers. India and New Zealand proposed to delete this requirement to have a free hand at protection. Wilcox saw that as a threat to the charter; the obligation to seek permission was crucial to cooperation in the ITO. A showdown vote in July defeated the amendment, but Wilcox was compelled to insert a paragraph that implied permission would be easily granted. Developing nations were also given one year after the ITO went into effect to use protective devices. The deal won over all but Chile, Lebanon-Syria, and China. Wilcox later admitted that "we put in a couple of things we don't like" to beat back the Third World revolt.[4]

But he also did not halt the rebellion against free trade multilateralism by

Clair Wilcox.
(Courtesy Friends Historical Library, Swarthmore College)

advanced nations. The Commonwealth sought liberal escape clauses and regulatory provisions for employment. Even the United States had promoted some of the 70 escape clause amendments that offset the 170 commitments to liberalism in the London Charter. As New Zealand's Walter Nash explained, a flexible charter would "recognise that free enterprise is not in all cases the best way to prosperity."[5]

America battled, vainly, to protect its principles and interests. For example, Wilcox accepted state trading as long as it did not evade general rules of nondiscrimination and could not prevent a requirement for prior approval of export subsidies. But the issue of freedom to impose quotas epitomized the American compromise in Geneva. America had acquiesced to foreign demands on quantitative barriers in London, but now nations sought to whittle away all limits, complained Wilcox. The United States wanted the International Monetary Fund, not the International Trade Organization, to have the final say over whether payments problems justified discriminatory trade practices.[6]

A majority, including Canada, backed Britain's proposal for the ITO to make the decisions. Not only would the transition from war to peace take more time than allotted by the International Monetary Fund, held the Board of Trade, but also the dollar crisis required a free hand in obtaining imports by "any form of discrimination." Until the economic crisis eased, Britain would not bargain on controls. An IMF observer summed up that nations desired more "flexibility in the Charter than the U.S. is willing to concede."[7]

Wilcox backed away again. In a "Geneva compromise," quotas were added to a list of articles in the draft charter that dealt with exceptions to the policy of lowering trade barriers. The nondiscrimination rule was made less stringent than the tough Article 9 of the loan agreement. Wilcox insisted that the U.S.-dominated IMF play a prominent role, however. In the Geneva compromise, the Fund had to be consulted. But import and exchange controls, frowned on in principle, would nonetheless be allowed after the transitional period.[8]

A bitter Anglo-American dispute over U.S. film exports showed the importance of such quotas. This conflict reflected cultural tensions as well as the depth of Britain's economic crisis in 1947. And it demonstrated Prime Minister Clement Attlee's ability to confront U.S. free trade principles.

The conflict arose from the British financial crisis. Along with tobacco, films represented 40 percent of the value of U.S. exports to Britain. The austerity plan of September 1947 targeted both; the Board of Trade put "food before fags" and "films."[9] And the people consented. Only 15 percent of those surveyed wanted the remainder of the U.S. loan to be spent on these luxury items. The government thus decided to enhance wartime regulations.

Restrictions on U.S. studios already were in effect. They were prohibited from taking home most of their earnings from Britain. In addition, the number of foreign films in Britain was limited by a quota. Of the films shown by theaters, 20 percent were required to be British. Because British exhibitors could not fill the quota, the restraint was not onerous for the Americans. But a proposed Cinematograph Act called for an even higher domestic quota. The government and film industry also sought to expand Britain's infinitesimal British movie sales in America, a market four times the size of Britain's. Big British producers like the Rank Organization negotiated better marketing arrangements. Because they were discriminatory, however, British screen quotas bothered the Americans more than the threat of competition.[10]

Because screen quotas amounted to discriminatory internal regulations, the State Department claimed that they violated Article 15 of the ITO Charter. The British had rejected the article on internal regulations in London, but it was referred to a drafting committee before the Geneva talks. Britain then attached an amendment that exempted films from the requirement of liberalization in Article 15. America stood alone in Geneva against this escape clause. The State Department recommended that Britain gradually end discrimination against U.S. movies. If that did not work, Wilcox could demand a freezing of discrimination at the current 20-percent-quota level.[11]

The battle was joined. The Motion Picture Association of America (MPAA), headed by Eric Johnston, formed an export group in 1946. A former president of the U.S. Chamber of Commerce, Johnston was a self-made businessman, a defender of free enterprise, and a Republican presidential hopeful. He had a plan to solve the film problem by promoting wider distribution of British films in America. Britain could earn $15 million in 1947 and double that the next year. Recognizing the predominance of U.S. studios, British producers viewed this idea as an empty promise and refused to negotiate.[12]

The U.S. delegation in Geneva then worked against the amendment to Article 15. The Republican Senate Finance Committee readied a retaliatory duty on film imports, but most of the Commonwealth still defended the exception. Don Bliss of the State Department suggested instead a three-year freeze on screen quotas in the nine nations that had them. This "breathing spell" would head off Congress and allow Britain to generate revenue from movie exports. The standstill was also consistent with America's acceptance of quotas during the transition period.[13]

Because the MPAA's Eric Johnston had little hope for the Bliss proposal, he sought a year's delay on the Cinematograph Act. That would save dollars and help Arthur Rank's distribution monopoly thrive. But small independent producers, who relied on protectionism, rejected the plan. Because they were backed by trade unions, the governing Labour Party listened to them. Bliss then proposed a deal through GATT. America would submit a supplementary tariff request on films to counter British offers on preferences. But this also had no support. Bringing tariffs and preferences into the picture would provoke domestic critics in both nations. The State Department conceded the fight in late July and backed a new provision in the draft charter, Article 19, that permitted an escape from discriminatory rules for screen quotas. Johnston grudgingly accepted but the British refused to give this inch. In fact, they got even tougher.[14]

The financial crisis prompted Attlee to declare a "second Battle of Britain," with tobacco and films as two battlefields. To America's chagrin, he hiked the tobacco tariff. Now he added an ad valorem tax on foreign movies to be applied on the highest possible value. The measure defied Britain's pledge at previous conferences not to raise tariffs. Eric Johnston was outraged.[15]

The Americans looked for ways to satisfy Britain. Johnston told top British officials that Hollywood not only backed Article 19 but also supported a plan to block 25 percent of film remittances to America. That is, no more than one-quarter of the receipts from U.S. movies would leave Britain until the payments account was in balance. The other three-quarters would be appropriated by the government to support the pound. That proposal was accepted, but the same day Parliament hiked film duties by 300 percent ad valorem.

Never before had the British government placed levies on the gross receipts of both producers and distributors. The Americans were shocked. "For the British to produce a new weapon at this time signals an intention quite contrary to the spirit at Geneva," complained the U.S. embassy in London in August 1947. American diplomats suspected a cynical attempt to increase British bargaining leverage at GATT and in the ITO Charter talks.[16]

The MPAA retaliated. After a three-hour meeting on August 8, Johnston announced a boycott on films to Britain to protest the prohibitive tariff. Yet British producers saw this embargo as an opportunity to seize a greater market share. And Attlee stuck by the import tax. Polls showed that 58 percent of the British people approved the duty even though the backlog of U.S. movies would eventually run out. The boycott proved more effective than the tax, but the ITO bore the brunt of the dispute. As nations looked ahead to a world trade conference in Cuba, President Truman told Johnston that America and England "might as well throw their whole Havana Charter into the waste paper basket" if they failed to solve their film feud.[17]

In Geneva, Article 19 to the charter became acceptable to Britain. Screen quotas would be granted but they could not be raised, nor could new ones be introduced. But Eric Johnston refused to endorse the article until the "confiscatory tax" was terminated. As usual, Clair Wilcox put the best face on compromise, claiming that the article swept aside discrimination against Hollywood. Yet the British tax and the American boycott continued to poison trade relations until Britain lifted the levy in 1948.[18]

The British tax was discriminatory. Only U.S. producers would be faced with the tariff, which amounted to more than their expenses in Britain. Worse, disguising a tariff as a tax set a dangerous precedent for nations seeking protectionism. Indeed, Australia and Argentina had raised duties on several items after the movie fee went into effect. Attlee's cabinet soon realized that the U.S. boycott hurt more than the tax helped. Theaters at home complained of declining audiences while British studios faced retaliation against their films in the United States. The burdensome tax was also ill-timed, for Republicans would look for any reason to reject the Marshall Plan in 1948.[19]

By February 1948 Britain offered to end the tax and allow the exhibiting nation to keep the proceeds earned from a limited number of films. At month's end, Chancellor of the Exchequer Stafford Cripps and Board of Trade president Harold Wilson met with Eric Johnston. Initially, Wilson refused to budge on the tax. But Johnston proposed that U.S. producers be allowed to keep a higher proportion of their British earnings as long as much of the revenue remained in Britain.[20]

On March 11 Britain repealed the tax and replaced it with permission for U.S. filmmakers to distribute 180 movies in the country and remit home 17 million pounds a year in income. Under this four-year accord, surplus earnings, estimated at 10 million pounds a year, had to be spent in the sterling area on projects approved by both nations. This would guard foreign exchange reserves. Furthermore, U.S. earnings sent home would rise only if profits from British films in the U.S. market increased. The agreement flooded Britain with films withheld during the embargo at the same time that second-rate Rank films were released in America. Johnston had continued Hollywood's dominance in British theaters, albeit due to audience preference.[21]

That the market seemed to decide the fate of the struggling British film industry prompted Harold Wilson to strike back with the Cinematograph Film Act of 1948. A provision required that 45 percent of the movies shown in Britain had to be domestically produced. In the face of American anger, Wilson defended this quota. Americans have "so long enjoyed a predominant position in this market that they have come to regard it as their right," he argued. Besides, the quotas would protect British reserves. The United States had no recourse but to protest the measure as detrimental to Anglo-American relations. In the following years, however, not even the British movie industry could defend the quota. It gradually fell to 30 percent, in 1950, where it remained for thirty years.[22] But it was clear to the Americans, in Geneva and beyond, that Britain would defend its right to impose quotas of any sort deemed crucial to its economy.

The film dispute, as well as the Geneva Charter and the Cold War, impeded U.S. free trade universalism. The ITO—a sort of economic United Nations —had been the ultimate objective of the American planners. Now they were resigned to a brand of universalism that permitted government intervention. But they still hoped that all countries, including the communists, would participate in the grand project.

Clair Wilcox held that America won "virtually 99%" of its aims in the Geneva Charter. His basis for this incredible claim was that the draft limited escapes from multilateralism. While preoccupied with the GATT crisis, Wilcox had presided over the longest period in diplomacy of intensive collaboration on a single document. A code now applied uniform rules to all sorts of commercial behavior.[23] That was an accomplishment.

But free-traders were prone to misrepresentation. That nations had recognized their interdependence for the first time was less meaningful when the dozens of exceptions in the trade code were taken into account. Provisions in the Geneva Charter might have been "clearer, more concrete, tougher, and more workable," but contrary to Wilcox's view, they betrayed free trade ideals.[24]

That was apparent to foreigners. Only leftists, with exaggeration, criticized the document as too market oriented. The Commonwealth was happy. The draft realistically addressed the recovery and development needs of the British nations. Careful scrutiny revealed, said Australia's minister of postwar reconstruction John Dedman, that "the only really important trading country which will be subject to all the restraints which it imposes on the conduct of commercial policy for a long time to come is the United States." These remarks were designed to sell the charter to the Australian Parliament. But Clair Wilcox had been very enlightened, indeed.[25]

In the United States, internationalists applauded the Geneva Charter, but members of the business community scorned it. Any accord, whatever its content, was a step forward in the current era of tension and uncertainty. Yet business commentators were nervous. To be sure, Wilcox had sensibly bent to foreign demands. The escapes showed "that the U.S. knows that any other kind of charter doesn't have a chance in today's world," wrote the editors of *Business Week*. But the Geneva compromise set a dangerous precedent for statist regulation.[26]

The charter irritated free trade purists. The U.S. Chamber of Commerce disliked the interventionist employment and development clauses, and the National Association of Manufacturers found many provisions "far out of conformity with American principles." Business hoped that exceptions would be cut, investments given more safeguards, and sections on cartels and commodity agreements rewritten to promote competition. For NAM, "the one thing worse than having no International Trade Organization" was "to have a bad one" that menaced the private enterprise system.[27]

That the charter demanded American sacrifices also inflamed protectionists. The American Products Council called it a "ridiculous document" that would get the administration laughed out of Congress. Many legislators believed that the document would undermine the welfare of their constituents. Combined purist and protectionist dissent further undercut free trade ideals.[28]

Even more ominously, the Cold War intervened in the drive for free trade universalism. The Soviets had not shown up in Geneva. Wilcox had decided to use a carrot-stick approach to coax the communists into the trade organization. It had included state trading provisions to lure them, but he also sought a "strong rule" against nonmembers to deny them the benefits of the charter if they refused to join. There were pitfalls in such a tough stance. Russian satellites might balk at the ITO or the Soviets might cut back commodity exports to Western Europe and prevent these nations from joining the Marshall Plan. But American diplomacy had already confronted the Soviets in Eastern Europe. The strong rule against nonmembers would either persuade the Russians to cooperate with the West or contain the communist bloc behind a wall of capitalist commercial discrimination.[29]

Although the Russian press covered the Geneva talks, Western observers believed that Joseph Stalin sought to upend the charter. Soviet theorists predicted an imminent American depression that would intensify class conflict and hasten a worldwide communist revolution. The capitalists would attack Russia as a ploy to divert attention from such domestic woes. Doing business with the United States to strengthen producers there was, therefore, not a Russian interest. Furthermore, the Geneva talks were merely an insidious effort by the Americans to dominate the world economy by demanding that vulnerable nations open their markets, believed Moscow. As Truman's executive order showed, however, the United States would willingly shut out imports from its own allies.[30]

By mid-July, after the Russians had attacked the ITO and the Marshall Plan, Wilcox abandoned hope of Soviet cooperation. Moscow claimed that it lacked personnel to send to Havana, although Stalin managed to send over one hundred delegates to the Marshall Plan conference in Paris as the Havana meetings got under way. He advocated the strong membership rule in the charter. Socialist-leaning nations like Australia wanted to woo the communists, but Wilcox claimed that economic interdependence did not interest the Russians. With British help, the United States offset a Czech proposal for a weak rule on nonmembers. The choice, said Wilcox, was between an ITO that excluded the communists or a weak trade organization that accepted all nations. He preferred the former, even if it meant giving up on universalism.[31]

The Geneva draft was completed on August 15, 1947, with the expectation that the United Nations would meet in Havana, Cuba, in November to perfect and sign the ITO Charter. Wilcox was prone to typical boosterism. He ignored the troubles posed by the communists, developing nations, and friends alike by exalting the draft as a fulfillment of American designs.

On November 17, the day before the Conference on Trade and Employment opened in Havana, President Truman convened a special session of Congress to seek passage of funding for the Marshall Plan. He did not mention the ITO but the relationship was clear. Multilateral trade would be a long-term replacement for aid. As Will Clayton explained from Havana, assistance to Western Europe "would be a temporary and emergency program" for the region "to help itself get back on its own feet, whereas tariff and ITO negotiations at Geneva are intended to produce results of a permanent character in putting the world back on the road to economic peace." The ITO Charter and the Marshall Plan were complementary.[32]

Several suggestions circulated to make the Marshall Plan conform to the charter. Western Europe should abandon trade preferences and move toward a nondiscriminatory customs union that fit ITO rules. Discrimination for balance-of-payments reasons and export controls for commodities in short supply under the Marshall Plan also had to adhere to limits allowed in the charter. The ITO's state-trading articles might be adopted by the European Recovery Program while allocation and production had to be consistent with the cartels and commodity chapters of the trade code.[33] Integrating charter principles into the recovery agenda would facilitate the smooth operation of the ITO once normal economic patterns had returned to Europe.

But the Marshall Plan also signified the harnessing of trade toward political ends, now even for diehard free-traders. "If the countries of Western Europe must resist Communism in conditions of cold and hunger and economic frustration, they will almost certainly lose the battle," warned Clayton.[34] Such an appeal sold the Marshall Plan, but at the expense of the ITO Charter. The American loan had just about run out, and GATT concessions would advance recovery too slowly. A more direct, concerted assistance package was needed. That made a universal trade code useless in a world in economic crisis, divided by ideological barriers.

As the Havana conference continued into March 1948, the Cold War increasingly loomed as a factor against free trade universalism. Military discussions drew up a Western European defense pact, the basis of the North Atlantic Treaty Organization (NATO) the next year. The fall of Czechoslovakia's democratic government in February, under Russian pressure, prompted the U.S. Senate to authorize $6.2 billion under the Foreign Assistance Act on March 13, 1948, to combat communism. In June, as the Soviets began the blockade of Berlin, Congress appropriated $12.4 billion in Marshall Plan aid. Meanwhile, America reversed its policy of reform in Japan, restoring the power of prewar industrial oligarchs in order to build Japan into a strong partner in the Pacific. At home, a search for supposed communist subversives intensified. The Cold War consensus put in question the notion that nations could be united by universal ideals.

Strategic, anticommunist realities slowly subverted free trade doctrine and politicized the world trade arena. Congress demanded a withdrawal of

GATT concessions to Czechoslovakia to protest the communist coup. Worried Western Europeans cringed at this appeal for economic warfare. France and Britain counted on trade with Eastern Europe for their recovery. But containment of Russia compelled the use of trade as a strategic weapon, insisted the Americans. For the time being, they did not pull back tariff cuts granted to the Czechs. But Truman imposed controls on exports to the communist nations.[35] The Cold War undermined the plans developed during the Second World War.

All but three of the fifty-six nations in Havana signed the Final Act of the Charter on March 28, 1948. Differences were so deep from the outset of the meetings, however, that the delegates missed the original termination deadline of January 15. Accord was largely a product of the Cold War. That is, America conceded ground because of a concern that the Soviets would make political capital out of a breakdown in Cuba.

In Havana, as before, the problem lay with exemptions to principles of free trade. The expansion of planning talks to several dozen nations resulted in a staggering eight hundred amendments to the Geneva draft. The developing world proposed most of these, attacking the notion that the big powers deserved to dominate the world economy. Clair Wilcox, deputy to U.S. delegation chief Will Clayton, believed that the Latin Americans saw Havana as a dress rehearsal for the Bogota Inter-American Economic Conference, at which they would demand a Marshall Plan for their region. They challenged every chapter of the Geneva draft and threatened its integrity, he complained. In response, Clayton summoned a group of nuclear club members to defend the work of the Geneva meeting.[36]

Led by the Latin Americans (particularly Argentina), Australia, and India, the thirty-nine developing countries in Havana had leverage. First, solutions to the European dollar gap hinged on trade with overseas territories and underdeveloped nations. Second, the Cold War made them important. The Soviets, who did not appear in Havana, claimed that Clayton had gathered the nuclear club to deal with the rash of amendments in order to extort good behavior from poor countries. Russia suggested adjournment, for America had "disclosed its imperialist designs." Indeed, the developing nations had felt excluded from the planning agenda of the rich countries.[37]

They provided the dramatics in Havana on nearly every issue. Allowances for taxes and preferential trade networks, reducing price disparities between raw materials and manufactures, and inclusions for social security guarantees were amendments aimed at fueling development. The chapters on cartels and investments were assailed for benefiting strong nations, the state trading section for not giving governments enough freedom. A Greek proposal called for special protection for key commodities (in Greece's case, tobacco and currants). That the Latin Americans led the revolt worried the United States. America believed that they would be susceptible to pressure because Brazil, Chile, and Cuba had been associated with earlier drafts of the charter. But with their "industrialization fixation," wrote J. Robert Schaetzel of the U.S. delegation, they sought "unequal and more onerous obligations" from advanced nations.[38]

The extremist Argentina, Uruguay, and Chile often did not agree with moderate Colombia, Cuba, and Brazil, but all the developing nations disdained the draft charter. Simply lowering trade barriers would not suffice for them. Instead, a philosophy of protectionism, government regulation, and resistance to imperialism must undergird the document, they demanded. Thus, Ramon Bateta, Mexico's secretary of finance and public credit and delegation chairman, argued that the ITO was "of a negative quality since it sought rules and methods of abolishing trade restrictions instead of accentuating the positive solutions" to development problems. He proposed eighty-five amendments to reshape the charter. Wilcox viewed most of them as a mockery of multilateral principles.[39]

Yet even developed countries sympathized with this assault on U.S. dogma. Britain criticized Clayton's opening speech as a disappointing rehash that free trade could overcome global ills. The dominions remained steadfast proponents of regulation. The Associated Chambers of Manufacturers of Australia sounded every bit the Third World critic. In January 1948 it campaigned for trade discrimination so that Australia would not "be swamped completely by the dominant, powerful nations" of the world.[40]

The Commonwealth and the Western Europeans rallied to the multilateral cause of the charter, but they also endorsed the use of quantitative barriers in development. The British joined the Americans to confront the more exorbitant Third World proposals. Yet because they had also asked for an exemption from the rule of nondiscrimination in Article 23, it was only fair to let the developing nations have similar protection. The Board of Trade authorized a limited escape clause to protect infant industries, under which the poor countries would have to seek prior approval before instituting import controls. That approach would save the Havana meeting but erode free trade principles a bit more.[41]

Wilcox focused on winning approval of the Havana Charter from a bare majority of thirty nations. He cultivated moderate southern dominions and Latin Americans and lashed out at many amendments as examples of self-pity, selfishness, and political grandstanding. He also used clever tactics to quell the Third World rebellion. For instance, Wilcox had the Mexican Bateta appointed chairman of an Economic Development Committee to consider exceptions to the charter. Wilcox gambled that Bateta would bring the Latinos into line and undermine the extremists.[42]

These countries looked to the Economic Development Committee to serve as an autonomous agent working on behalf of the Third World within the ITO. Advanced nations refused them, but they did agree to place decision-making power over tariff rates in the ITO's executive board, on which the developing countries won substantial representation. Latin Americans also managed to revise the charter to prevent punishment of those nations that did not fulfill their commitments to reduce tariffs.[43]

The developing countries got additional concessions. The Havana Charter safeguarded investments, allowing expropriation only on just terms, subject to the review of the ITO. Mexico's amendment to deny foreign investors access to diplomatic aid was turned away. But America received no positive guarantees; hosts retained sovereign rights over property and could interfere with investments. In addition, they were granted leeway to create regional tariff networks, replete with preferences approved by the ITO. These countries were also satisfied with the economic development chapter.[44]

Squabbles between rich and poor countries threatened to derail the six-week-old Havana talks by the New Year. Wilcox lamented his inability to "obtain general acceptance for anything approaching the Geneva draft." Further delays would not give Congress time to ratify the charter in the 1948 session. In June, moreover, the Republicans would consider their own version of the Reciprocal Trade Agreements Act. That legislation, along with the Marshall Plan and tax and price control bills, would tie up Congress. But the possibility that high-ranking officials had lost interest in the charter was even more alarming than bad timing. The campaign for the Marshall Plan in Congress took top priority. If difficulties persisted at Havana, the administration might simply abandon the ambitious ITO Charter, especially as the presidential election neared.[45]

But disputes continued into March 1948. One major point of contention, a carryover from earlier talks, dealt with treatment of the former Axis powers. The United States sought to extend the charter's rules to Germany and Japan so that these occupied nations would enjoy the benefits of multilateralism. Both were crucial to trade in their regions and a burden on the American treasury, which financed the occupation forces. The United States had suggested in Geneva giving them equal trade treatment or most-favored-nation status. France, Britain, New Zealand, Australia, Czechoslovakia, and Poland had opposed the idea. At Havana, the U.S. delegation looked for alternatives, eventually proposing an amendment to Article 99 that called for the ITO to study the issue of most-favored-nation treatment.[46]

Tired of paying occupation costs, the U.S. army advocated such an approach. American general Lucius Clay's German occupation government would comply with the provisions of the charter as long as the ITO recognized two circumstances. First, a uniform exchange rate did not yet exist to provide for stable commodity prices. And second, there was a moratorium on new foreign investment in Germany until the creation of a government. Both situations were temporary but would require exceptions to the charter's payments and investment provisions. In Japan's case, occupation supervisor General Douglas MacArthur approved of the charter. Quota controls were necessary to correct a payments imbalance, but Japan would abolish state trading, endorse the provisions on subsidies, welcome higher levels of investment, and revise the country's tariffs to adhere to GATT.[47]

Other nations were edgy, however. Adherence to the charter was a political act that entailed recognition of the pro-Western zone of Bizonia in Germany, which might anger the Soviet Union. Britain and France thus hesitated. Economics was also a concern. That Germany and Japan would get access to markets frightened neighbors who had been victims of their autarchic aggression in the past. Holland, Denmark, India, Belgium, and most of Latin America supported most-favored-nation treatment for Germany. But America's proposal challenged the security of France and Britain. They preferred that Allied Control Authorities remain in command over the trade of the occupied nations and that the issue be deferred at Havana until experts could study the problem.[48]

The Americans adamantly stressed that most-favored-nation status was critical. German trade was critical to European recovery. It was better to risk angering the Soviets, and the withdrawal of their satellites from the ITO, than not have such potential Cold War allies as Germany and Japan adhere to the charter. Secretary of the Army Kenneth Royall reminded George Marshall, moreover, that Congress would not ratify "a charter containing such discrimination against the areas for which we are financially responsible."[49]

But the opponents prevailed. Under Article 99, the Havana delegates decided to give the ITO merely investigatory powers to explore German and Japanese trade. The extension of most-favored-nation treatment would be included, perhaps, in the European Recovery Program and in the China Aid Program.[50] Unable to overcome wartime fears of the Axis powers, the United States lost this battle in Havana.

This issue typified the difficulty the United States had with its allies, especially the Commonwealth. The Canadians, for instance, came up with a means of preserving export subsidies in certain cases, yet Wilcox was not so lucky in preventing exceptions to the rule of nondiscrimination under Article 23. America tried again to require nations with balance-of-payments deficits to seek approval for controls from the International Monetary Fund. Worried about a backlash in Congress against the Marshall Plan, the Americans wanted Britain to honor its commitment not to discriminate in trade and finance. But in Havana, all nations except the United States endorsed a Czech proposal to allow ITO members to resort to controls.[51]

The British held to the Geneva compromise. They wanted ITO rules and Article 9 of the loan accord superseded by the Marshall Plan, which extended the period of discrimination into 1952. They also opposed prior approval. Wilcox defended the principle of nondiscrimination as a cardinal doctrine of the charter, but the Bank of England's Lucius P. Thompson-McCausland hoped that "more senior officials capable of wider vision than is found in the lesser priesthood here" would rule in Britain's favor.[52] That stance caused a crisis in Havana so serious that the charter's completion was delayed until mid-March 1948.

When Wilcox held to his position, the Board of Trade's Harold Wilson gave U.S. ambassador Lewis Douglas an aide-mémoire that protested American rigidity. But administration officials let Wilcox decide policy on Article 23. In early March he announced that the matter was closed; if Britain persisted, then the United States would exit from the conference. Some British officials angrily claimed that Article 23 "still smells too strongly of I.M.F. dictation" and hence American free trade dogma.[53]

But the ensuing accord afforded a way out of the stricture on nondiscrimination. As the final arbiter of escape clauses for balance-of-payments reasons, the IMF would dictate policy after March 1, 1952. Under Article 23, however, nations could choose the proposal of the London draft that used the transitional era set by the fund (the American preference) or the Geneva version, in which the recovery period would last until the fund intervened. Britain took the "Geneva option." The country would, therefore, enjoy much freedom to impose trade and exchange controls. The elastic Article 23 permitted an escape hatch that undercut free trade principles.[54]

Article 21, which limited the general use of quotas for balance-of-payments reasons, was similarly flexible. America sought a prohibition on import and exchange controls but conceded that the only option was deflation and its attendant negative social and political consequences. The provision thus limited quotas "to cases of real financial necessity," under the watchful eye of the IMF, wrote a U.S. delegate. But Articles 21 and 23 reflected an American retreat necessary to convince Britain, France, and others to sign the Havana Charter.[55]

Wilcox traded principles for expediency in Havana. If he had not done so, the talks would have broken down and thus subverted the anticommunist alliance, or so administration officials feared. Warned State Department analyst Joseph Coppock, the West "would be without a rudder in the international economic sea" without the ITO. Delighted by the trade warfare within the Free World, Stalin would coax disgruntled nations to his side. Truman would respond by directing the U.S. economy with controls. Such state intrusion would undermine the American way of life because of "the close affiliation of capitalistic economic arrangements and political and civil liberties." The menace to democracy, as well as the tensions among Western allies, would give the Republicans a platform from which to attack the president in the election campaign of 1948. Coppock advised that by compromise, threat, or pleading, some sort of ITO Charter had to be completed.[56]

Wilcox took this advice. In early February 1948 he reported that some delegations had given up hope. The Canadians and British were depressed; Australians wanted to adjourn. Talking like "a football coach with his team before the last game of the season," he urged solutions to outstanding issues. Joined by Will Clayton in backroom negotiations later in the month, Wilcox conceded on nondiscrimination. He also acquiesced to a "weak" rule on membership to appease allies with a stake in trade with Eastern Europe. Refusing some Latin American amendments, but giving in on others, Wilcox wound up the discussions.[57]

Wilcox believed that the document promoted multilateralism among dozens of nations as best as could be expected. The Havana Charter did not alter the basic provisions on cartels, commodity agreements, state trading, and employment that had been accepted in years past. Articles regarding

Clayton signs the Havana Charter, March 23, 1948.
(Courtesy Department of Public Information, United Nations Photo Archives)

commercial policy leaned toward discrimination, but the United States had
achieved most of its objectives. Wilcox claimed that he had defended the
charter from distortion; the tarnish of protectionism could be wiped off
once normal economic conditions returned. America's "views about a free
economic world are not universally held," he confessed to business advisers. Regulation of trade unfortunately represented "the kind of a world we
live in."[58]

At least when the dire economic conditions of that world had ended, a
code of rules would be in place, held Wilcox. Nations would then have a
blueprint to guide them toward liberalization, although the Havana Char-

ter would zigzag around discriminatory obstacles. One day, exceptions would be banished and ITO members would reclaim the free trade doctrines that underlay America's original proposals of 1945.

Liberal traders lauded the Havana Charter. Comprised of 9 chapters and 106 articles, this code of rights, obligations, and procedures balanced a plurality of interests. Principles of fairness, interdependence, and tolerance for various national practices and philosophies provided a framework for profitable trade expansion. The charter would be reviewed in five years, once the transitional recovery period had ended, to get rid of the exceptions. Wilcox described it as "the most comprehensive international economic agreement in history." Signing the document on March 24, 1948, President Truman viewed it as "a code of fair dealing in international trade" needed to enhance prosperity, the Marshall Plan, and global cooperation.[59]

Wilcox prepared to resign from the government and write a book to explain the charter's significance and urge ratification by Congress. He would show that this far-reaching document served U.S. interests, honored congressional wishes, and ensured American leadership over the global economy. He left Havana content. An interim commission of the ITO would oversee procedural matters until the fifty-three nations ratified the code.[60]

In some respects, the Americans had good reason to be happy. The arduous planning process had resulted in a weighty document that addressed all aspects of commercial relations. The Havana Charter was complex. It reflected the difficult circumstances of the times and accounted for the diverse economic systems of its signatories. Multilateralism was still the goal, albeit in a far-off future. And the United States had shown leadership befitting its stature as a powerhouse and defender of the West.

Britain had provided the original blueprint for the charter during the war, but the Americans had seized the initiative by 1943. Since then, the United States had directed the show in two meetings in Washington, two nuclear club preparatory conferences, and the world gathering in Havana. A commercial code—a dream for years, if not decades—was now a reality. Considering that the ITO code had been negotiated in a chaotic era, its completion was a remarkable feat.

The ITO Charter was not now, however, an American document. It did not uphold the principles of market-driven trade and private enterprise. In fact, it fell far left of these marks. The charter was so ridden with exceptions to free trade that much of its original meaning had been eroded in a morass of discriminatory measures. Government regulation and protectionism served as its foundation. This development owed much to the acceptance of big government during the Great Depression and the Second World War, as well as to the instability of the postwar economy. The rise of the Labour Party and collapse in Britain highlighted these factors. Britain and the Commonwealth, as well as the developing nations, muffled and modified free trade principles to suit their interests.

Above all, the Cold War had an overriding impact on the outcome of the Havana conference. The British collapse and the European dollar gap pointed to the need for trade cooperation. These crises influenced diplomacy and international security. The Marshall Plan aimed to return the Western nations to solvency in order to strengthen the front against Soviet expansion. Likewise, the Americans conceded many elements of multilateralism so that trade partners, rich and poor alike, would not be further weakened. On the grounds of national security, free-traders retreated in the Geneva and Havana Charter discussions, just as they had in the GATT negotiations.

And therein lay the demise of the ITO Charter. Free trade idealism was a dim memory; universalism was based on regulated, not free, markets. This brought the charter into conflict with American capitalist ideology, which government and business leaders defended against socialism. For the latter in particular, planning had betrayed their ethic of private enterprise and the market. They readied an assault on the charter when Wilcox brought it home for congressional ratification. Havana had been trying for him. But he was in for an even ruder awakening in the United States.

CHAPTER 9

The End of Idealism
1948–1950

During the Christmas holidays, which interrupted the Havana meetings, the American delegates had written a poem for comic relief from the acrimonious talks. They had devoted a stanza to each nation. The reference to the United States had urged that the ITO Charter be kept secret so as not to arouse domestic critics.[1]

The point was well founded. Protectionists and free trade purists had disparaged earlier drafts of the charter, and they sharpened their criticism as a tough containment policy emerged in the late 1940s. Universalism faded; ideology intruded in the trade agenda. The business community and Congress viewed the charter's exceptions to free trade as a retreat from private enterprise, the bedrock under American economic tenets and democracy. The interventionist trends abroad, as well as at home, had to be halted or the Cold War would be lost.

Although all nations debated the merits of the charter, the spotlight was on the United States. The Soviets ridiculed the Havana conference as a failure, and the usual dissenters—empire isolationists and leftist critics—complained that America had gotten its way. But most Commonwealth observers applauded the exceptions to the rule of nondiscrimination as a victory for their side over American free trade designs. Still, as the Soviets noted, no nation had ratified the charter as of late Summer 1948. They all awaited action by the United States.[2]

Yet many Americans were hostile. Protectionists lashed out with standard denunciations of State Department giveaways and bureaucratic elitism. Some claimed that the term "reciprocity" meant one-sided American concessions. Senator Eugene Millikin warned that the charter readied U.S. producers for "destruction as payment for obscure or unknown diplomatic

147

advantages." Like the Reciprocal Trade Agreements Act, the ITO Charter bolstered the institutionalization of executive power over trade. Congressman Bertrand Gearhart called the charter and the General Agreement on Tariffs and Trade—the "little ITO"—unconstitutional intrusions by foreigners on domestic policy. Senator George Malone, an erstwhile GOP protectionist, proposed to place policy under the nonpartisan Tariff Commission. The plan never took hold, but it showed the enduring nature of protectionism and the threat from the Right.[3]

Farm policy did, too. Protectionists rejected the International Wheat Agreement of 1948, designed to stabilize prices and cut surpluses. Arthur Booth of the United Farmers of America claimed that both the Wheat Agreement and the ITO subordinated "the people of this Nation to the dictates of foreigners, whose standard of living and ideologies are as foreign to our way of life as the inhabitants of Mars and Venus." During debate over the farm bill of 1948, the Department of Agriculture compelled Truman to broaden import quotas to commodities not covered by Section 22 of the Agricultural Adjustment Act. The president refused, perceiving a clash with GATT/ITO principles, but farm protectionism was clearly on the rise.[4]

Right-wing extremists saddled the protectionists but they cleverly exploited the Cold War climate. Reactionaries lumped the ITO with the North Atlantic Treaty Organization (NATO) of 1949 as a conspiracy to encourage totalitarian ideologies. Daniel Reed of New York also ridiculed the terms of the ITO Charter, which, to him, disguised the free trade agenda. For example, "protectionism" at home was called "development" abroad. Archprotectionists zeroed in, moreover, on national security concerns. Czech shoe imports competed with his state's factories, complained New Hampshire Republican senator Styles Bridges. His constituents did not understand "why we should be extending to a country with which we are fighting a total diplomatic war, a cold war, the privilege of exporting shoes to this country and taking bread out of the mouths of the American workers."[5]

The administration countered that the Cold War compelled freer trade. In May 1950 President Truman declared that his foes were out-of-touch isolationists who "would cut down international trade, force down the living standards of other free peoples—and ours, too—and let the Communists take over." Affixing the label of fanatic to opponents weakened their appeal.[6] Yet the protectionists had a card they could play: they enjoyed an unholy alliance—wholly unintentional—with free trade business purists who also denounced the charter.

Most worrisome to the administration was the response of business ex-

ecutives to the Havana Charter. Allies in the cause of freer trade and leaders respected in Congress, they had endorsed the Marshall Plan and RTAA.
But even the business advisers who had attended the Havana conference
were guarded. For instance, Wilbert Ward of the National City Bank of
New York proclaimed that "we all dislike the Havana Charter" but recog-
nize that the ITO was a useful consultative and negotiating body. By 1949 all
of the major business organizations had turned on the code.[7]

That the charter might curb exports was one reason that the perfectionists criticized it. The numerous exceptions to free trade created "more holes
in the cloth than there is cloth," said W. H. Stanley of the Wrigley Company; there were more "loopholes than rules" in the document, echoed another businessman. The State Department argued that such discrimination
was temporary, but purists countered that every nation but their's endorsed
trade controls. Thus, discrimination would remain well after the transitional
recovery period. The exceptions simply excused protectionist restraints on
U.S. sales abroad.[8]

The one-sided obligations demanded of the United States were also grat-
ing. Protested Curtis Calder of Electric Bond and Share Company, it was as
if a town had a penal code to which a citizen would adhere as long as he
could commit murder on Mondays. Like other business purists tired of
compromising on principles of free trade, he preferred to move out of
town. The administration's reliable ally, the National Foreign Trade Council, refused to support the charter because of the escapes from multilateral
commitments. No wonder other nations liked the charter; America would
be unable to retaliate against their protectionism.[9]

The business community also scorned the investment article. Instead of a
"bill of rights," it seemed to give host nations total control. The charter
confirmed the fears of bankers that Latin Americans would constrain the
freedom of investors. Like the recent Inter-American Charter, the trade
code appeared to require U.S. credit and loans to any depressed nation of
the region. General Motors Corporation, an automaker interested in overseas production, claimed that the provision would deter the flow of venture
capital abroad by removing diplomatic protection for investments. The National Foreign Trade Council warned that investors might even be forced to
hand over part of their stock ownership to local nationals. Business leaders
advised junking the article, for its present form was unacceptable.[10]

The charter was just unworkable. Unrestricted trade was simply irrecon-
cilable with full employment. Multilateralism was also impossible as long as
the monetary system did not provide adequate credit facilities and currency

stabilization. Nations understood that the Marshall Plan was a realistic approach to their problems. They therefore "relegated the International Trade Charter to the field of remote and ideal aspirations," wrote Paul Wohl in *Barron's*.[11] The Havana Charter was, in other words, premature.

At a deeper philosophical level, however, business leaders opposed the charter because they saw it as a threat to the foundations of capitalism. It veered from its original intent of promoting unfettered commerce, favoring instead economic planning and deriding values of private enterprise. This approach would be fatal in the Cold War, a conflict as much over ideology as territory.

Free trade was a weapon against the Soviets, a notion that supporters of the charter as well as detractors acknowledged. William Batt of the Citizens Committee for the ITO, for instance, urged Congress to ratify the charter by a large majority to make "quite clear both to those people throughout the world who look to us for leadership and those beyond the Iron Curtain who would destroy it, that we are determined to continue our war for international cooperation and peace." The ITO stood "against the menace of an alien ideology," added policy planner Paul Nitze.[12] But such comparisons of capitalism to communism caused purists to denounce the charter's statist elements all the more.

The planners vainly defended their actions in Havana before the critics. Clair Wilcox noted that the ITO would discourage interventionism; purists had to be patient. As he explained, "we can't just go off to the North Pole and be fine and pure just by ourselves; we have to come to terms with the actual situation that we find in the world and put as much restraint on it as we can, and that is what the Charter does."[13] Perfectionists took little solace from his words, however.

For business leaders, the code was a product of mistaken New Deal thinking. Price controls, sympathy for labor unions, and full employment programs had drifted the nation toward socialism, they claimed. Once elected, Truman embraced "incentive-destroying and competition-destroying collectivism," charged General Electric head Charles Wilson. Under his Fair Deal, the president sought to enlarge the welfare state by pursuing national health care, public housing, and deficit spending. Business leaders urged General Dwight D. Eisenhower to run for the presidency to halt creeping big government statism, which he also feared.[14]

The charter was a typical example of the slide down the slope of regulation, regimentation, and statism. Controls turned off the business community. America stood for the idea of "an economy of free prices, free markets, free competition and free enterprise," declared a National Industrial Conference Board publication in late 1948. But the entire document undermined that philosophy. It represented a huge planning mechanism, a global bureaucracy that sullied the principles that had built the United States into a great and powerful nation.[15]

The charter was, in short, flawed by statist provisions. Exceptions and the investment clause were good examples, as was the employment article. The latter went no further than U.S. law, yet purists argued that it implied a return to New Deal–type work agencies that had intruded in the private sector. Others held that the state-trading chapter too weakly constrained government cartels, frowned too slightly on monopolies, and perpetuated controls over the economy. Quite obviously, socialist principles had shaped the Havana code. As a result, opined the National Association of Manufacturers, "American free enterprise might find the trade tribunals stacked against it."[16]

Philip Cortney, chief of Coty Inc. and a member of NAM's International Relations Committee, became the major spokesman for the purists against the charter. In 1949 he published *The Economic Munich*—a pointed allusion to the earlier diplomatic sellout to the Nazis—to excoriate the code and doom it in Congress. Cortney likened the document to a girl presented for marriage to a young man. Describing the wonderful qualities of the bride, the matchmaker added that her only fault was that she was slightly pregnant. "We shall drift into Communism and finally to war," Cortney warned, with an ITO that fostered discriminatory protectionism and "socialism the world over."[17]

To Cortney, regulation was the danger. Incredibly, the State Department had consented to discrimination against U.S. trade. In January 1950, when the British announced that they would retain controls as permanent instruments, Cortney saw an opportunity for Secretary of State Dean Acheson to abandon the charter in protest. The administration seemed not to realize, he warned, that multilateralism, Western prosperity, and NATO unity were impossible if allies rejected private enterprise.[18]

Cortney found Wilcox's adulatory account of the ITO highly instructive. A typical economist, Wilcox had "swallowed hook, line and sinker, without any critical mind, Keynes' theories" on employment and consumption. Keynes, more for political than economic reasons, had claimed that because governments could not cure depression, they should attempt to counteract

Philip Cortney (far right) with members of the U.S. Council of International
Chambers of Commerce. (Courtesy U.S. Council for International Business)

its symptoms. Freedom was replaced by intervention in the economy as a
"quack" cure for disorder. But such intrusion, demanded by the domestic "intrigues of ignorant, stupid people and of people who are always
ready to fish in troubled waters," would lead to "the loss of our individual freedom" and ultimately to "the destruction of our free society," argued Cortney.[19]

Because there was no viable middle way between communism and capitalism, Cortney rejected the charter as an "Economic Munich." Americans
had sold out democratic market capitalism to regulatory "grave-diggers of
our human liberties." Cortney's book and his testimony at the House hearings in April 1950 represented the fatal censure of the ITO by conservative
business leaders.[20]

That is, usually dependable allies of administration trade programs, the
purists stood in the charter's way. "I believe this is about the first time in
history that I have not been willing to wholeheartedly work for your policies and achievements," wrote a banker in March 1949 who refused Will

Clayton's request to help the effort. Business opposition to the ITO, noted lobbyists, had grown more extensive, vigorous, and vocal.[21]

The opposition dealt a severe blow to the charter. The ITO, simply, would not usher in an era of free trade. In fact, most business leaders viewed it as obsolete. The Marshall Plan was working and statist Labour governments in Australia, New Zealand, and Great Britain watched their popularity decline. A comprehensive code of trade rules, riddled by regulatory controls that debased market capitalism, was now an unwanted, and even unnecessary, element of the world economy.[22]

The ITO was in trouble. As free-traders defected, the administration had to decide whether to save it, and if so, how and when to present it to Congress. These decisions, along with the circumstances of the Cold War, lessened the odds that Congress would ever ratify the document.

In the fall of 1948, the administration decided not to submit the charter until the next year. Judging Americans preoccupied with the election and the Cold War, financier Bernard Baruch suggested that ITO legislation be delayed until the international climate improved and the world economy was more conducive to multilateralism. "If the ITO Charter is adopted, it will be like a new plant, struggling to come up in a weed-choked garden" full of trade restrictions and Cold War tensions. The administration should let the ITO lie.[23]

Truman took this advice. He postponed action on the charter in the hope that the return of the Democrats to power in Congress in 1949 would facilitate its ratification. A delay would also cancel the ITO as a presidential election issue. The decision threw cold water on the charter's proponents, however. Led by the business-run Citizen's Committee for Reciprocal World Trade, they had been at work since the Havana conference drumming up backing for the code. But they met so much opposition from fellow executives that the campaign had stalled. They switched their focus to the RTAA renewal in 1948.[24] Meanwhile, Truman held back the charter.

His victory and the Democrats' recapture of Congress might have given him a green light. But criticism of the charter had not abated when Truman's second term began in 1949. The president therefore proceeded with caution.

In January 1949 the State Department sent the charter to Capitol Hill as a joint resolution, to be treated as a foreign policy initiative. Senator Arthur Vandenberg complained that because the ITO touched on matters of na-

tional sovereignty, it should be considered as a treaty. But the ruling Democrats knew full well that a trade treaty would face a very close vote in the
Senate, where just one-third of the members could defeat it. The joint resolution, which required a simple majority, was referred to the House Foreign Affairs Committee. The Committee on Ways and Means, however,
would have to determine the changes in domestic law required for adherence to ITO rules. That laborious process consumed valuable time.[25]

And most notably, the Cold War intruded on planning. The successful
test of a Soviet atomic bomb and the impending victory of Chinese communism made the program of military aid and pact building under NATO all
the more crucial. The Western alliance also added the Federal Republic of
Germany to its ranks. These developments in national security compelled
the administration to turn from the charter. The time had passed for universalism, especially under a code vilified even by free-traders.

The administration's lack of commitment to the charter worried its advocates. Dean Acheson would not sabotage the ITO, but he would not be
a great help, either. Unpopular in Congress, he lacked authority to win this
piece of legislation. But above all, Acheson did not hold the convictions of
the free-traders. His approach to the world integrated foreign economic
policy into the national security agenda. Free trade idealism was not an objective but a means to face the immediate crises of Cold War. In short, trade
was subordinated to diplomacy. Compared to NATO, mutual aid bills, and
domestic measures in 1949, the charter was way down the list of priorities.
Besides, with Will Clayton and Clair Wilcox gone from the administration,
nobody of influence remained to push Acheson on the ITO.[26]

Advocates tried to sidestep this complacency. Wilcox's book on the charter appeared in January 1949; Clayton sent it to the press, Congress, and
representatives of the business community. He also helped form the Committee for the ITO, a lobby that worked with the State Department (like the
Committee for the Marshall Plan a year before) to stimulate public interest
in the charter. Republican William Batt, head of SKF Industries, assumed
leadership of the Committee and Clayton served as vice-chairman. Fanfare
accompanied the May 2 launching of the group, which was composed of
124 business, banking, education, labor, farm, and civic leaders.[27]

The committee believed that sound argument could win back the
purists. Clayton pointed out that the United States was as guilty of sin as
others. America was the world's second largest state trader, for example. In
addition, the cartel clause at least provided a means to protest restrictive
business practices. The employment provisions were harmless, and excep-

tions for quotas honored IMF rules. These barriers, as well as the investment clause, were not some slick trick to obtain foreign support. No British consumer, on strict rationing under the austerity program, desired controls to continue. Instead, discrimination was a necessary element of the crisis period.

Despite the code's imperfections, a trade charter was better than none at all, claimed its proponents. Tied to the Marshall Plan, monetary system, and GATT, the ITO would promote recovery. "Instead of seeking a perfectionism that is unattainable, we should do well to lay hold on the measure of order that is within our grasp," urged Clair Wilcox. Business and Congress should give the ITO a try, for, he cautioned, the only alternative was unbridled economic nationalism.[28]

That purists were unreasonable emerged as a major argument for the advocates. High-minded economic accords after the First World War had been so general that they had dissolved under nationalistic pressures. The charter took this into account. Qualifications were the only way for fifty-three nations with diverse economic systems and long histories of protectionism to reach agreement. The charter did not encourage discrimination; rather, it limited controls. Free trade purism was "as helpful in solving today's very pressing problems as hoping that the entire Russian Politburo will somehow drop dead," concluded Clayton.[29]

But the mission for the ITO foundered. Hearings convened in 1950, a year behind schedule, thus hurting momentum. Also, Batt learned from Democrats and aides that the president did not consider the charter to be an urgent matter. Truman reportedly held that the reciprocal trade program fit perfectly with GATT, and both were sufficient bases for commercial policy. Truman's tepidness disappointed Batt, who decided to deactivate the Committee for the ITO in September 1949 and await the next session of Congress, when hearings would take place.[30]

There was reason to complain about Truman's action. After all, he had campaigned for the Point Four program of aid to the Third World in 1949. But ever since the ITO was placed in the Democratic platform of 1948, he had not aggressively backed it. The president gave three major foreign policy addresses in the summer of 1949 but mentioned the charter in only one, in Arkansas. He passed up opportunities in August before the Veterans of Foreign Wars and the American Legion, speeches focused almost entirely on trade objectives that included references to the RTAA, Point Four, and regional ties. His midyear economic report omitted discussion of the ITO. "In light of this record it is understandable that some people might have the impression that the Administration is no longer solidly behind the ITO," concluded Melvin Fox, Batt's assistant in the Committee for the ITO.[31]

But the administration had not abandoned the project. After Truman transmitted the charter to Congress on April 28, 1949, Acheson followed with a speech to the U.S. Chamber of Commerce devoted entirely to the ITO. Acknowledging the business leaders in the audience who frowned on the compromises at Havana, the secretary of state asked them to shun the unrealistic and self-righteous free trade purists who wanted all barriers to fall. He placed the code in the larger context of foreign policy, linking the Marshall Plan, the monetary system, the United Nations, containment of "the aggressive conspiracy of the Communists of all countries," and NATO to the progress promised by the ITO. The charter was the "capstone of the economic structure" of the Free World, he proclaimed.[32]

In reality, the administration showed a lack of enthusiasm, rather than disregard, for the charter. Its agenda was too full of important business in 1949. Yet on February 10, 1950, Truman told his cabinet to promote the ITO, and Acheson followed with his endorsement. Still, the State Department did not grant the charter the same priority as other economic issues, such as Point Four and the dollar gap. As officials later explained, trade was not "our primary purpose" in diplomacy. Most acknowledged that GATT took care of U.S. commercial aims, which made efforts to obtain business and congressional acceptance less pressing.[33]

The administration also tried to round up votes, yet few legislators showed a familiarity with the ITO or thought it important. In the House, Robert Doughton, Wilbur Mills, Ways and Means Committee chairman Jere Cooper, and Republicans Jacob Javits and James Fulton, both of whom had served as advisers in Havana, would be effective lobbyists. But no senator could debate the intellectual Republican Eugene Millikin, who opposed the charter. The cause was hurt further by the indifference of Senator Walter George, chairman of the Finance Committee, and the lack of influence of such newcomers as Senators Estes Kefauver of Tennessee, Lyndon Johnson of Texas, and Russell Long of Louisiana. Advocates hoped that Wilcox, Clayton, Batt, Paul Hoffman of the Marshall Plan, Acheson, and others would be able to persuade Congress to pass the charter at the House hearings scheduled for April 1950.[34]

The timing of the charter in Congress was also crucial to its sagging fortunes. Jack McFall, the assistant secretary of state for congressional relations, predicted a split in the Senate Foreign Relations Committee if this controversial item came up first in the 1950 session. That might prejudice the

Marshall Plan renewal, a Korean aid program, and the Military Defense Assistance Program. Truman agreed. He did not press for the charter's early consideration, settling for hearings four months into the 1950 session. The charter then languished, lamented a free trade bureaucrat, with "neither the Secretary of State, nor the White House, willing to expend any time, effort, or bargaining power to jimmy it out of committee."[35]

This lack of will to wheel and deal for the charter hurt its prospects. Many legislators were as skeptical as purists about the code. Some denounced the exceptions that watered down its meaning, others feared that the ITO would increase imports to their states. A survey of House members in February 1950 found many potential adherents either uncommitted or lukewarm. Meanwhile, the clerk of the Senate Finance Committee reported that Eugene Millikin was trying to bring the ITO under that committee's jurisdiction so he could take a whack at it.[36] Truman asked his cabinet to lobby for the charter. But low-intensity campaigning, rather than direct presidential pressure, was no match for the opposition.

The House hearings on the charter in April and May 1950 revealed daunting obstacles to ratification. Free-traders jumped ship in droves. Within business sectors, splits were apparent. Whereas bankers Wilbert Ward and Randolph Burgess sanctioned the charter, for instance, National City Bank opposed it. Other firms refused to commit one way or the other. But the testimony of the National Foreign Trade Council was devastating. This longtime ally of multilateralism advised Congress to let the charter die. The planners had worked courageously against foreign protectionism, but their code would not result in a system of nondiscriminatory trade.[37]

The purists offered counterproposals to the charter. Most ideas centered on trimming the code so that it embraced the basic components of commercial liberalization. Such "fringe" elements as provisions for employment and development should be erased to render the charter consistent with market precepts. Business leaders insisted on honing down the document, even as advocates explained that few nations would consent to excisions. Philip Cortney recommended a bold slashing of tariffs and a return to the gold standard as the best route to multilateralism. ITO proponents faced an uphill climb with their own free trade allies.[38]

In testimony before the Foreign Affairs Committee, advocates focused on the perfectionists' complaints. Acheson and Secretary of Defense Louis Johnson discussed exceptions in a diplomatic context. The charter was linked to European integration, NATO, and Point Four development assistance. The General Agreement on Tariffs and Trade would soon invite West Germany into its ranks. This nation, considered a linchpin of European security, would also join the ITO but only if its domestic needs were met. Provisions for escaping from obligations also allowed America to take necessary measures in times of national emergency. International cooperation in the Cold War, testified charter supporters, hinged on a flexible approach to deviations from trade liberalization.[39]

The Cold War now drove trade ideology. A range of ITO backers, from actor Douglas Fairbanks Jr. to economic interests and religious, civic, youth, and academic organizations, believed that trade fostered peace. But that meant a peace without Soviet cooperation. That Moscow had opposed the ITO plan from its inception was a good reason to ratify the charter, said Dean Acheson. "As freedom is hanging in the balance in many parts of the world, and millions of people are looking in our direction for assurance that we really mean what we say," he said, the United States could send the right signal "in the basic field of trade." Universalism was dead; the Free World against the Iron Curtain was reality. The charter, concluded Congressman Jacob Javits, was "an instrument in the cold war."[40]

The dollar crisis in Western Europe gave credence to this view. On his resignation as secretary of the army, Gordon Gray became special assistant to the president. In April 1950 Truman asked him to find answers to the dollar gap and build "economies against communist subversion or aggression." The United States was a creditor that exported $16 billion worth of goods in 1949 but imported only $10 billion. It must address the imbalance or face "a substantial shift of power from the democratic to the Soviet sphere," warned Acheson. Gray recommended a boost in European exports to the United States as well as higher levels of American investment and tourism in the region and simplification of U.S. customs procedures. Estimates showed that tourist and investment revenues, and an increase in imports by $400 million (one-third of 1 percent of America's total production), could balance European payments accounts. Issued on November 10, 1950, the Gray Report included just a sentence on the charter but advised U.S. membership as integral to solvency in the alliance.[41]

The report encouraged charter advocates. To be sure, Gray's staff found the public unaware of the ITO. And business leaders, like Hollywood's Eric Johnston, had reservations about it. But proponents, like Gray, had made a case that Congress must ratify the code as a national defense measure. The document, concluded Batt, was "our baby, good, bad, or indifferent, and the rest of the world looks at it that way."[42]

But in the summer of 1950 trade allies were cooling to the ITO. The British Parliament was less inclined to consider the charter before the Conservatives returned to power. Because the Canadian Parliament had been dissolved in 1949, the government was forced to resubmit its ITO Charter bill. Clearly, Canadian business free-traders also took cues from their American counterparts in denouncing the code. The United Nations had chosen a site near the World Bank in Washington, D.C., to locate the ITO but could not move until Congress had acted.[43]

But the Cold War soon overwhelmed the ratification process. The United States had steadily militarized the containment policy in the late 1940s. In April 1950 the National Security Council issued NSC-68, a review of U.S. policy toward the Soviet Union. Its findings were alarming. Possessing a large military, the atomic bomb, and a budding alliance with Mao Tse-tung's communist Chinese, the Russians had the capacity to overrun Western Europe, drive toward the oil-rich Middle East, and influence Asia. The Americans and their allies were vulnerable. To counter this weakness, NSC-68 called for more spending on defense, more military and economic aid, and improved internal security and intelligence gathering. The rise of Joseph McCarthy in early 1950 and the onset of the second Red Scare then raised the political stakes of being soft on communism at home and abroad. Democrats and Republicans, looking toward the 1952 elections, contested each other on foreign policy.

These developments spelled trouble for the charter. Truman refused to launch a high-profile campaign, and leading Democrats were unwilling to push the ITO in Congress. Others looked to GATT and the pooling of French and German coal and steel resources under the Schuman Plan as the road to reconstruction.[44] But above all, the Cold War atmosphere undercut universalist projects. The outbreak of war in Korea on June 25, 1950, conclusively proved that point.

As the House Committee on Foreign Affairs began its hearings just before the Korean War began, the charter actually did not appear to be in bad shape. The committee's chairman, John Kee of West Virginia, was too ill to attend the hearings at great length but he was a firm advocate. Jacob Javits would try to pull Republican members of the committee along. Advocates testifying for the ITO doubled the number of opponents, leading the clerk of the committee to predict that the charter would get to the House floor by a comfortable margin by early June 1950. The ratification process had received a boost in May, when Democrats on the Ways and Means Committee announced their unanimous endorsement. The measure was not under their purview, but they deemed it such an integral part of the reciprocal trade program that they rallied to the cause.[45]

Yet ratification was really a longshot. Few ranking Democrats attended the hearings. And even if the House passed the joint resolution, Senator Millikin lay in wait with protectionists to whom he had taught the intricacies of the charter. They vowed to report the document out of the Foreign Relations Committee as a treaty and send it to the full Senate. The administration knew that ploy would ruin the ITO's chances, for nearly one-third of the Senate opposed the charter. Democrats would vote for a joint resolution, but Republicans and skeptical Democrats could team up to block the measure.[46]

Democrat Tom Connally, of Texas, the chairman of the Senate Foreign Relations Committee, agreed. As the House hearings ended in mid-May 1950, he balked at bringing the ITO before the Senate during the session. Truman would likely be embarrassed by the indifference of his own party. And surely, other matters were more pressing. Five members of the Foreign Relations Committee served on the Tydings Subcommittee that at present was handling the charges made by Senator Joseph McCarthy about communism in the government. Even "some Democrats feel that on account of the pressure of other legislative matters, it would be unwise to undertake consideration at this session," noted Connally.[47]

Faced with such meager support, Kee's House Foreign Affairs Committee sat on the ITO ratification resolution in late May. Adviser Jack McFall urged the president to proceed, arguing that further delays would provoke foreign criticism. Truman asked Kee to report out the measure to the House floor, but the chairman, believing that it would fail, refused. William Batt was convinced that the fight was now over, for the Democrats had stalled their own president's legislation. As 1950 was also a congressional election year, many legislators did not want to vote for an item that was so unpopular among the articulate public. With House subcommittees also investigating the linkage of unemployment and imports, it was better not to take a stand on trade issues. The Senate would not consider the charter during the 1950 session.[48]

The onset of the Korean War nailed the coffin shut on the charter. As the nation riveted on the defense of South Korea in early August, Chairman Kee of the House Foreign Affairs Committee wrote Truman, "it seems clear that pressure of other urgent business, and particularly legislation of an emergency nature, has made it impossible for the Congress to act upon the bill before the contemplated date of adjournment." Kee recommended reserving the joint resolution for the next session, even though that would mix it with the RTAA extension. Truman concurred, and the State Department informed Britain, France, and Canada in mid-August 1950 of the decision to postpone the charter.[49]

The ITO's fate was sealed. By the fall, the administration planned to drop it and incorporate many of the code's provisions into a broadened General Agreement on Tariffs and Trade. Setting the legislative agenda for 1951, Acheson wrote Truman that trade was "an indispensable part of our total effort to create strength and unity in the free world." The Korean War showed how trade and aid fueled the military machine. Yet the Reciprocal Trade Agreements Act, which granted authority for negotiations at GATT and simplified customs procedures, would more than suffice in defense plans. Anyway, the ITO was bound to be rejected.[50]

And Congress, wary of supranational bodies, was amenable to GATT. Lacking an executive board or secretariat and enjoying only a informal relationship with the United Nations, the General Agreement had no legal standing. Participants were contracting parties, pledged only to confer on trade matters on a haphazard schedule. Acheson advised that the administration ask Congress, in connection with the RTAA renewal, to approve participation in the forum. This would not invest GATT with any powers not already held by members but would give it a permanent status and bring U.S. laws into line with GATT rules.

The tariff body was a good alternative to the ITO. Indeed, the National Foreign Trade Council had endorsed a proposal by business to jettison the charter and build up GATT to end the council's uncomfortable opposition to administration trade policies. Protectionists could then be handled by the concerted efforts of the liberal trade camp. Such unity was imperative. In 1951 the trade agreements program faced a another stiff battle in Congress, Acheson reminded the president. The GATT idea would "help to float the program over the shoals of the opposition of individual protectionist groups" and achieve foreign policy objectives.[51] In short, Acheson recognized that idealistic thinking in U.S. foreign economic policy must cease.

Recognizing the tough fight ahead in Congress over the RTAA of 1951, as well as the need for approval of new taxes to pay for war mobilization and civil defense measures and for price controls to keep inflation in check, Truman took Acheson's advice. In late November the dramatic military reversal in Korea had occurred as Chinese troops drove back the United Nations in a brutal retreat. The president was in no mood to proceed with risky legislation. He would inform legislators who frowned on the RTAA (some in his own party) that he had abandoned the charter in return for their support on the trade program in 1951. Even Millikin might be persuaded on these grounds. The State Department announced the change in policy on December 6, 1950, closing the curtain on the ITO era.[52]

The move was expected overseas. The British Commonwealth nations accepted GATT as a permanent body and canceled plans to send the charter to their parliaments. At the Torquay Round of GATT in early December, U.S. officials asked Britain and Canada to help establish a GATT executive committee and examine ways to administer GATT so that the forum would become a permanent entity. Sir Stephen Holmes of the British delegation noted that the bailout would shock many nations. Even though they had had no illusions about the charter's prospects, "there was quite a difference between knowing somebody was dying and knowing that he was dead." A few nations would accuse the Americans of betrayal and would use their hurt feelings to win amendments to GATT rules. Indeed, some even sought to insert the ITO employment provisions in the General Agreement. Britain, Canada, and the United States beat back that effort so as not to reignite the opposition of American free trade purists.[53]

In the United States, the reaction was generally favorable. Protectionists welcomed the shelving of the charter, viewing it as an absurd product of do-goodism. Many internationalists were disappointed that the United States had seemingly forfeited its leadership during a period of crisis, when allies counted on American resolve. Yet more commonly heard was the opinion that realism had prevailed. The charter had been badly timed. The nation was preoccupied with the Korean War, alliance building, and European recovery. GATT provided an opportunity to integrate some of the charter's less ambitious parts into international trade rules. American leadership was imperative to make this forum effective.[54]

The Cold War reached a dangerous peak in 1950, just as Congress was considering the Havana Charter. The business purists' position was important because it prevented unity in the free trade ranks necessary to the campaign for ratification. The perfectionist critique was also significant because it

Truman and British prime minister Clement Attlee discuss NATO in
December 1950, just days after the president set aside the ITO Charter. Secretary
of State Dean Acheson and Secretary of Defense George Marshall look on.
(Courtesy National Archives)

highlighted the ideological struggle of the Cold War. By imposing regulations on open competition, the charter contradicted the precepts of market capitalism, now under attack by the Soviet Union. That was unpalatable
in the Cold War, a contest between capitalist and communist ways of life.

The conflict over ideology coincided with an escalation of tension
throughout the world. Joseph Stalin probed and expanded, Harry Truman
condemned and responded. The determined Americans decided to defend
the West, first by economic means and then by military containment. For
the United States, the conflict in Korea crowned that effort, elevating the
pursuit of Western security over global collaborative commercial planning.

No matter how qualified by exceptions to multilateralism, a commercial
code bent on a world order of trade cooperation had no place in a war at-

mosphere. By the 1950s, for that matter, the charter no longer had a place in American foreign policy or in the global trade system. The Marshall Plan had stabilized Western Europe, and GATT worked behind the scenes, in essence, to open U.S. markets to allies. The time had long passed for universalist thinking. That was why the grand design of the ITO lay stillborn in the halls of Congress.

Trade idealism had succumbed in the arena of Cold War commercial relations. American officials realized that multilateralism would occur only in the Western alliance, and gradually at that. The ITO Charter fit neither into Cold War ideology nor strategy. But GATT served national security interests. It promoted economic stability in Western Europe, promising to build a strong defense structure by providing revenue for rearmament and stability for recovering allies. It was also consistent with American capitalist principles. Thus, GATT replaced the Havana Charter. It supplanted free trade, universalist dreams with a pragmatic liberalization program, moderated by protectionism. Undergirding an alliance of Western nations, GATT now presided over the international trade system.

CHAPTER 10

Trade Liberalism on Track
1949

In 1949 Truman and the Democrats drove the Republican majority from Capitol Hill. Fiscal conservatism and protectionism were not dead, but the president seized the opportunity to extend the welfare system and the other New Deal programs that had been attacked by the GOP Congress. He also restored the powers of the Reciprocal Trade Agreements Act and coaxed GATT partners to liberalize their trade barriers. In trade policy, the Cold War prompted him to shove aside ITO universalism for GATT pragmatism.

The RTAA of 1949 and GATT's Annecy Round were shaped by the Cold War. The administration prioritized these endeavors as key elements of national security policy. Free trade was not the goal. Rather, an acceptance of moderate protectionism would ensure that trade served the agenda of containment.

The immediate task at hand after the president's election focused on restoring the Reciprocal Trade Agreements Act. Truman hoped to rocket the repeal of the GOP law of 1948 through both Democratic houses of Congress in time to provide negotiating authority for the second tariff negotiating session of GATT, the Annecy Round. These talks were scheduled for April 1949. Canceling out the 1948 RTAA's peril point provision, which hindered tariff cuts on U.S. products, was, therefore, imperative.

The Democrats acted swiftly. On January 8 Truman asked Congress to extend the RTAA without the "hampering restrictions" of the peril point process. Ways and Means chairman Robert Doughton promptly held hearings and reported out a three-year extension, retroactive to June 1948, when the Republican law took effect. Peril points were eliminated. Not only a duplication of the escape clause, they were also a gimmick that gave blanket protection to undeserving producers, argued the liberal traders. They would also delay the GATT talks until the Tariff Commission investigated each concession, as well as sour trade partners on American offers. Under the new bill, the Tariff Commission was returned to its advisory role and the Committee for Reciprocity Information resumed its place as a complaint forum.[1]

Protectionists did not go quietly. Watchmakers, independent oil producers, and textile manufacturers were among the interest groups that lobbied for peril points. That U.S. tariffs had been halved since the inception of the reciprocal trade program gave credence to their pleas. In defending peril points, they also claimed that the Annecy Round and currency devaluation would increase import competition. Even Democrats chimed in. Senator Walter George, chairman of the Finance Committee, wondered if foreigners, aided by the Marshall Plan, would seize Georgia's textile sector. Senator Theodore Green, a Rhode Island Democrat, added that U.S. aid had built modern plants abroad, while Americans were "losing our mills" to competition. Beyond the usual charges of economic destruction and executive branch tyranny, protectionists also attacked GATT as a substitute for the ITO Charter.[2]

But in an era when the health of the Western alliance was crucial, the protectionists were playing a losing hand. The trade agenda, undergirded by the RTAA, served U.S. interests. Imports promoted recovery, a high standard of living, and low prices, said government officials. If imports rose less than 1 percent of America's $254 billion in production, the dollar gap, now at −$2.5 billion, could be closed. This would lessen Europe's dependence on aid and strengthen the NATO alliance. And American exporters, of course, would profit. The Reciprocal Trade Agreements Act, declared the *New York Times*, was the "indispensable other half of the Marshall Plan."[3]

There was, in sum, no alternative to freer trade. Americans would reject high taxes to subsidize exports or fund foreign aid. Imports were the least painful way of "balancing the books," said Senator Ralph Flanders of Vermont. Opposed to another loan, the British wished instead to stand on their own feet by selling goods for dollars in an open market. The U.S. trade surplus of $6.8 billion, therefore, had to be narrowed.[4]

The American economy was at issue, too. A recession in 1949 led to price hikes, unemployment, and bankruptcies. The output of goods and services dropped by over $10 billion from normal production times. The trade agreements program could help combat inflation. Thus, Truman wanted the trade law restored not only to help dollar-starved nations but also to stimulate the U.S. economy.[5]

Still, the protectionists moved on to exploit the temper of the times. The Red Scare was in full swing in 1949. For years, right-wingers had denounced the supposed presence of subversives in the government, Hollywood, and labor unions. The Cold War milieu undermined appeals to reason. In 1947 the Taft-Hartley Act had purged communists from unions and Truman had instituted a Federal Employee Loyalty Program, subjecting government workers to background checks. And witch-hunts grabbed headlines. Most notable was that against Alger Hiss, the former State Department official who was accused of passing secrets to Russian spies. He also directed the citizens' group that campaigned for the RTAA, while suspects Victor Perlo and Henry Wadleigh had worked in the State Department's Trade Agreements Division. Accused Congressman Daniel Reed, "Communists who helped write our trade agreements" had attended the GATT talks in Geneva and thus threatened U.S. security.[6]

Most critics did not use smear tactics, but the allusions to communism highlighted the presumption that free enterprise was under attack. "We are off on a great international movement toward state socialism" in trade, wrote Senator Eugene Millikin. Foreign discrimination was inimical to market capitalism. Yet U.S. tax dollars supported socialist states that perpetuated colonialism (Britain and France), menaced domestic interests (Swiss watches), or adhered to the Soviet line (Czechoslovakia). The United States should not jettison trade barriers to such violators of American principles, argued protectionists.[7]

Liberal traders responded that the trade law discouraged statism. Without the removal of barriers, the United States would face a world rife with commercial controls that would force America to regiment its own business. And red-baiters were just plain ignorant. The charge that the RTAA was communist-inspired was illogical and ridiculous, said Louisiana Democrat Hale Boggs. Free-traders were "promoting something which is the antithesis of communism and planned economy." That the trade agreements program had provoked the wrath of the Russians validated the point, he concluded.[8]

Truman adopted this anticommunist line. Western nations had to cooperate to repair the damage of the war by reviving international trade. They would then demonstrate that "the economic system of the free nations is better than the system of communism" with its "fake" rhetoric. This was not charity, but prosperity through private enterprise. The president rationalized the RTAA as a key part of capitalist doctrine on which Cold War ideology was based.[9]

Officials and interest groups followed his lead. Secretary of Defense James Forrestal told Congress that the military considered the Reciprocal Trade Agreements Act to be "a step in the interest of national security both in the immediate and in the long-term sense." It encouraged imports and exports deemed crucial to national security like machine tools and communication equipment. Interests as diverse as the National Farmers Union, the National Women's Trade Union League, and the Brotherhood of Railway Clerks agreed that the best defense was to buy goods rather than seek self-sufficiency by tariffs. Seymour Harris of the Americans for Democratic Action added that the protesters crudely drew on the national security argument to appeal for unjustifiably high tariffs.[10]

"What is the cold war about?" asked Senator A. Willis Robertson, a Democrat from Virginia. "It is over trade. The Russians put a blockade in Berlin and say, 'You cannot ship any of your goods in or out. You cannot go behind the iron curtain with your railroad trains and your goods.' We say, 'All right, Mister. You cannot come over on our side with anything you have.'" The confrontation was "something of a trade war." In short, reducing barriers promoted prosperity, curbed political friction, encouraged democracy, all essential to the fight against international communism.[11]

A majority of Americans embraced that view. In contrast to its treatment of the Havana Charter, big business applauded the RTAA as a boon for exports and U.S. leadership. In general, business, industry, labor, and agriculture backed the law, to the acclaim of the press. Pollster Elmo Roper concluded that "the American people see reciprocal trade as having a permanent place in the scheme of American international commitments. It now looks as though our high tariff days are behind us."[12]

Economics, diplomacy, and the Democratic majority in both houses of Congress won the RTAA of 1949 by an impressive margin. The House passed the bill by a large 319–69 margin on February 9, with many Republicans joining Democrats. The Senate Finance Committee then held hearings until mid-March. But the illness of committee chairman Walter George delayed action. Ratification of the North Atlantic Treaty Organization during the summer pushed the bill further back on the legislative docket. Once the Finance Committee did deliberate, the protectionists gave the administration a scare by reporting the RTAA to the Senate by a narrow 7–6 vote.

The Senate did not pass renewal until mid-September 1949. Again, protectionists lobbied to restore peril points and impose several other restraints on the president's authority. They ultimately failed, but in many cases not

Truman restores the powers of the RTAA in 1949. Seated is an aging Cordell Hull. Behind are Undersecretary of State James Webb, Tariff Commission chairman Oscar Ryder, Senate Majority Whip Scott Lucas, House Speaker Sam Rayburn, Senate Finance Committee chairman Walter George, House Ways and Means chairman Robert Doughton, Senator Tom Connally, second-ranking member of the Finance Committee, and Congressman Jere Cooper, second-ranking member of the Ways and Means Committee. (Courtesy National Archives)

by much. Millikin's peril point amendment, designed, he said, "to judge the extent to which our domestic producers have become the pawn of diplomacy," lost by a narrow 38–43 margin only because eight Republican backers were absent. Joseph McCarthy of Wisconsin initially won quotas on fur and fur products, but his amendment was later rejected. Import quotas on petroleum fell short by one vote. The Senate then tallied 62–19 for the RTAA, and President Truman signed the legislation on September 26, 1949.[13]

By doing so, he ended two trying years of managing the Republican insurgents. But protectionism had not been obliterated. Indeed, the *Economist* claimed that the Senate's vote on the peril point showed that "the protectionist spirit in the United States is by no means dead." Yet the argument that reciprocal trade served Free World interests weakened the protection-ist cause.[14]

By late 1949 managing protectionism became easier for the administra-tion. Growing internationalism (the Republicans had endorsed the NATO treaty) and the view that defense in the Cold War depended on increasing imports added allies to the liberal trade side. Congress was also content with GATT, which carefully lowered tariffs. Thus, State Department negotiators proceeded to the second round of GATT talks in Annecy, twenty-five miles across the French border from Geneva, discussions that had actually begun months before the RTAA of 1949 had passed.

Thirty-four nations met at Annecy from April to August 1949 and negoti-ated 147 bilateral agreements, including accords with new nations that ac-ceded to GATT. The significance of the Annecy Round lay in its timing more than its accomplishments. It ended just as a new British dollar crisis led to devaluation of the pound and as U.S. opinion hardened against the ITO Charter. The GATT talks tested international cooperation and American leadership in the world economy.

Talks on procedures and rules preceded the actual tariff negotiations at Annecy. On April 8 twenty-three contracting parties and eleven acceding nations began discussions. Working parties were established to address major problems regarding procedural matters and issues ranging from import re-straints to customs unions.[15]

Although unassuming relative to the dramatic Geneva Round of 1947, the Annecy talks did have some controversy. For one thing, Cuba protested America's plans to reduce preferential tariffs on products bound at the Geneva negotiations, particularly sugar. Havana contended that no margins created under the U.S.-Cuban trade agreement could be touched without its permission. Opposed to the demand for such prior consent, the United States recognized that the agreement legally tied its hands. But Cuban in-flexibility, warned U.S. delegation chief Woodbury Willoughby, would counter the spirit of GATT, as well as take pressure off the British nations to eliminate their preferences. Cuba refused to discuss the sugar preference, however. The contracting parties voted 14–1, with several abstentions, against the request for prior approval, which prompted Cuba to withdraw from the Annecy Round.[16]

Quantitative barriers were also contentious. GATT allowed quotas to safe-guard monetary reserves, but now developing nations, and many advanced ones, sought exemptions to protect infant industries. South Africa announced that it did not want to consult other countries prior to imposing import controls. Willoughby warned that discrimination, the "old friend (or enemy) of the drafters of the General Agreement and the ITO Charter," had returned. The Commonwealth still favored the discriminatory sterling bloc, disregarding multilateral ideals, he complained.[17]

But the dollar gap compelled an exemption from GATT rules, replied the Commonwealth. Thus, South African and U.S. officials struck a deal in June. GATT would require an exchange of views, but not formal consent, on import controls. The process allowed the United States to voice its opinion, yet South Africa got its way in this first application of GATT's consultation procedure on quantitative barriers. Import controls, despised by the Americans, would remain in effect to protect, in particular, British and Commonwealth industries and payments balances.[18]

The Annecy participants considered other issues carried over from Geneva. Brazil agreed to amend its internal consumption taxes that widened discrimination against foreign products. This revenue measure placed higher taxes on imported watches, spirits, and cigarettes than those levied on similar domestic goods. In addition, because the Geneva accord had validated the Benelux and Lebanon–Syrian customs unions, the contracting parties explored the feasibility of similar fusion for South Africa and Southern Rhodesia; the Scandinavian nations, France and Italy; and four Latin American countries. America supported these arrangements, even though they might discriminate against outsiders, for such economic integration promoted political unity within the Western alliance.[19]

The Cold War hovered over the talks. European integration was one proof, problems with Czechoslovakia another. The Czechs protested U.S. export controls, claiming that the requirement for exporters from communist nations to obtain licenses to trade was inherently discriminatory. America defended its policy, however. Czechoslovakia would be denied coal mine drills because the equipment was obviously intended to extract uranium for use in Soviet atomic bombs. Surely, high-quality ball bearing exports that had already been sent to Czechoslovakia were headed for aircraft factories. Controls thus related only to exports that contributed to war potential. Besides, GATT's national security provisions certified the licenses. America's Free World partners among the contracting parties fully agreed.[20]

Another Cold War issue, and a holdover from the Havana talks, was whether to grant Japan equal treatment in trade. By 1949 America viewed Japan as a link to containment in Asia, hoping that the nation could stand on its own once the occupation was over. The Commonwealth countries had refused most-favored-nation trade for Japan at Havana, but at talks with the United States in London in November 1948, they decided to discuss the idea again.

In 1948 the Commonwealth and Japan had signed an agreement to raise Japan's exports to the sterling area, but most British countries opposed more help. They all feared that once the U.S. occupation ended, Japan would revert to prewar patterns of autarchy. They sought freedom to protect themselves by discriminatory measures against a future commercial powerhouse.

The Commonwealth thus argued against the U.S. request for most-favored-nation status. First, equal treatment could never be retracted once given, even if the need arose. Second, Japan needed a firm exchange rate to prevent unfair currency manipulation that would give it price advantages. Third, Britain worried about the renewal of the sort of vicious competition in textiles that had existed before the war. Fourth, domestic politics factored in, for war-engendered hostility toward Tokyo persisted. Besides, multilateralism would have little effect on Japan's strictly controlled trade. The Commonwealth nations were unconvinced that most-favored-nation status was necessary. As the Association of British Chambers of Commerce summed up, "a constant watch on Japanese competition" was imperative.[21]

America answered all of these arguments. Conferring equal status would prevent arbitrary discrimination and would provide a psychological boost to the occupation forces, easing the burden of U.S. subsidies. The occupation recorded a taxing annual trade deficit of about $400 million. Anyway, many allies had extended multilateral treatment to the occupation force in western Germany in 1948. Also, Japan would establish stable exchange by the summer, and an Anglo-American textile mission could discuss arrangements concerning exports.

Above all, argued the Americans, by denying Japanese exports fair treatment, Commonwealth nations were violating GATT principles and undermining the goal of expanding international trade. Congress would frown on aid recipients, especially from the Commonwealth, that refused to give nondiscriminatory status to others. Ten of the 23 members of GATT discriminated against Japan. That created "the basis for dangerous economic and political frictions in the future," wrote Assistant Secretary of State for Economic Affairs Willard Thorp.[22] He alluded, of course, to national security concerns.

Japan was a key player in the Cold War. Since the war, it had lost $3 billion in Asian assets, much in the lucrative Manchurian market seized by the Chinese communists. Most-favored-nation status would reorient Japan toward Southeast Asia, Western Europe, and North America to meet ambitious export targets of $1.5 billion by 1953, levels necessary for its self-sufficiency. As the Annecy Round began, a Ministry of International Trade and Industry was created to coordinate export promotion. Rehabilitated by the occupation, Japan would become a stable, democratic, and powerful ally in the Pacific, or so the security-conscious Americans hoped.[23]

In Annecy, however, the Commonwealth, as well as Western European, remained unmoved. Economics took precedence over diplomatic strategy. A textile mission might soothe Manchester producers, and progress on exchange rates was encouraging. But most-favored-nation treatment for Japan must be postponed until the signing of a peace treaty. By then, the dollar gap would be closed and the terms of Japan's postoccupation policies would be clearer. The United States must either drop or postpone the proposal, relying, in the meantime, on the RTAA to help Japan. The British were particularly adamant. Because of approaching national elections, Prime Minister Attlee was hesitant to confront domestic textile interests. The southern dominions, France, and other countries were in accord.[24]

America lost the argument. By mid-May 1949 Acheson chose to postpone the request until the end of the Annecy talks. Yet delegation chief Woodbury Willoughby conceded that the issue was dead. Further effort against the bloc of opponents, including the usually amenable Canadians, would hurt U.S. prestige. And time was short at Annecy. Facing angry friends and foes, Acheson abandoned the plan. He agreed with the Department of Defense to try again at the next round of GATT talks beginning in 1950 and lobby for Japan's accession to the tariff forum thereafter. Tokyo gained admittance into GATT in 1955, but America would battle for fair treatment of Japanese exports for decades.[25]

The Japanese case heightened the importance of granting West Germany equal treatment. Marshall Plan nations already accorded it most-favored-nation status, and America had persuaded fourteen of the twenty-three contracting parties to follow this lead. But at Annecy, some nations—wary of renewed German power—sought a review of West German tariffs. Holland circulated a memorandum that focused on lowering German barriers. Despite efforts to conform the West German tariffs to Benelux duties, there was a move underfoot by France, Belgium, and Britain to deny most-favored-nation status in Berlin and the western zone of Germany until tariffs fell. By July the Europeans had halted progress on the issue.[26]

America countered their effort. The Bipartite Control Office had found Holland's claim to be erroneous. Zonal tariffs did not limit or bar imports; bilateral talks at Annecy should go forth. The United States advised that until the Council of Foreign Ministers had met and clarified German security issues, West Germany should be allowed to take part in multilateral tariff negotiations. Present rates would be bound until 1951, the new Federal Republic of Germany could seek entrance into GATT, and negotiations would be based on future tariff levels. Such an approach would integrate West Germany into the GATT system, boost European recovery, ease occupation costs, and, most important, unify this pivotal country with the NATO alliance.[27] It was not until the Torquay Round in 1951, however, that the Federal Republic got equal treatment by acceding to GATT.

These debates preceded the actual Annecy Round of tariff negotiations. Liberalization was modest in comparison to the Geneva Round; indeed, America was the only participant eager to cut tariffs. Yet obstacles stood in the way. The RTAA of 1948 remained in effect during the Annecy Round, thus limiting U.S. concession offers. Meanwhile, Britain faced another financial collapse. The GATT talks of 1949 thus treaded water.

A problem weighed on President Truman. The delay in the Senate vote on the RTAA of 1949 forced him to adhere to the Republican law, which required the Tariff Commission to review U.S. offers and decide on peril points. The Tariff Commission gave its peril point findings to Truman on March 4, and a report followed to account for additional offers made to GATT newcomers Colombia and Liberia. The Tariff Commission curbed some offers, raising the hopes of protectionists. Senator Millikin asked for disclosure of the minutes of the Committee on Trade Agreements to prevent sweeping tariff cuts. The administration refused but was frustrated. Truman hoped that the Senate would act quickly on the trade agreements program, but its vote actually came after the Annecy Round.[28]

Considering the constraints, U.S. offers were reasonable. Tariff cuts would amount to $39 million; additionally, nearly three-quarters of the $103 million in offers would maintain imports on the duty-free list. The offers covered over half of the total value of U.S. imports from the acceding nations. Meanwhile, the United States requested foreign tariff reductions of $341 million, the bulk of this aimed at the new nations. To be sure, the American schedule was modest relative to the Geneva Round. Peril point findings forced the withdrawal of some offers. But many offers were of particular importance to trade partners and would likely provoke U.S. protectionists. The *Economist* urged the United States to remain generous at Annecy.[29]

The dollar gap made generosity a foremost American aim. The State Department viewed the Annecy Round as a means to build dollar reserves and restore equilibrium in world trade. The Commonwealth nations especially counted on expanded trade with the United States. They had increased their share of world exports 28 percent by 1948, whereas America's share had dropped to less than 23 percent. Yet the U.S. share of global imports had also fallen. To close the dollar gap, American imports had to rise.[30]

This was particularly true in regard to imports from Britain. In 1948 British productivity and exports had risen, helped by U.S. aid and the suspension of currency convertibility and rules of nondiscrimination. But the dollar drain persisted. By 1949 U.K. imports again outpaced exports. Britain's export drive faltered, hurt by the onset of the U.S. recession that cut purchases of British goods, and Attlee considered a devaluation of the pound to make goods more competitive abroad and imports less attractive. American business and political leaders welcomed devaluation as a step toward fiscal responsibility and away from socialism.[31]

The issue of currency devaluation had political and economic importance. It would hurt Attlee's political standing and impair relations with the dominions, where the move was unpopular. But the Americans held that depreciation was a better option than protectionism, which would close the sterling area. Like Western Europe, Britain must liberalize trade and payments to guard tumbling reserves. A large internal European market would solve the payments dilemma, argued the United States. Devaluation would be a start toward multilateralism.[32]

Throughout much of 1949, however, Attlee resisted the move. He preferred to restrict imports, develop nondollar sources of supply, target North American markets, and ease intra-European import controls. Many cabinet ministers supported discrimination instead of depreciation, which they predicted would not boost exports because the Americans would not cut tariffs enough to help. But the government could not hold the line. In late July figures showed a −$1.51 billion dollar gap, much higher than previous estimates. Marshall Plan aid of $780 million and Chancellor of the Exchequer Stafford Cripps's plan to cut dollar imports by 25 percent, or $400 million, would temporarily cover the deficit. But a more drastic solution was in order.[33]

Britain, America, and Canada signed a tripartite financial agreement in September 1949, a month after the Annecy Round had ended. Under the accord, the discriminatory sterling bloc would be allowed to continue pending devaluation of the pound. Britain would maintain discrimination, including Ottawa preferences, and would be exempt from the liberalization plans of the Organization for European Economic Cooperation, which directed Marshall Plan aid. Some American free-traders sought a wholly unilateral elimination of U.S. tariffs to raise imports from Britain. Given the breadth of protectionist sentiment in the United States, however, the proposal was totally impractical. Attlee and Cripps acted instead. Devaluation, and the Korean War's kindling of exports and aid afterward, helped the British payments balance. By the end of 1950, the European dollar famine ended and America experienced its first quarterly trade deficit in thirteen years.[34]

The tripartite accord rendered British concessions at the Annecy Round meaningless, but the State Department understood that such was the sacrifice necessary to avoid Britain's economic collapse. Besides, the moderate U.S. import policy was partly to blame for the dollar gap. Thus, at Annecy, the Americans were primarily concerned with keeping multilateral principles alive and bringing new nations under the GATT umbrella. There would be plenty of time after the dollar crisis ended to attack discrimination.[35]

The pound crisis—and its impact on a major Cold War ally—prompted the Americans to forge ahead with liberalization. The 147 accords at Annecy expanded GATT's coverage to four-fifths of world trade. Two-thirds of the contracting members' imports were now subject to GATT schedules. The United States granted $167 million in concessions to the acceding nations, on 44 percent of their exports, and received in return concessions amounting to $637 million on 46 percent of its exports to them.

American gains were more apparent than real. These numbers did not reflect that concessions were generalized to all GATT members, which raised the value of U.S. imports from the acceding nations to $259 million. Furthermore, because the dollar gap and availability of Marshall Plan funds so distorted trade, many nations imported at abnormally high levels. Italy, for instance, bought much more wheat and cotton from America in 1948 than it did in 1938. Thus, the results did not really favor the United States. And, considering the constraints of the RTAA of 1948, the United States had done well to cut tariffs at all.[36]

All nations were responsible for the modest results at Annecy. Bilateral accords were delayed as new contracting parties proposed to raise tariffs. Colombia's projected hikes were so enormous and its concession offers so pitiful that it actually left the talks. Uruguay pondered a 20 percent rise in duties. Farm protectionism was also rampant. Nicaragua refused concessions on U.S. milk exports, and Sweden resented America's meager offers on a number of agricultural items. Meanwhile, the United States resisted halving tariffs on Danish butter until Denmark promised to meet all U.S. requests. And talks with Italy stalled when America initially refused concessions on lemons.[37]

The lemon issue was so serious that the U.S.-Italian bilateral agreement was reached just two days before the end of the Annecy Round. Lemons were a key export for Italy. The State Department wanted U.S. tariffs cut to stabilize the Italian economy, guard against a peasant revolt in Sicily, and promote Italy's allegiance to NATO. Yet producers and legislators in California and Arizona lobbied the president, through the sympathetic Department of Agriculture, to withhold concessions. Producers held that the eventual offer to reduce lemon tariffs was made to coax Italy to sign the Annecy agreement (which Italy did not do until mid-1950). Besides, even the State Department agreed that Italian lemons had competed well in North America for over a decade.

But Truman felt that the threat of Italy's withdrawal from the talks outweighed domestic concerns. A concession would better the nation's dollar position; anyway, America could absorb the competition, for its lemon industry was profitable, even as an exporter. Truman sided with the diplomats. He disregarded peril point limits and slashed the lemon tariff in half. U.S. growers were furious. Senator Carl Hayden, an Arizona Democrat, spent months asking Truman to limit Italian lemons by a quota. The president refused, seeking to close out the Annecy Round and aid an important Cold War ally.[38]

The impartial Tariff Commission concluded that, like Italy, U.S. allies gained at Annecy. Seventy-five percent of Italy's dutiable imports into the United States and 99 percent of those of Finland, Nicaragua, and Uruguay won concessions. Roughly 95 percent of America's dutiable imports were now subject to agreements, and tariff reductions accounted for 90 percent of the concessions. Quotas and customs restraints limited the effect of the reductions. But the aggregate U.S. tariff cuts from the Geneva and Annecy Rounds roughly halved the country's pre-GATT rates. From 1934 to 1949 duties on commodities plummeted by 37 percent; on manufactures, by half.

Truman also authorized cuts in rates below the peril points on several items for the benefit of foreigners.[39]

For that reason, the Annecy Round garnered the usual comment. Commonwealth nations were content that no alterations in imperial preferences were required. In the United States, protectionists lamented that the tariff vanishing act had carried over from Geneva. But most commentators agreed that the talks had broadened the Geneva agreement and aided European dollar balances. A *New York Times* survey of industrial leaders uncovered few complaints. Such import-sensitive industries as machine tools, textiles, and jewelry expressed no dismay about the concessions. The Annecy Round, proclaimed the National Foreign Trade Council and the National Council of American Importers in September 1949, was a "step down the path toward the goal of multilateral trading and currency convertibility."[40]

The modesty of the Annecy results signaled that moderate protectionists kept their hold on the GATT process. According to free-traders, protectionism in world trade seemed stronger than ever at the end of 1949. Controls on trade remained. Thus, Canada's Dana Wilgress, who chaired the Annecy meetings, warned that it would not be "too pessimistic to predict that before long nearly half of the [contracting parties] will be intensifying import restrictions." Woodbury Willoughby echoed this worry, that the concessions were tempered by discrimination.[41]

For the Americans, that criticism was doubly serious not just for pointing out the restraints on trade liberalization but also because of the campaign for the ITO Charter. The Annecy Round had revealed the pervasiveness of regulatory controls on trade. Such statism validated the arguments of free trade purists, hurting the chances of ITO ratification.

The constrained Annecy talks and the holdup of the ITO in the United States also raised fears among nations that America was abdicating its position of leadership over the international trade system. In response, the administration renewed its campaign to link the Havana Charter, GATT, and the Marshall Plan into the web of foreign economic policy. The results at Annecy, officials argued, promoted Western European productivity. And complex trade problems demanded more permanency to the provisional GATT, especially as the charter went down the tubes.[42] Thus, even before shelving the ITO, GATT became America's substitute.

The administration considered steps to strengthen the General Agreement. Over the objections of allies and U.S. veterans, West Germany, Japan, and Korea were to participate in the next round of GATT talks. Concessions by these nations, claimed the Committee on Trade Agreements, would boost European recovery. By late 1949 West Germany and Korea prepared for accession to GATT at the Torquay Round, which would convene the following September in England. Over Commonwealth protests, Japan was invited as an observer. The Torquay talks would expand GATT membership from thirty-four to forty-one nations and include over three hundred bilateral agreements. By May 1950, just months after the Annecy Round had ended, hearings on concession lists were already under way in the United States in preparation for the next round of GATT, which had become the centerpiece of the global capitalist commercial order.[43]

In 1949 Harry Truman cared more about recouping losses in trade policy than in making bold policy moves. Liberal traders breathed a sigh of relief as the Democrats returned to dominance in Washington. They restored the powers of the Reciprocal Trade Agreements Act during the year, excising the peril point. Protectionists persisted in their campaign to limit free trade, however. Yet the Cold War atmosphere undercut their fight. The RTAA made sense for a Western alliance enfeebled by struggling trade partners.

Maintaining momentum for trade liberalization was another job for the administration. The Annecy meetings did not transform the commercial system. In fact, no GATT discussions until the 1960s would equal the Geneva Round in significance. Yet Annecy's modest tariff concessions and the admission of several new members further legitimized the GATT forum. Discrimination still abounded; the British crisis over devaluation ensured that it would remain a guiding force. But America, like before, accepted moderate protectionism as a key element of GATT.

In 1949 the United States continued this compromising approach to appease domestic interests and strengthen the economies of allies abroad. GATT business indicated that the drive toward trade liberalization was alive, although not kicking vigorously. But no nation endorsed radical action. Instead, trade partners sought moderate, steady progress toward the ultimate objective of multilateralism.

CHAPTER 11

Cold War Ideals
1950–1953

The idealistic belief that goods exchanged under a universal code of rules would bring a millennium of peace had been laid to rest by 1950. The realism embedded in national security policy pushed the General Agreement on Tariffs and Trade to the fore. The transformation in ideology was completed. Free-traders now adapted to circumstances; they became Cold Warriors. As protectionism mounted overseas and at home, they replaced peace with the containment doctrine as their rationale for trade liberalization. By the early 1950s free trade undergirded a Free World.

Even before the Annecy talks had concluded, the GATT parties were planning another round of discussions. These took place in Torquay, England, a resort town 150 miles west of London. Six acceding nations and twenty-seven contracting parties began negotiations on September 28, 1950. The talks, however, did not go well for the Americans or, for that matter, the GATT system.

To be sure, there were positive developments at Torquay. For instance, a special session addressed the disparity of tariff levels among Western European nations, which were months away from creating the Coal and Steel Community. The differentials impeded the creation of a common tariff, held up integration, and caused discrimination against the United States. These talks focused on the regional economic community that led to the European Common Market, which flourished for decades afterward.

Another gain at Torquay was the progress made toward trade liberalization, excepting the British Commonwealth. America secured concessions valued at $1.2 billion, covering 20 percent of its exports to the seventeen nations with which it concluded accords. In return, the United States cut or bound duties amounting to $478 million, or 7.2 percent of its imports.

America got much less than this apparently great deal, however. The figures included shipments of U.S. farm goods not normally exported to GATT nations. Also, over half of America's tariff cuts were in the high 25–50 percent range, but few foreign reductions came near this level.[1]

The issue of quantitative barriers also limited U.S. gains. GATT made allowances for quotas under certain circumstances, but import controls now seemed permanently entrenched in the discriminatory sterling area. The International Monetary Fund reported a better dollar position for most nations in 1950, and, in accordance with their membership in the European Payments Union, seventeen countries of the Organization for European Economic Cooperation eased their quotas by late 1950. But the Commonwealth feared that progress would be temporary; the dollar gap might grow again once Korean War rearmament spurred imports and spending. At Torquay, these nations thus denied American requests for relaxing controls.[2]

The Commonwealth also dealt a severe blow to GATT and U.S. trade policy. In April 1950 America handed in its tariff offers and requests, adding more items in May and August. The offer list was designed to close the dollar gap by granting duty reductions even on sensitive items like wool and cheese. In return, the United States expected, once and for all, progress toward ending imperial preferences. But the British remained tough, refusing to narrow margins without more American concessions. America must slash tariffs while Britain, wrote Board of Trade president Harold Wilson, "would sell preferences very dearly with the idea of preserving as far as possible the structure of the Imperial preference system." Australia and New Zealand were in accord.[3]

By August 1950 the British embassy told American officials that Prime Minister Clement Attlee would insist on unilateral action by the United States. Notably, Britain acknowledged that its offers were inadequate by any standard. But in part, this reflected pressure from Parliament. The British also believed that creditors owed debtors generous concessions to make GATT work effectively and balance the world economy. Britain prepared to prune back offers. "We were out to secure an agreement which was somewhat, at least unbalanced in our favor," noted U.K. delegation chief Stephen Holmes after the Torquay Round.[4]

Not surprisingly, then, American-Commonwealth negotiations quickly reached an impasse. In September Foreign Secretary Ernest Bevin had asked that the trade talks not be allowed to bog down again over preferences, but the United States insisted that margins be reduced. To move the Commonwealth, Truman approved a controversial offer to cut the raw wool tariff by 25 percent, over the objections of the Department of Agriculture. Like the Geneva Round, failure to conclude agreements with the southern dominions would bolster Britain's stubbornness in Torquay.[5] But as it turned out, nothing would sway the British.

Once again, political and economic concerns were the reasons. Holding a slender majority in Parliament, Attlee would not expose himself to charges before the 1951 elections that he had weakened the Commonwealth. The unity of the British nations was even more important now that the Korean War put a spotlight on containment in Asia, a foundation of the empire. Business leaders and politicians alike had an emotional commitment to preferences. The dollar shortage also discouraged free trade. Stephen Holmes found that the American offers were "unexpectedly generous," covering all British demands to the maximum extent. Yet he would not trade preferences or commitments under the Ottawa Agreement for a wool deal, no matter how significant, and the southern dominions backed him up.[6] There was a sense of déjà vu in the Anglo-American negotiations.

The U.S. delegation responded with vigorous counterarguments. First, politics should not dictate trade policy. Second, the dominions wanted preferences reduced. And America's offers were far superior in terms of import coverage, concessions, and items affected. Britain had offered no major cuts in margins and no concession at all for the benefit of U.S. farmers. Of Britain's $130 million in offers, the large majority amounted to "worthless" bindings. Meanwhile, almost all of America's $122 million concessions were in the form of duty cuts. British offers covered only 11 percent of imports from the United States; America's covered 55 percent of imports from Britain. The U.S. delegation repeatedly pledged to expand its offer list and radically curb requests on British tariffs. It also played the political card, reminding Britain that progress would strengthen solidarity among the Western nations. But the United Kingdom made no move to open its markets.[7]

Its pleas for compromise falling on deaf British ears, the State Department warned the Foreign Office in March 1951 of an imminent collapse in the talks. Without getting concessions on preferences, America would leave the negotiations and withdraw the wool offer to the dominions to boot. But the British still balked, willing both to accept a limited agreement and to risk a breakdown, which would not be disastrous in their eyes. Attlee would not "tamper with the preference system."[8]

The Americans then turned to the dominions to break the jam. They approached Australia, but the new Liberal government faced a labor crisis and an election in the near future and was unable (or unwilling) to release its empire partners from their Ottawa Agreement obligations. Only Canada criticized the political motivation behind British policy. Still, the British refused to make the concessions, as nations other than Canada would be affected. Delegation head Holmes did drop below the minimum margin level on dried figs, but only because Britain bought scarcely any imports of the commodity from Commonwealth nations. Faced with this refusal, America dramatically withdrew its offers to Britain and aborted the Anglo-American talks. Because the wool offer was withdrawn in the process, Australia, New Zealand, and South Africa also did not conclude an agreement with the United States at Torquay.[9] Unlike the Geneva Round, the American warnings on preferences turned out to be no bluff at Torquay.

Domestic politics was a major impetus to the Department of State's stance. Protectionists might interpret the breakdown, along with the ITO debacle, as evidence that the free-traders were on the run. But above all, British offers were simply poor, wrote Carl Corse of the Committee on Trade Agreements. The Senate's vote on the Reciprocal Trade Agreements Act of 1951 was nearing. There was no need to add to its substantial opposition by angering legislators with a bad deal. America did sign a solid agreement with Canada. President Truman then approved the Torquay results on April 17, 1951, and this third GATT round came to an end.[10]

The Torquay Round was another setback for American free-traders. To be sure, most nations had exhausted their bargaining power in previous rounds, so the results were bound to be minimal. But the perpetuation of import controls and the lack of American-Commonwealth accords undermined the campaign for multilateralism. "In this uncertain and dangerous world it seems still to be the British policy to pull down the shutters," claimed the *Economist*. Yet along with other British analysts, the journal believed that the country had done well. After all, discriminatory barriers had been left untouched. The Foreign Office would accept the risk of political damage to Anglo-American relations, although in the tense atmosphere of the Cold War, the British were safe from U.S. recrimination.[11]

Many nations worried about the Torquay Round's implications. They realized that the talks had discouraged further attempts at large multilateral trade negotiations. Was GATT simply irrelevant? When the International Trade Organization had been jettisoned in December 1950, a working party had been tapped to consider the formation of a permanent committee to administer GATT. But a review was put off until late 1954. Also, the Reciprocal Trade Agreements Act seemed to be in trouble in Congress. The United States had walked out on the Commonwealth in Torquay and now might sour on trade liberalization. Thus, many foreign observers viewed the Torquay Round as a failure.[12]

The Americans were also worried about the stress on GATT. Carl Corse claimed that the situation at Torquay had been hopeless; no deal had ever been possible except on British terms. As the State Department concluded, Torquay revealed that "the difficulties encountered in lowering rates of duty are probably greater today than at any time since the end of the war." The White House disguised the failure by focusing on the agreements with other nations and stressing its toughness in refusing to grant concessions to the Commonwealth without reciprocity. But this GATT round signaled the staying power of protectionism. Indeed, although Britain tried but failed to win Commonwealth consent for a waiver on the GATT rule that prevented new preferences in 1952, the British, as well as the Americans, sought exemptions within GATT to protect certain sectors. Significantly, moreover, no major tariff negotiations occurred for almost a decade. And even this Dillon Round of GATT, in 1960–61, proved disappointingly modest in its results.[13]

The Commonwealth had jarred GATT, and for the first time America had not granted concessions without assurances of something in return. But the United States itself was not immune from the protectionist bug. During the Torquay Round and afterward, domestic resistance grew to freer trade. The administration responded by relying on the linkage between trade and security.

In August 1950 Senator Theodore Green, of Rhode Island, a Democrat who supported the trade agreements program, had sought a postponement at Torquay. His state produced cotton textiles, and Green objected to the number of these manufactures on the American offer list. He considered offering a resolution to delay the talks, using the Korean War as an excuse. Bargaining over tariffs while economic conditions were unsettled by war, he argued, was unreasonable. Also, GATT members (and the acceding South Koreans) were preoccupied with the conflict. Reminding the administration that the Reciprocal Trade Agreements Act was due for renewal in 1951, Green demanded protection. The State Department predicted that many southern Democrats and most Republicans would engage in similar pressure tactics. Indeed, even Ways and Means chairman Robert Doughton, from the textile state of North Carolina, leaned toward Green's view.

Secretary of State Dean Acheson scrambled to head off the resolution. His figures showed that Rhode Island could absorb the tariff cuts, but he preferred to emphasize security instead. "The invasion of Korea has greatly increased, not lessened, the need for economic strength and unity in the nations of the free world," asserted a press release. The Torquay Round would further cooperation by establishing formal trade links between West Germany (which was acceding to GATT) and the NATO alliance. It would also raise American imports, dampen inflation, help balance foreign accounts, and thus bolster containment. Defense "against aggression is not exclusively a military" issue, concluded Acheson. Senator Green met with Truman and agreed to withdraw his resolution on the condition that he receive a letter that pledged fair treatment for domestic interests at Torquay.[14] The specter of the Cold War, and the existence of a hot one, managed protectionism in this case.

The administration also invoked the escape clause for the first time ever, in December 1950. The Tariff Commission advised the president to withdraw concessions on women's fur felt hats and hat bodies. Allowed by GATT, the action affected many European nations that demanded more proof that their exports had hurt American employment and industry profits. Indeed, the State Department found the case for hat bodies inconclusive. The Tariff Commission had cited a mere 3 percent decline in production as grounds for escape from prior agreements. Belgium quickly retaliated by withdrawing concessions to the United States on industrial wax. But even State Department officials stomached the decision because it showed Congress that Truman listened to industry complaints.[15]

The Cold War also abetted protectionism. Truman had struck a blow against communist Czechoslovakian hat exporters, while he also tightened the system of export controls against the Soviet bloc. And, in the further politicization of world trade, he signed a proclamation on August 1, 1951, that ordered the suspension of trade agreement concessions with members of the Soviet bloc, including Czechoslovakia, the People's Republic of China, and nations that might fall under communist control, such as Vietnam. The year before, Red China had withdrawn from GATT. By late 1951 America had canceled most of its GATT accords with communist nations.[16]

Other protectionist actions ensued. Congress curbed imports of competitive commodities in June 1950 by reauthorizing quotas under Section 22 of the Agricultural Adjustment Act. Senator Warren Magnuson of Washington later attached an amendment to the Reciprocal Trade Agreements Act that required that future agreements enforce quotas, which could be imposed in emergencies resulting from the perishability of a food product. Magnuson sought more expansive powers for Section 22. For instance, he suggested that the protectionist-leaning Department of Agriculture, rather than the Tariff Commission, investigate complaints by farmers regarding imports. Producers of lemons and nuts welcomed the measure, whereas exporting nations protested it as a threat to dollar reserves. Other restrictions on foreign commodities were imposed under Section 104 of the Defense Production Act of July 1951. The administration swallowed the measures, which it deemed too popular in Congress to oppose.[17]

This slide back toward protectionism was quickened by the renewal of the Reciprocal Trade Agreements Act in 1951. The administration calculated that its tough stance at Torquay, as well as the escape clause action, export controls, and quotas for agriculture, would sway Congress to extend the legislation. That proved true, but problems arose for the liberal traders nonetheless. The RTAA was a middle-rung priority. The Korean War, the Japanese peace treaty, NATO rearmament, and McCarthyism, among other issues, occupied the Eighty-second Congress. But it remained a key element in recovery programs. For that reason, the fact that the RTAA of 1951 embodied some major protectionist elements was worrisome for the foreign policy establishment.

The very success of the reciprocal trade program increased resistance to the bill in 1951. To be sure, there was no rush to renew the law, as no GATT rounds were planned for the near future. And in the climate of the Korean War, reciprocal trade was not a chief concern. Yet the State Department urged Democrats in Congress to press forward on the basis that the trade agreements program had been so effective over the past seventeen years. Average tariff rates on dutiable imports had been 52.8 percent in 1933 under the Smoot-Hawley Act. In 1949 they stood at a strikingly low 13.8 percent and would fall to around 5 percent once the Annecy Round schedules were fully in effect. The momentum would continue if Congress granted fresh authority to reduce tariffs.

But Congress was in no mood to maintain the streak of trade liberalization. Boosted by the Marshall Plan, foreign competitors were starting to move in on markets that had been the domain of American producers. Furthermore, many imports—glass, shoes, furs, and textiles—came from such unpopular sources as the communist bloc and Japan. Raised to record postwar levels by the recession of 1949, unemployment heightened awareness of the impact of imports at home. Despite the fact that trade played a minor role in their troubles, stagnating industries still had powerful representatives in Congress who believed that protectionism could remedy their problems. Even exporters complained that the RTAA had done little to open markets abroad.[18]

Faced with these obstacles, the administration adopted a clever tactic. To reinvigorate support for the Reciprocal Trade Agreements Act and muffle dissent and perhaps to appear as hardheaded traders before the 1952 elections, congressional allies of the administration inserted such procedural safeguards as escape clauses, agricultural quotas, and even the dreaded peril points into the legislation.[19] Unfortunately for liberal trade advocates, the idea turned out to be too clever by half after Truman sent a simple renewal bill to Congress in January 1951.

The bill was notable not for the debate over time-worn issues, but because procedural safeguards became its centerpiece. The extension so diverged from Democratic Party policy that several commentators called the measure the most protectionist tariff bill since Smoot-Hawley and certainly worse than the Republican law of 1948. An alarmed Secretary of State Dean Acheson testified against the version that exited the House Ways and Means Committee because it was so rife with restrictions.[20]

Congress did not listen to him. After four days of Ways and Means hearings, the bill arrived on the House floor with peril points, restrictions on imports from communist nations, mandatory escape clauses for agreements, quotas on foreign commodities, and a two-year time limit. By a large margin in February, the House accepted all of these revisions but renewed the law for three years. A vote of 225–168 restored the peril point measure, which prevented concessions below a certain tariff rate. Only 4 of the 187 Republicans opposed the provision, and 42 Democrats voted for it. The escape clause, similar to Truman's Executive Order of 1947, passed 191 to 89. Protectionism had gained in popularity.

The reinstatement of peril points was the biggest change in the bill. Protectionists had pushed for such action since the procedure had been eliminated in 1949. In Summer 1950 they had been stymied after the Senate Finance Committee shelved a copper tax bill with a peril point clause offered by Eugene Millikin. Now they had won back their prize.

The trade bill went to the Senate Finance Committee, which modified the measure by tightening up escape clause and peril point procedures, widening the use of farm quotas, and reinstating the two-year time limit. Interruptions extended consideration by the committee until early April 1951, but the Finance Committee then unanimously reported out the bill. Among some of the changes from the House version was a provision declaring that passage of the law did not mean that Congress approved of GATT. The full Senate passed the bill on May 23 by a margin of 72 to 2. A conference committee revised it further, and the president signed the Reciprocal Trade Agreements Act on June 16, 1951.[21]

Disgusted bureaucrats tried to stop the changes, but the administration figured that a renewal of the law was good enough. Truman was preoccupied with European rearmament and the aftereffects of firing Douglas MacArthur from his command in Korea. The Republicans had turned up the heat on the administration, viciously denouncing Truman for having supposedly "lost" China to communism, bogging down in the Korean War, and wasting taxpayers' money on fruitless defense programs. They also began investigations into alleged political corruption by the president's associates. Moreover, McCarthyism was all the rage. Bipartisanship in foreign policy had vanished by 1951. Truman watched his public approval rating sink as the GOP strived to unseat the Democrats from the Oval Office in 1952. In this poisoned atmosphere, just renewing the trade program was good enough.

The White House thus viewed the vote on the RTAA as a victory, declaring that its principles were more widely accepted than ever before. That was true, but the fact that the law won in both houses by huge margins is instructive. The votes showed the appeal of protectionism. Many legislators, and not just rabid opponents of reciprocal trade, endorsed the bill because it seemed reasonable.[22]

Both parties had backed the peril point and escape clause. These measures, they argued, blocked the cadre of insensitive free-traders, while honoring the principles of reciprocal trade. Lyndon Johnson, a rising star in the Senate, voted for the RTAA of 1951. In his view, tariff cutting had gone far enough. He thus believed "that the time has come to stop, look and listen before making further concessions because trade barriers in the countries with which we trade have been growing and growing." Another Democrat, John Kennedy of Massachusetts, also voted for the law because he worried about the "assassination of [the groundfish fillet] industry" by foreign competition. Later he explained that free trade was an ideal, possible only after domestic industries were safe from bankruptcy. Indeed, the Reciprocal Trade Agreements Act of 1951 was not a party issue. Both sides of the aisle deserted the administration.[23]

Liberal traders made the best of the situation. President Truman noted that "some of the new procedural provisions are cumbersome and superfluous," for protective safeguards already existed. And the legislation ig-

nored the needs of the Western alliance. "We cannot win the cold war" by
seeking refuge in protectionism, announced Will Clayton. "We should do
everything within reason to strengthen the economies of these powers by
allowing them to trade with us on a fair basis," echoed owners of a pho-
tography company.[24] Yet over the next decade, protectionism played a
growing and more influential role in trade policy.

The Korean War, militarization, and the gradual recovery of competitive
allies led to the scaled-back Reciprocal Trade Agreements Act. The Torquay
Round had been, at best, a meager success; the march toward lower barriers had slowed appreciably. The ITO Charter was a discard of history. With
a lameduck and unpopular president in office, free-traders were, in short,
on the defensive, hopeful that the presidential election of 1952 would spur
liberalization efforts. But what little planning there was in 1952 involved
setting the groundwork for the next president, looking ahead to the renewal of the trade law in 1953 and perhaps trying again to create a trade institution. All such efforts were ensconced in the Cold War; all were a
response to rising protectionist pressures.

A host of bills pending in Congress spurred protectionism in 1952. Congress considered several measures to restrict trade. These included a bill to
halve imports containing any materials that enjoyed a priority status in government allocation, one to require that half of Mutual Security Program
goods travel in American ships, tariff hikes on several products, and a law
that would lower the amount of foreign chinaware from $500 to $35 that
could be brought in duty-free by tourists. When added to the sixteen applications for relief under the RTAA's escape clause, it was clear that protectionism was much more than a specter.[25]

Congress also touched off a threat of retaliation from five allies, including Canada, when it restricted dairy products late in the year. The protest
was prompted by Section 104, a rider tacked on to the Defense Production
Act that imposed quotas of up to 40 percent on imported dairy products,
fats, and oils. The president despised this "Cheese Amendment," for it was
"the kind of law which makes the job of the Kremlin's propaganda experts
a great deal easier." Free-traders argued that protectionism was not consistent with the expensive policy of shoring up foreign economies to assure allegiance to the Free World.[26]

The administration tried to have commercial policy reflect diplomacy.
Britain protested the number of applications by U.S. producers for relief

under the escape clause, and the Board of Trade led a major review of British trade policy, undertaken in part to answer rising American protectionism. The study considered GATT's future and the feasibility of multilateralism, the dollar gap, and whether to strengthen the imperial preferential trading network in light of growing economic unity in Western Europe. Word of the review, and mounting U.S. protectionism, prompted Dean Acheson to warn that if "we and our partners in the free world are to build the kind of economic and military strength we need for our security, we must all cooperate to reduce and minimize the barriers to trade between us." In July and August 1952 Truman ruled on three recommendations by the Tariff Commission.[27] He raised tariffs on dried figs but refused increases on watches and to impose quotas on garlic. His reasons related to national security.

Watch imports from Switzerland had long been a point of debate, but they did not appear to the administration to be the main cause of the domestic industry's downturn. Besides, Truman wished to maintain the exports of a nation that received no aid from the United States but leaned toward the West. The Swiss recognized this, as they rejoiced over the decision that was of "tremendous importance in reaffirming the confidence between his country and the free nations of Europe," exalted the Swiss *Journal de Genève*.[28]

Cognizant of southern Europe's importance to containment, the president nevertheless acted on garlic and figs. He had doubted that California garlic growers were injured by imports, and he refused to slow imports from Italy, a NATO ally. But he curbed foreign figs, claiming that abnormal crop and seasonal factors dictated the action. Yet Truman also pledged to keep a close watch on the product so he could lower the duty as quickly as possible. Furthermore, he deemed the move temporary until he could convince exporters like Greece to curb their sales. *Business Week* hoped so, for the tariff issue "brought home to us in the cold war that it is to our own interest to help make the nations of Europe self-sufficient."[29]

As protectionism reared up, free-traders held that Congress did not think of foreign policy when acting on trade matters. If not discouraged, noted *Time* magazine in an April 1952 article entitled "Buy Free World," protectionism could "play havoc with the weak economies of America's partners abroad, and the greater the dollar gap, the greater the peril to the free world's security." Those claiming injury due to a flood of imports were crying wolf, charged liberal traders, for the annual surplus of exports over imports since 1946 had averaged about $5 billion. Simply, U.S. allies could trade with America or, tariff cutters warned, turn to the communist world.[30] This recognition of the prominence of the Cold War served as the basis of the Bell Report, commissioned by President Truman in July 1952.

Named for banker Daniel Bell, the chairman of the United States Public Advisory Board for Mutual Security, the report that was published in March 1953 reflected the meshing of national security and trade policies. Concerned about the rash of protectionist measures he faced, Truman had asked the board to keep in mind that "[w]e are working night and day to build up the military and economic strength of our friends and allies throughout the free world." The Gray Report of 1950 had pushed for freer trade but had been buried by the Korean War. Success in the Cold War now made the Bell Report imperative.[31]

The commission delighted the free-traders. It advocated an agenda "that will meet the needs of the present world situation and that will be in the national interest rather than in the interest of small groups of producers who fear foreign competition." The Bell Report essentially opted for the sacrifice of American industry to imports for the purpose of strengthening Cold War allies. Aimed at liberalizing the Reciprocal Trade Agreements Act in 1953, this sweeping proclamation of free trade put protectionists on alert that a new administration might give them trouble.[32]

Both presidential candidates in 1953 were free-traders; both viewed commerce in terms of the Cold War and capitalist ideology. The Democrat, Adlai Stevenson, was an avowed internationalist who despised protectionism and warned that the Republican Old Guard would rear up and wreck the reciprocal trade program if his opponent took office. The front-runner and eventual winner, Dwight D. Eisenhower, was also a free-trader, even a dogmatist in the mold of Cordell Hull and William Clayton. Wisely playing politics, Eisenhower reserved his support for the RTAA out of respect for Robert Taft's forces of protectionism in his party. But he steadfastly determined to encourage trade with all noncommunist nations. Ike pushed for free trade, particularly in the Third World, where he saw international communism hard at work. As president, he would ensure that global resources did not pass into Soviet hands and that nations friendly to the United States and its way of life would remain allies. Indeed, in his administration during the 1950s, liberal trade would serve as an instrument of national security in the Cold War.[33]

Eisenhower would have been a free trade universalist in earlier times,

but, like other security-conscious leaders, he had become a Cold War realist when it came to trade. Protectionism would have no place in his administration because it undercut containment efforts. He cited Joseph
Stalin's last public political speech, in October 1952, which predicted a
breakup of the Western alliance. According to the Soviet dictator, American allies would rebel against U.S. domination, for they were eager to trade
with the Soviet bloc. West German businessmen had already initialed deals
to exchange goods with China, Southeast Asian businessmen looked to
Russia for scarce industrial supplies, and the Milan Chamber of Commerce
had criticized America for frowning on trade with the communist world.
At the Moscow economic conference in Spring 1952, the Soviets had called
for expanded East-West trade, which now amounted to $10 billion. Britain
responded by negotiating a multimillion dollar textile deal with the Soviet
Union and the People's Republic of China. France had also renewed its
trade accord with Russia in September 1951. Eisenhower thus urged that
America allow its friends to sell more of their goods in the U.S. market to
lure them away from the communists.[34]

And he accused legislators in his own party of seeking a ruinous return
to the days of the Smoot-Hawley Tariff Act. Writing Secretary of State–
designate John Foster Dulles a few days before the inauguration in January
1953, Eisenhower declared his readiness to confront the new Republican
Congress's bills, "each sponsored by some pressure group and each seeking
to establish some new kind of obstacle to throw into the path of international trade." His motto "trade, not aid" had the endorsement of big business free trade purists, who also comprised his cabinet. He borrowed the
saying from the British chancellor of the Exchequer Richard Butler, who,
like the new president, wanted to push for free trade now that the Marshall
Plan and recovery period had finally come to an end.[35]

President Eisenhower would subsume trade policy under a national security agenda. Also, as a strong believer in market capitalism, he would
insist on lowering barriers that burdened the economy. Yet despite his fer-
vent views, protectionism grew steadily stronger throughout the 1950s.
Like Truman, Ike would also commission a major study of trade policy
under the direction of industrialist Clarence Randall. But Eisenhower
made one thing clear. In the Cold War, there was room neither for idealistic dreams of trade universalism nor for protectionism. The former was
now but a distant dream; the latter continued to plague him throughout
his administration.

Trade, not aid, believed the incoming Eisenhower administration, would bolster
the Free World. (*Collier's*, November 22, 1952, p. 78.)

It is easy to conclude that in the early 1950s, trade liberalization was on the
wane. But in reality, the Torquay Round and the Reciprocal Trade Agreements Act of 1951 simply indicated that a new context had developed in the
GATT system, in the Cold War, and in the United States. The crisis of European recovery was passing, although trade partners still worried about
competing once again. Reconstruction overseas and the emboldened Republican critics of the Truman administration at home provided the impetus for protectionism. The superpower conflict became more dangerous as
militarization replaced economic containment. In America, an unpopular
president struggled with international and domestic problems that eventu-

ally chased him and the Democrats from power. Liberal trade ideology and policy could hardly be expected to thrive in this atmosphere. Yet they persisted all the same.

The postwar trade system wavered but did not collapse. GATT faltered as the Torquay Round severely tested the multilateral precept. Protectionism was more prevalent as nations compromised in their trade relations. But GATT survived. Its flexibility, its forgiving nature, permitted all sorts of deviations from free trade. Likewise, for the seventh time in its history, the reciprocal trade program was renewed. By the time Dwight Eisenhower took office, the Reciprocal Trade Agreements Act was almost two decades old. Battered by protectionists and revised to suit Congress's will, the law still guided trade liberalization. The quest for multilateralism, however modified and adjusted, was still alive.

Eisenhower faced many of the same problems in trade policy that confronted his predecessor as well as new ones. Protectionism was increasing at home and abroad. Momentum for major strides toward liberalization in GATT had slowed appreciably. Congress had grown more unruly, insisting on an array of safeguards for constituents. Yet the inexorable pull of containment prevented a retreat from a liberal trade agenda. Imports had to rise into the United States to strengthen allies. World trade had to expand to bolster the capitalist system. National security was the bottom line. The Cold War compelled the leader of the Free World to pursue free trade in the 1950s, and well beyond.

Conclusion

Despite the role played by the General Agreement on Tariffs and Trade in postwar recovery and in the security of the Western alliance, the initiative to cut trade barriers fell dormant after the early Cold War. Indeed, the negotiations at Torquay were such a disappointment that observers feared that GATT itself was in jeopardy. Some, like an Australian manufacturers' association, argued that the General Agreement had been "a complete failure."[1]

By the mid-1950s a review of GATT was under way. Some of the provisions of the Havana Charter were integrated into GATT rules. The contracting parties then created an institution, the Organization for Trade Cooperation, to administer GATT. But again, as in the case of the International Trade Organization, the president withheld from Congress an agreement to create a formal international trade body because of protectionist dissent. It would take four decades before Congress accepted a global commercial charter called the World Trade Organization in 1994, which subsumed GATT. What had been an informal forum of, initially, 23 members in 1947 had grown into an organization of over 130 nations a half century or so later.[2]

In the meantime, GATT forged onward. Denied recognition by national legislatures and bereft of formal status (it was never ratified by nations), the General Agreement nonetheless championed trade liberalization within the Western alliance for a half century. That it persisted owed to its flexible nature—primarily its very lack of universality—and to the penetrating impact of the Cold War. That is, GATT thrived because nations recognized the politics embedded in international trade policy. Politics compelled compromise acceptable to all.

International trade policy cannot be divorced from its political context. This is common sense, but it is nonetheless crucial to understanding the creation of the trade system under GATT. In the period under review, ideology, domestic politics, and diplomacy supplanted pure economic considerations and theories of efficiency in commercial relations. In pursuit of trade liberalization tempered by protectionism, the United States shaped a GATT order that promoted a moderate form of multilateralism. Free trade ideals were left behind, victims of domestic regulatory practices, the influence of protectionism, and, above all, the Cold War. The politics of trade took precedence over theoretical constructs and lofty dreams.

America condoned forms of economic nationalism out of sheer pragmatism. First of all, protectionist pressure at home turned the United States away from free trade. Second, trade partners adopted discriminatory trade and exchange measures in an effort to recover from the world war and meet domestic planning goals of full employment. At successive meetings with these nations, U.S. free-traders tried to moderate discrimination, but American foreign policymakers wisely accepted it. Without protectionist devices to regulate their economies, Cold War allies would have collapsed. Furthermore, no nation would have joined a system that did not allow freedom to resort to protectionism. Without cooperation, the alliance against global communism might have fallen into disarray.

Cold War realpolitik ultimately shaped the trade system, but protectionism in the United States and abroad signaled that free trade was simply not acceptable. The Reciprocal Trade Agreements Act authorized cautious tariff cuts, becoming more burdened with restrictive measures in nearly every renewal. And from the compromise on imperial preferences in the Atlantic Charter through drafts of the ITO Charter to the Torquay Round of GATT, multilateralists retreated under fire from statism and nationalism. By then, in any case, the superpower conflict had undermined universalism.

Ideology thrust GATT to the fore. The heady era of the United Nations' founding had given way to the antagonism of the Cold War, which made no room for universalist ideas. Americans now defended market principles in the face of perceived threats from the regulatory state at home, socialism among allies, and international communism. Unlike the ITO Charter, the malleable GATT did not pretend to embrace free trade multilateralism. As Dean Acheson wrote in his memoirs, "Wilsonian liberalism and a utopian dream" based on "classical economic goals" had no place in the Cold War.[3]

Free trade universalism was a goal for the far-off future when the superpower struggle had abated. This became clear when the United States gave rigidly antiprotectionist advice to the Russians in the 1990s, after the breakup of the Soviet Union, as they labored to convert from socialism to market capitalism. Back in the early Cold War, however, GATT's plan for modest tariff cuts sufficed. American policymakers regarded GATT as a supplement to the Marshall Plan. The forum was also tolerable to free trade purists who chafed at corruptive statist influences, as reflected in the Havana Charter. Furthermore, although no country ever ratified the General Agreement, every country supported it because it allowed for protectionism. In sum, GATT did all things for all nations but especially served U.S. purposes. GATT aspired to the philosophy of market capitalism, maintained pressure for trade liberalization, permitted protectionism, and united the Western powers into an anticommunist trade bloc that economically undergirded the NATO alliance.

To be sure, the Cold War forced the United States to concede major objectives at GATT. At the level of tariff bargaining, Americans usually gave more than they received. At the level of defending cherished principles and goals, they were forced into a wholesale retreat. During the first three GATT rounds, Britain and the Commonwealth resisted a commitment to end imperial preferences and import and exchange controls. American anger at this obstinacy did not shake these allies. Top officials, who placed a priority on diplomacy rather than economic principles, would not risk Western European security by needling the Commonwealth. For the benefit of the Western alliance, America sacrificed its principles and, to some extent, its markets.

In short, Great Britain was hardly a victim of American policy. Its structural weaknesses actually provided substantial bargaining chips, causing the United States to curtail the campaign for free trade. The Commonwealth revised U.S. plans and, therefore, had a major hand in shaping the GATT order. That resistance, moreover, puts in question the scholarly critique that decries U.S. hegemony run rampant over the world economy. American trade partners were at least as dominant in policy-making as the United States.[4]

These outcomes should not be interpreted as a defeat for U.S. interests, however, as protectionists (commentators as well as interest groups) have argued. GATT successfully policed the world commercial system for decades after the Second World War. Global trade soared, spurred by huge export growth in Western Europe, Asia, and the United States. Expansion led to the recovery of Western Europe and Japan, and to the creation of a customs union—the European Common Market—that harnessed the might (and suppressed the militarism) of West Germany. As a result, the economic boom prompted in part by the GATT order cultivated peace among two historic antagonists: the French and the Germans. And European integration raised U.S. exports. Trade growth, encouraged by GATT, brought stability

and prosperity for Cold War allies. And after the Cold War, GATT liberalization helped usher in the dynamic age of globalization. Ironically, the free
trade idealists, many of whom had experienced the evils of the Great Depression and the rise of fascism, could be proud that their ultimate objectives of peace and prosperity had largely come to fruition.

Certainly, the United States opened its markets to foreign imports. Jobs
were lost as a result. But not all difficulties at home could be blamed on trade.
Outmoded plants, an untrained workforce, lack of business-government co-
ordination, a consumer (rather than production) culture, the burden of defense spending, and inflation were significant factors in America's troubles
from the late 1960s onward. And most important, protectionism remained
as influential as ever.

Even during its reign as the so-called hegemon over the world economy,
the United States was no unilateral free-trader, like Britain during its era of
dominance in the nineteenth and early twentieth centuries. The reciprocal
trade program authorized only selective cuts in tariffs, a prudent—but most
unbefitting—policy for a world leader. Not until the Trade Expansion Act
of 1962 was the RTAA's procedure changed to allow the slashing of duties
across entire sectors, as the Commonwealth had demanded in the 1940s.
But even in 1962, significant safeguards, including escape clauses and retraining programs, were inserted in the law to cushion the effects of this
change and win over reluctant interests.[5]

The constraints on trade policy reflected the power of protectionism, of
which the Republican Right represented only a most virulent expression.
The undercurrent of resistance to imports never disappeared. A majority of
Americans endorsed internationalism and, by association, trade liberalization. But they did not accept free trade. Renewals of the Reciprocal Trade
Agreements Act showed the popularity—among Democrats and Republicans alike—of a wide range of protectionist measures. Presidents, all of
whom have advocated liberal trade, have been unable to exorcise these provisions from trade law. Over time, many endured, many were incorporated
into other devices, and many became the basis of even more effective methods of protectionism. Franklin Roosevelt and Harry Truman, in fact, did re-
markably well in handling dissent to their liberal trade agendas.

Truman, in particular, proved to be politically dexterous when it came to
trade. Sometimes by confrontation, more often by compromise, he managed protectionism skillfully enough to offer meaningful tariff concessions
to foreigners. Most important, he eased the country away from its previous
trade isolationism that had exacerbated the Great Depression. He put the

United States on a road of a nominally liberal trade policy. Considering America's historic protectionist record, the steady drop in the tariff rates of the United States under the impetus of the Reciprocal Trade Agreements Act and GATT was quite an accomplishment.

In general, American trade policy of the time has been misunderstood by many observers. The extent to which trade partners reshaped the charter, defied State Department objectives, and opened U.S. markets puts in question the supposed imperialistic selfishness of American policy. Furthermore, only in a narrow economic sense did officials sacrifice domestic producers to imports. In the larger contexts of Britain's financial crises, European recovery, and the Cold War, concessions at GATT were mandatory. In any case, protectionism remained a prominent feature of policy. There is no better evidence of this than the constraints on free trade that were inherent in GATT negotiations, rules, and principles, or in the increasing influence of Congress over the American trade agenda.

Faced at home with a public that focused on protectionism and abroad with trade partners who united in the call for regulated commerce, the Truman administration leaned toward trade liberalism while it embraced national demands. This compromise of free trade and protectionism, with the former taking precedence, epitomized the elasticity of GATT. Protectionism was integrated into the forum so that members could address their economic problems and political pressures but still aim for multilateralism. To be sure, GATT fell short of free trade. Thus, its incorporation into the World Trade Organization will not likely bring an end to trade restrictions and loopholes to liberalization. A fixture in international trade history, protectionism will endure in the future global commercial order.

GATT was the product of the clash between free trade and protectionism. If only to bear light on this elemental debate, the story of its birth is important. But its significance went far beyond this. GATT arose at a crucial point in history. The Second World War had transformed the global balance of power, as much as the defeat of the Spanish Armada or Napoleonic Wars had changed the rank of nations centuries before. America was now one of two great powers; GATT was a tool in its exercise of leadership. GATT developed as the Soviet-American rivalry emerged, a conflict that defined the second half of the twentieth century. A weapon in the arsenal of democracy, the General Agreement on Tariffs and Trade built international cooperation and prosperity throughout the epic Cold War. Its humble beginnings and modest nature belie that fact that GATT proved crucial to the Free World's victory in this great conflict.

Notes

ABBREVIATIONS

AA	Australian Archives, National Office, Canberra
AANSW	Australian Archives, New South Wales
AAV	Australian Archives, Victoria
AFBF	American Farm Bureau Federation
AFL-DL	American Federation of Labor, Department of Legislation Files, Silver Spring
ASSCR	Assistant Secretary of State for Congressional Relations, NA
BCNEA	Office of British Commonwealth and Northern European Affairs Records, NA
BPRO	British Public Record Office
BT	Board of Trade document (Britain)
BWTA	Boston Wool Trade Association Records, North Andover
CAB	Cabinet document (Britain)
CFR-R	Council on Foreign Relations Archives, New York
CO	Colonial Office document (Britain)
CQ	*Congressional Quarterly*
CRI	Committee for Reciprocity Information
DO	Dominions Office document (Britain)
DSB	*Department of State Bulletin*
ECEFP-R	Executive Committee on Economic Foreign Policy Records, NA
ECOSOC	Economic, Social, and Cultural Agency of the United Nations
FDRL	Franklin D. Roosevelt Library
FO	Foreign Office document, BPRO
FRUS	U.S. Department of State, *Foreign Relations of the United States*
HCL	Henry Cabot Lodge II Papers, MHS
HHL	Herbert Hoover Library
HSTL	Harry S. Truman Library
ICC	International Chamber of Commerce
ITF	International Trade Files (RG 43), NA

LBJL   Lyndon B. Johnson Library
LC   Library of Congress
LSE   British Library of Political and Economic Science, London School of
                Economics
MHS   Massachusetts Historical Society, Boston
MRC   Modern Record Centre, University of Warwick, Coventry
NA   National Archives of the United States
NAC   National Archives of Canada
NACIM   National Advisory Council on International and Monetary Policies Rec-
                ords, NA
NAM-A   National Association of Manufacturers Archives, Wilmington
NAWM   National Association of Wool Manufacturers
NFTC   National Foreign Trade Council
NGEMG   National General Export Merchants Group
NICB   National Industrial Conference Board Archives, Wilmington
NLA   National Library of Australia
NORC   National Opinion Research Center Records, Chicago
NWGA   National Wool Growers Association Papers, Laramie
NZA   New Zealand National Archives
OH   Oral History
OIT   Office of International Trade Records, U.S. Department of Commerce, NA
OPOS   Office of Public Opinion Studies Records, NA
PAB   Public Advisory Board Records, NA
POF   President's Office Files, HSTL
PPP   *Public Papers of the Presidents*
PSF   President's Secretary's Files
RES   Records of the Executive Secretariat (Dean Acheson), NA
RG   Record Group
RTAA-House   U.S. House Committee on Ways and Means, *Reciprocal Trade Agreements
                Act*
RTAA-Senate   U.S. Senate Committee on Finance, *Reciprocal Trade Agreements Act*
SBR   U.S. Senate Bills and Resolution Files, NA
TUC Records   Trade Union Congress Records, MRC
USCC   U.S. Chamber of Commerce Records, Wilmington
USDA   U.S. Department of Agriculture
WHCF   White House Central Files, Harry S. Truman Library
WWGA   Western Wool Growers Association Papers, Laramie

INTRODUCTION

1. *UN World* 2:5 (June 1948): 53.

2. Woods, *A Changing of the Guard*, 1–8 (transformations; Kennedy, *The Rise and Fall*, 291–390; Kunz, *Butter and Guns*, 1–2.

3. U.S. Department of Commerce, *Historical Statistics: I*, 228, *II*, 884.

4. Cohen, "General Agreement," 204.

5. Bairoch, *Economics and World History*; Eckes, *Opening America's Market*; Irwin, *Against the Tide*; Krauss, *How Nations Grow Rich*; Krugman, *Pop Internationalism*; Landes, *The Wealth and Poverty of Nations*. In the 1990s conservatives, liberals, unions, scholars, and environmentalists targeted their wrath on the North American Free Trade Agreement (NAFTA) and the World Trade Organization (WTO). See Kaplan, *American Trade Policy*, 125–54, and Buchanan, *The Great Betrayal*.

6. Shutt, *The Myth*; W. A. Williams, *The Tragedy*; McCormick, *America's Half Century*; Hogan, "Corporatism."

7. Goldstein, *Ideas, Interests*; Ikenberry, Lake, and Mastanduno, *The State*; Pastor, *Congress*; and Milner, *Interests, Institutions*. Corporatist, neo-Marxist, pluralist, and endogenous tariff theories counter that private interests dominate the state. See Hogan, "Corporatism"; Jessop, *State Theory*; Bauer, de Sola Pool, and Dexter, *American Business*.

8. Sally, "International Trade"; Goldstein, "Creating the GATT Rules"; Finlayson and Zacher, "The GATT"; Lipson, "The Transformation"; Bhagwati, *Protectionism*; Rhodes, *Reciprocity*; Jackson, *World Trade*, 17–21. Ruggie ("International Regimes") calls this compromise "embedded liberalism."

CHAPTER I

1. Eckes, *Opening America's Market*, chaps. 1–5; Lake, *Power*; Schatz, "Cordell Hull," chap. 2; Pratt, *Cordell Hull*, 29–30, 107–18; Hull, *Memoirs*, 320–74.

2. Kottman, *Reciprocity*, 79–215; Muirhead, *Development*, 9–10.

3. Schatz, "Anglo-American Trade Agreement."

4. Dallek, *Franklin D. Roosevelt*, 19–20, 54–61, 82–93; L. C. Gardner, *Economic Aspects*, 24–33, 40–61.

5. "Tariffs and Trade Pacts," *Nation*, January 13, 1940, 33.

6. Memorandum Concerning Certain Current Fallacies Regarding Our Foreign Trade and Tariff Policy, n.d., box 315, Hoover, HHL; Export-Import Group, November 16, 1938, V.IX, 1938–39, CFR (Thompson and Lippmann); Rosenberg, *Spreading*, 172 (Beard).

7. U.S. Department of State, "Five Years of the Trade Agreements," 1939, box 16, Sayre, LC; U.S. Department of Commerce, *Historical Statistics, II*: 884–87.

8. Carl Kreider, "Democratic Processes in the Trade Agreements Program," *American Political Science Review* 34:2 (April 1940): 317–32 (CRI); Cantril, *Public Opinion*, 122–24 (polls); Trade Agreements Report, February 5, 1940, box 85, RG 16, NA.

9. *RTAA-Senate*, 1940, L. J. Taber [Grange], 571, and Earl Smith [AFBF], 415.

10. Young to Doughton, January 10, 1940, box 855.2, NAM-A.

11. Ickes, *Secret Diary*, 113.

12. Darilek, *Loyal Opposition*, 9–13.

13. *Congressional Record–House*, February 21, 1940, Earl Michener (R-Mich.), 1740, and Henry Dworshak (R-Idaho), 1767–68.

14. *Congressional Record–Senate*, April 3, 1940, O'Mahoney, 3906; Moley, "Perspective,"

Newsweek, January 22, 1940, 52; John Day Larkin, "The Trade Agreement Act in Court and in Congress," *American Political Science Review* 31:3 (June 1937): 498–507; *RTAA-Senate,* 1940, O'Mahoney, 185–210 (ratification).

15. *Congressional Record–House,* February 21, 1940, Reed, 1732–33. By 1943 only Finland of the twenty-seven trade agreement countries was at war against the Allies, and the Finns fought Soviet imperialism, not the United States.

16. *RTAA-House,* 1940, Hull, 8–11.

17. Ibid., *Boston Herald,* 1720; Jeffreys-Jones, *Changing Differences,* 94–95 (women's groups); *RTAA-House,* 1940, 1535–38, 1674–79, 2216, 2294 (other interest groups).

18. *RTAA-House,* 1940, "Are You There, Mr. Elephant?," January 15, 1940, *Iowa Register,* 2840–41; "White for Hull Pacts," *Kansas City Times,* January 19, 1940, 2839.

19. *RTAA-House,* 1940, Doughton, 2058.

20. *RTAA-House,* 1940, 5–6.

21. Annual Message to Congress, January 3, 1940, *PPP, 1940,* 5–6.

22. "Trade Agreements Upheld," *Nation,* March 2, 1940, 297 (vote); *Congressional Record–Senate,* April 3, 1940, 4014; Willkie, "We, the People—A Foundation for a Political Platform for Recovery," *Fortune,* April 1940, 4278.

23. U.S. Tariff Commission, *Operation . . . II,* 12–13; R. N. Gardner, *Sterling-Dollar,* 5–7, 14–18; Woods, *A Changing of the Guard,* 12–24.

24. Darilek, *Loyal Opposition,* 41–82.

25. Joseph M. Jones, "The State of Public Opinion," November 25, 1942, box 3, Pasvolsky, NA. See also NORC, Studies for the Department of State, 1945–57, Surveys 202 and 210, January 1943, and Survey 212, May 1943.

26. Millikin address, July 14, 1942, box 3, book 1, Millikin Collection, Boulder.

27. Speech in the Senate, May 20, 1943, roll 8, Vandenberg Papers, Ann Arbor.

28. Speech in Congress, May 12, 1943, quoted in Dalunay and Phillips, *Speak,* 96–97. See also *RTAA-House,* 1943, Hull, 3–7, 50–56, 69.

29. Press release, June 3, 1943, *DSB,* June 5, 1943, 494; *Congressional Record–House,* May 13, 1943, 4378 (the House vote was 343 for, 65 against, and 25 not voting); *Congressional Record–Senate,* 89:5, June 2, 1943, 5202. See also Hull memorandum, May 12, 1943, reel 51, Hull, LC.

CHAPTER 2

1. Woods, *A Changing of the Guard,* 16–30; Irwin, *Against the Tide,* 189–206.

2. Drummond, *British Economic Policy,* 103–22; Pincus, "Evolution," 68.

3. Barnes and Nicholson, *The Empire,* 757. See also Woods, *A Changing of the Guard,* 34–41, and Louis, *In the Name,* 106–8, 232–59.

4. Addendum to note for Ambassador Winant, [1942], box 2, Pasvolsky, NA (Dalton). See also Woods, *A Changing of the Guard,* 41–48, and Dobson, *U.S. Wartime Aid,* 8–9.

5. Sir Owen Chalkley's Proposals, November 1940, BT 11 1474, BPRO; Moggridge, *Collected Writings,* 47.

6. Moggridge, *Collected Writings,* 143–46.

7. Ibid., 139–40. See also Dobson, *Politics*, 26–27.

8. Moggridge, *Collected Writings*, 172; Keynes to Acheson, July 29, 1941, box 18, Acheson Papers, New Haven. See also Woods, *A Changing of the Guard*, 30–32.

9. Moggridge, *Collected Writings*, 203–6. See also Dominions Office to UK High Commissioners, May 31, 1941, FO 371 26252, A4191/2354/45, BPRO.

10. Hawkins to Acheson, August 4, 1941, box 71, PSF, FDRL.

11. "History of Negotiations with Respect to Point Four," January 16, 1945, box 13, Notter, NA. See also Dobson, *U.S. Wartime Aid*, chap. 3, and Harper, *American Visions*, 262.

12. R. N. Gardner, *Sterling-Dollar*, 51; Memorandum of meeting at State Department, July 9, 1941, BT 11 1695, BPRO (reexports).

13. Pasvolsky, "Possibilities of Conflict of British and American Official Views," December 12, 1941, box 2, Pasvolsky, NA.

14. Woods, *A Changing of the Guard*, 58–61.

15. Jean-Charles Harvey, "North American Customs Union," *Living Age*, July 1941, 459–61; CFR, "International Control of Trade Policies," box 81, Feis, LC; Woods, *A Changing of the Guard*, 191–92.

16. Institute of International Affairs, Balliol College, "The Functions and Structure of an International Economic Authority," February 12, 1941 (BT 11 1680), and Hurst Committee minutes, August 11, 1941 (CAB 87 60), BPRO.

17. Meade, "A Proposal for an International Commercial Union," July 25, 1942, Meade Papers—Correspondence, LSE.

18. Dalton, "Project of a Commercial Union," November 5, 1942, FO 371 31531, U1395/1395/79, BPRO.

19. Playfair to D. H. Lyal, November 9, 1942, FO 371 31512, U1254/20/70, BPRO. See also Wood to Dalton, November 16, 1942, FO 371 31531, U1395/1395/79, BPRO.

20. Meeting of Interdepartmental Committee on Postwar Commercial Policy, November 24, 1942, FO 371 31531, U1546/1395/70, BPRO.

21. Report of the Committee on Postwar Commercial Policy, January 6, 1943, ibid.

22. TUC, Postwar International Trade Policy, March 8, 1944, MSS 292/520.3/7, TUC Records. Unions and the FBI supported the World Trade Alliance Organization, the former to regulate business and boost employment, the latter to raise exports to the United States. See also E. P. Thomas [NFTC] to Guy Locock [FBI], January 18, 1943, MSS 200/F/3/D2/2/7, ibid.

23. Henderson comment on David Waley's Note, January 7, 1943, and Henderson to Keynes, January 13, 1943, T 247 2, BPRO.

24. Keynes to Meade, December 15, 1942, ibid. See also Keynes to Overton, February 3, 1943, ibid. Interest groups (London Chamber of Commerce, National General Export Merchants Group, International Chamber of Commerce, and British Federation of Industries) in Summary of Opinions and Ideas on International Postwar Problems, July 15, 1942, box 65, Berle, FDRL.

25. Stirling to Ronald Fraser, July 10, 1942, FO 371 31494, U 328/328/73, BPRO.

26. Keynes, Postwar Commercial Policy, January 15, 1943, T 247 2, BPRO.

27. Nigel Ronald minute, February 21, 1943, FO 371 31531, U1546/1395/70, BPRO. See also Notes by president of Board of Trade, January 9, 1943 (FO 371 31531, U1546/

1395/70), and Johnstone to John Anderson, January 15, 1943 (FO 371 35351, U260/251/70), BPRO; London Chamber of Commerce, NGEMG minutes, January 8, 1942, MS 16613, vol. 1, Guildhall Library.

28. Cherwell to Churchill, January 12, 1943, PREM 4, 18/4, BPRO.

29. Coombs, "Keynesian Crusade," 1, also 3–4, 21–22. See also J. L. Knott, Notes on Ottawa Agreement, August 22, 1946, 43211 pt. 1, A9790/1, AA.

30. Butlin and Schedvin, "War Economy," 631–52, 742–67; Beresford and Kerr, "A Turning Point," 8–14.

31. Summary of discussions in London, June 1943, FO 371 35348, U2301/190/70, BPRO.

32. Dalton diary, September 2, 1943, I-29, Dalton Papers, LSE.

33. Howson and Moggridge, *Wartime Diaries*, 93–111.

34. Informal economic discussions, September 21, 1943, box 19, ITF.

35. Committee on Measures for Stimulating Commerce, September 23–24, October 9, 1943, box 19, ITF.

36. R. N. Gardner, *Sterling-Dollar*, 106–7; Liesching Report, October 21, 1943, FO 371 35358, U5690/251/70, BPRO.

37. Committee on Measures for Stimulating Commerce, September 27–28, 1943, box 19, ITF. See also *FRUS, 1943*, 1:1119–20.

38. Committee on Measures for Stimulating Commerce, September 27, 1943, box 19, ITF.

39. Committee on Measures for Stimulating Commerce, September 27–28, 1943, ibid.

40. Committee on Measures for Stimulating Commerce, September 28, 1943, ibid.

41. Howson, *Meade*, 3:42; Liesching Report, October 21, 1943, FO 371 35358, U5690/251/70, BPRO.

42. Memorandum on informal exploratory conversations and 4th plenary meeting, both October 16, 1943, box 19, ITF.

43. Liesching Report on Commercial Policy Discussions, October 21, 1943, FO 371 35358, U5690/251/70, BPRO. See also discussion in Ottawa, November 2, 1943, BT 11 2247, BPRO, and Norman Robertson to King, October 14, 1943, reel H-1473, vol. 237, J4, King, NAC.

44. Interim Report of Special Committee on Relaxation of Trade Barriers, December 8, 1943, box 20, ITF.

45. Liesching memorandum, December 15, 1943, and Meade to Liesching, December 18, 1943, BT 11 2247, BPRO.

46. Cripps to Law, December 30, 1943, CAB 127 91, BPRO; Cabinet 18th Conclusions, minute 4, February 11, 1944, PREM 4 18/1, BPRO (isolationists); Attlee to Law, December 23, 1943, BT 11 2247, BPRO (Labour); Winant to Hull, April 29, 1944, box 18, ITF (business).

47. Law memorandum, February 7, 1944, PREM 4 18/1, BPRO. See also MacLeod, "The Promise," and Cherwell to Prime Minister, February 10, 1944, PREM 4 18/1, BPRO.

48. "The Commonwealth Conference," *Canadian Forum* 24:281 (June 1944): 51.

49. Richard Law to Secretary of State, February 24, 1944, DO 35 1216/WR 254/47, BPRO (quotation); "New Zealand: War on Two Fronts," *Round Table* 34:134 (March 1944):

179–85. See also "The Australian Government and Post-War Planning," *International Labour Review* 49:6 (June 1944): 651–53.

50. War Cabinet 18th Conclusions, minute 4, February 11, 1944, and Note by Prime Minister, March 3, 1944, PREM 4 18/1, BPRO; Churchill speech, April 21, 1944, quoted in James, *Churchill,* 6919–20.

CHAPTER 3

1. "The State Department Speaks," *DSB,* January 22, 1944, 104–5; Harry Hopkins to Grace, July 11, 1944, box 138, Hopkins, FDRL (Democratic platform); Clayton to Randolph Crew, October 28, 1944, box 13, Clayton Papers, Houston. See also "Public Attitudes on Foreign Policy," June 16, 1944, box 1, OPOS.

2. Great Britain, *Parliamentary Debates,* May 25, 1944, Elliott, 998–1000; Ralph Robey, "A British Postwar Plan Which Demands Attention," *Newsweek,* April 10, 1944, 70 (*Economist*). See also Meade memorandum, June 6, 1944, T 247 2, BPRO.

3. *FRUS, 1944,* 2:40; Conversation with Law, July 20, 1944, box 22, BCNEA.

4. ECEFP meeting, October 7, 1944, box 18, Notter File, NA.

5. Committee on Trade Barriers, "Multilateral versus Multilateral-Bilateral Action," [October 1944], box 23, ITF.

6. Howson and Moggridge, *Meade,* 4:22–23. See also Meade to Robbins, November 27, 1944, FO 371 40949, UE2419/143/53, BPRO.

7. Wilfrid Eady note of conversation with Hawkins, November 29, 1944, FO 371 40991, UE2438/2429/54, BPRO.

8. *FRUS, 1945,* 2:1328–34; Cornish, "Full Employment"; Note for the President, January 15, 1945, box 18, ITF.

9. "The Story of the International Business Conference," November 10–18, 1944, box 81, NAM-A; Final reports of the IBC, box 854.1, Horsch Papers, NAM Archives; "Public Attitudes on Foreign Policy," August 16, 1944, box 1, OPOS.

10. Dobney, *Selected Papers,* 1–9, 21–136; Dryden, *Trade Warriors,* 9–11; Fossedal, *Our Finest Hour,* Clayton OH, Clayton Reminiscences, Houston.

11. Woods, *A Changing of the Guard,* 208. See also Hogan, "Rise and Fall," and Stinebower OH, HSTL, 13–15, 36.

12. Churchill to Roosevelt, February 13, 1945, box 18, ITF; *FRUS, 1945,* 6:29–30.

13. Woods, *A Changing of the Guard,* 220–21; McCormack to Roosevelt, box 232, Stettinius Papers, Charlottesville; Murans, "Reciprocal Trade," 49–50.

14. NORC report no. 8, June 4, 1945, box 169, SBR. See also Cantril, *Public Opinion,* 128; Summary of Opinion Developments, May 11, 14, 1945, box 2, OPOS; Foster, *Activism,* 94; and Taft to George Stringfellow, June 21, 1945, box 772, Robert A. Taft Papers, LC.

15. *RTAA-House,* 1945, Walter Cenerazzo, 1119, and Alfred Gaunt [small business], 2453–55 (interest groups); Minority Report, 1945, 2–12 (GOP); Tri-State Consolidated Mine and Mill Union to George Schwabe, April 17, 1945, box 6:38, Schwabe Collection, Norman; Earl Pedely [beet sugar union] to Bourke Hickenlooper (R-Iowa), April 30, 1945,

box 47, Hickenlooper Papers, HHL. See also Public Attitudes on Foreign Policy, July 30, 1945, box 1, OPOS.

16. *RTAA-House*, 1945, Curtis, 635, and Gearhart, 700–701.

17. Truman to Rayburn, May 25, 1945, box 898, POF. See also Meade diary 1/3, April 15, 1945, LSE; Leffler, *A Preponderance of Power*, 21, 23; and Truman, *Memoirs*, 153.

18. Wallace, *Sixty Million Jobs*, 14; Paterson, "The Economic Cold War," 46 (business); Marion Folsom to Millard Brown, June 22, 1945, box 409:19:5 (Colmer), Colmer Papers, Hattiesburg; U.S. House Special Committee on Postwar Economic Policy and Planning, *Economic Reconstruction* (Colmer Report), 18; *American Farm Bureau Newsletter*, May 15, 1945 (RTAA support); Minutes of AFL Meetings, Executive Council 91 (April 1945), Silver Spring; Proceedings of the 29th Annual Meeting of the Conference Board, "Foreign Trade Practices After the War," May 17, 1945, box 25, NICB; A. H. Conrad, "Foreign Trade Visions and the Facts," *Barron's*, July 30, 1945, 3; E. P. Thomas [NFTC] to Stettinius, February 5, 1945, box 47, Clayton Papers, HSTL; *RTAA-House*, 1945, Benjamin Marsh [People's Lobby], 1822, and Mrs. Harvey Wiley, 1080; Almond, *The American People*, 160–82; "Consider the Consumer," *Fortune*, May 1945, 107. See also Woods, *A Changing of the Guard*, 224–25.

19. Paul Fratessa to Wallace, January 26, 1945, reel 28, Wallace Papers, Iowa City; Roscoe Fleming, "Horseradish and World Peace," *Harper's Magazine*, May 1945, 533.

20. Acheson address, March 23, 1945, *DSB*, March 25, 1945, 512. See also *RTAA-House*, 1945, Stettinius, 10, and *Washington News*, April 25, 1945, 861.

21. Doughton to David Lavietes, May 25, 1945, box 35, folder 1285, Doughton Papers, Chicago; Acheson, *Present at the Creation*, 107; *CQ-Almanac* 1 (1945): 308–14 (votes). All 10 Republicans and Milton West (D-Tex.) opposed the bill in committee. All but 12 of 217 Democrats passed it. Some closely defeated amendments were a two-year extension, reducing tariff authority to 25 percent, textile quotas, and congressional approval for agreements. A recommittal lost by just 181–212.

22. O'Mahoney to Truman, May 28, 1945, box 898, POF; *CQ-Almanac* 1 (1945): 305, 314–17. Democrats Edwin Johnson (Colo.), David Walsh (Mass.), and Peter Gerry (R.I.) voted for Taft's amendment in committee. It lost 33–47, as 9 GOP crossovers offset 8 Democrats. Then, 38 Democrats and 16 Republicans passed the RTAA.

23. Woods, *A Changing of the Guard*, 225–28; Dobson, *Politics*, 81–83; *FRUS, 1945*, 6:56–60; Magowan to Liesching, May 21, 25, 1945, BT 11 2741, BPRO.

24. *FRUS, 1945*, 6:45 (proposal); Halifax to Foreign Office, June 25, 1945, BT 11 2741, BPRO; Meade diary, June 25, 1945, LSE.

25. W. Manning Dacey, "British Reconversion and Trade," *Foreign Affairs* 23 (January 1945): 249–54; U.S. House Special Committee on Postwar Economic Policy and Planning, *Economic Reconstruction* (Colmer Report); Hathaway, *Ambiguous Partnership*, 26–28; "Export or Die," *Economist* 148:5292 (January 27, 1945): 101–2; "The Hambro Plan," *Scope*, June 1945, 96–98.

26. Lippmann to Keynes, April 2, 1945, FO 371 30655, A4574/60/45, BPRO. See also Halifax to Foreign Office, June 12, 1945, BT 11 2741, BPRO, and Attlee address, June 12, 1945, Attlee Papers, Bodleian Library.

27. Howson and Moggridge, *Meade*, 4:105–6; Keynes to E. Bridges, July 11, 1945, T 247

2, BPRO. See also TUC, Economic Committee, "The Regulation of Foreign and International Trade," June 20, 1945, MSS 292/522/1/1, TUC Records.

28. *FRUS, 1945*, 6:61–62, 66–68; L. Rasminsky, "Anglo-American Trade Prospects: A Canadian View," *Economic Journal* 55:218 (June–September 1945): 161–78. Britain ended sterling bloc discrimination against Canada in July to help rid Canada of its inconvertible pounds that plagued its external payments balance.

29. *FRUS, 1945*, 6:74–76, 88–90.

30. Office of European Affairs, Division of British Commonwealth Affairs, "Implication of the Labor Landslide in Great Britain," August 1, 1945, box 2, U.S. Department of State, Clayton-Thorp, HSTL.

31. Estorick, *Cripps*, 96–347; Memorandum by president of Board of Trade, August 16, 1945, FO 371 45680, UE3692/113/53, BPRO.

32. Dobson, *Politics*, 88 (Dalton). See also Meade diary, September 1, 1945, LSE; Keynes to R. H. Brand, August 15, 1945 (T 247 2), and meeting of ministers, August 31, 1945 (FO 371 45698), UE4080/1094/53, BPRO.

33. "Loan to Britain," *New Republic*, December 24, 1945, 855 (Keynes); U.S. Commercial Policy Group meeting, September 28, 1945, box 82, ITF.

34. Leddy to Wilcox, October 26, 1945, box 83, ITF; Halifax to Bevin, October 11, 1945, FO 800 512, BPRO.

35. Cripps memorandum, September 13, 1945, FO 371 45699, UE4353/1094/53, BPRO; T. A. Stone to Hume Wrong, October 23, 1945, vol. 5773, 200(s), NAC; Department of the Treasury memorandum for Prime Minister, December 7, 1945, NASH 80/0689-1418, NZA.

36. Committee on Commercial Policy, October 1, 1945, box 82, ITF.

37. Committee on Commercial Policy, October 2, 1945, ibid; Howson and Moggridge, *Wartime Diaries*, 225.

38. Cripps to Liesching, October 27, 1945, and Liesching to Helmore, October 28, 1945, BT 11 2802, BPRO.

39. Draft Joint Report, November 6, 1945, box 83, ITF; Howson and Moggridge, *Meade*, 4:164–65.

40. R. N. Gardner, *Sterling-Dollar*, 148–49; Committee on Commercial Policy, October 5, 16, 1945, box 82, ITF.

41. R. N. Gardner, *Sterling-Dollar*, 147–48; Pollard, *Economic Security*, 24; Committee on Commercial Policy, October 5, 16, 1945, box 82, ITF. See also Report of FBI International Trade Policy Committee, June 13, 1944, MSS 200/F/3/D2/2/7, MRC.

42. Committee on Commercial Policy, October 4, 16, 1945, box 82, and State Department Division of Commercial Policy, "Agricultural Policy," January 1945, box 1, ITF.

43. Committee on Commercial Policy, October 5, 1945, box 82, ITF. See also Havinden and Meredith, *Colonialism*, 227–75, and Fieldhouse, "The Labour Governments," 83–120.

44. Berge speech, "The Challenge of Cartels," January 18, 1945, Cartel File, McClellan Collection, Arkadelphia. See also Corwin Edwards address, June 30, 1944, *DSB*, July 2, 1944, 25–31; Taylor, "Debate"; and "Cartel Foes, Inc.," *Business Week*, November 17, 1945, 22.

45. Board of Trade brief, December 1944, CAB 123 96, BPRO. See also Howson and

Moggridge, *Wartime Diaries*, 230; Note by Robbins, January 20, 1945, CAB 123 96, BPRO; *FRUS, 1945*, 6:152; and Comments Received from Firms and Associations on Chapter IV (Restrictive Business Practices), BT 64/307, BPRO.

46. Committee on Commercial Policy, December 1, 1945, box 82, ITF; Wilcox to Joseph Coppock, October 8, 1945, box 2, Coppock Papers, HSTL.

47. Keynes to Dalton, November 2, 1945, BT 11 2802, BPRO; John Minter to Byrnes, November 17, 1945, box 2417, 560.AL/11-1745, NA; Penrose, *Economic Planning*, 112–13.

CHAPTER 4

1. Bullock, *Ernest Bevin*, 202–3; James, *Boothby*, 319–20.

2. F. Williams, *A Prime Minister Remembers*, 133–34; Dalton, *High Tide*, 68–89; "The British Loan," *Fortune*, February 1946, 91; Churchill speech, December 13, 1945, in James, *Churchill*, 7280.

3. *PPP, 1946*, 45. See also Clayton, *DSB*, March 31, 1946, 515–24.

4. Gaddis, *The United States*, 299; Woods, *A Changing of the Guard*, 378–94; Doenecke, *Not to the Swift*, 59–66.

5. Leffler, *A Preponderance of Power*, 31.

6. *FRUS, 1945*, 2:1337–39, 1350–51.

7. Ibid., 1355–58.

8. *FRUS, 1946*, 1:1266–67, 1274–75, 1314–17; News conference, February 15, 1946, folder 557, Byrnes Papers, Clemson.

9. *FRUS, 1946*, 1:1271–92.

10. Ibid., 1280–83, 1328.

11. Ibid., 1292–1325; Board of Trade to Washington Embassy, April 26, 1946, FO 371 52983, UE1648/38/53, BPRO.

12. U.S. Opinion on Foreign Trade Trends, August 20, 1946, box 48, OPOS. See also *FRUS, 1946*, 1:1329–32.

13. R. Carroll [General Motors] in conversation with NFTC, April 8, 1946, box 4, U.S. Department of State, Clayton-Thorp, HSTL. See also proposals for expansion of world trade, June 19, 1946, box 20, NAM-A; W. K. Jackson [U.S. Chamber] address, May 21, 1946, box 19, USCC; Final Declaration of the 32d NFTC, November 12–14, 1945, box 79, PSF, HSTL.

14. Jackson address, November 6, December 4, 1946, box 19, folder W. K. Jackson, USCC; "Headaches in Export Boom: The Fight for Scarce Goods," *United States News*, March 8, 1946, 47–49 (export controls).

15. Cantril, *Public Opinion*, 129–30, 844; *PPP, 1946*, 168; Almond, *The American People*, 189–90 (polls); NORC Surveys, September 1, 15, October 13, 20; November 3, 1946, box 310, Charles P. Taft Papers, LC; Operation New Brunswick, June 6, 1946, Clayton Papers, HSTL.

16. *FRUS, 1946*, 1:1332–35. See also Wilcox, *A Charter*, and Brown, *Restoration of World Trade*.

17. Coppock to Wilcox, July 3, 1946 (box 13), and Wilcox to Acheson and Clayton, July

8, 1946 (box 5), ITF; Minutes of ECEFP meetings, June 14, July 19, 1946, box 7, Edminister Papers, HSTL.

18. Minutes of ECEFP meetings, June 5, 12, 17, 19, July 19, 1946, box 7, Edminister Papers, HSTL.

19. Minutes of ECEFP meetings, June 21, 1946, ibid.; FRUS, 1946, 1:1335–36.

20. *FRUS, 1946*, 1:1336–49; Summary of Foreign Reactions, October 1, 1946, box 13, Edminister Papers, HSTL.

21. Telegram to Dominions and India, August 26, 1946, FO 371 53049, UE3358/690/53, BPRO; Cabinet Trade Negotiations Committee minutes, September 25, 1946 (UE4649/690/53), September 30, 1946 (UE4726/690/53), FO 371 53049, BPRO.

22. Henry Chalmers Preliminary Analysis, July 17, 1946, box 3, ITF. See also "How Canadian Government Plans to Help Build Dominion's World Trade," *Export Trade and Shipper* 54 (August 5, 1946): 6–7; Department of External Affairs, ITO Project, October 3, 1946, vol. 3845, 9100-C-40, NAC.

23. South Africa High Commission to Dominions Office, October 8, 1946, New Zealand and Australian Agents Association, Proposals for Consideration by an International Conference on Trade and Employment, September 1946 (DO 35 1227/WT980/9), and Board of Trade notes, July 23, 1946 (FO 371 53047), UE3304/690/53, BPRO; Crisp, *Ben Chifley*, chap. 14 (Bretton Woods).

24. Report of Discussions on Draft Charter, August 30–31, September 2, 1946, 9391/18, A9879/1, AA. See also Ritchie, *Australian Dictionary*, 412–19, and Crisp, *Ben Chifley*.

25. E. H., ITO, August 15, 1946, 271, A9913/1, AA; Cabinet Agendum 1019A, January 22, 1946, 20/2/8, AA1974/156/1, AA; Notes of Board of Trade meeting with Coombs, April 26, 1946, FO 371 53047, UE2066/690/53, BPRO.

26. Board of Trade Report on views of industry and Annex I, October 15, 1946, BT 11 3239, BPRO. See also conversation with Indian delegation, August 30, 1946 (box 2421, 560.AL/8-3046), and Samuel Fletcher to Byrnes, June 10, 1946 (box 2420, 560.AL/6-1046), NA; Trade Negotiations Committee, Note by India Office, November 11, 1946, FO 371 53050, UE 5338/690/53, BPRO.

27. Allan G. B. Fisher, Summary of European Views, July 1946, box 5, ITF; British Industries Association, *Monthly Bulletin* 70 (December 1946), MSS 221/4/2/1, MRC. See also R. B. Dunwoody [British Chambers of Commerce] to Bevin, May 13, 1946 (FO 371 52983, UE2094/38/53), London Chamber of Commerce, Proposals for International Conference on Trade and Employment, March 1946 (FO 371 52983, UE1292/38/53), Meeting with Federation of British Industries, February 20, 1946 (BT 11 3254), and A. D. V. Leigh [NGEMG] to Undersecretary for Foreign Affairs, September 18, 1946 (FO 371 52985, UE4339/38/53), BPRO; Leslie Gamage [General Electric Co.] speech, January 29, 1947, MSS 200/F/D3/3/2, MRC; *Journal of the National Union of Manufacturers*, June 1946, BT 11 3242, BPRO; TUC, Economic Committee, 1st meeting, January 9, 1946, MSS 292/520.9/2, TUC Records.

28. Note by president of Board of Trade, British Commonwealth Talks, October 24, 1946, FO 371 52984, UE4093/38/53, BPRO.

29. U.S. Opinion on Foreign Trade Trends and American Attitudes on World Trade Issues, October 1946, box 48, OPOS.

30. *PPP, 1946*, 461. See also Wilcox address, October 17, 1946, *DSB*, October 27, 1946, 757–60.

31. Wilcox to Clayton, October 26, 1946, box 2423, 560.AL/10-2646, NA. See also R. N. Gardner, *Sterling-Dollar*, 269–71.

32. Coombs speech, October 17, 1946, 14, M448/1, AAV. See also Department of External Affairs, Trade, and Employment Conference Report, January 1947, 711/1/3/2, A1838/1, AA, and Division of Biographic Information, Herbert Coombs, box 111, ITF.

33. Wilcox to Clayton, October 26, 1946, box 2423, 560.AL/10-2646, NA.

34. R. N. Gardner, *Sterling-Dollar*, 283. See also George Luthringer to Camille Gutt, November 6, 1946, box 16, NACIM; Walter Gardner notes to Edward Bernstein, November 1, 7, 1946, I 231, IMF; L. P. Thompson-McCausland to G. L. F. Bolton, October 16, 1946, OV170/1, Bank of England; and Brown, *Restoration of World Trade*, 69–89.

35. Wilcox to Clayton, October 26, 1946, box 2423, 560.AL/10-2646, NA; *FRUS, 1946*, 1:1361–64; Diebold, Results of the London Conference, December 5, 1946, box 5, ITF; Matusow, *Farm Policies*, 84–91; R. N. Gardner, *Sterling-Dollar*, 271–79 (employment). FAO director-general Sir John Boyd Orr proposed the World Food Board's buffer stock, surplus disposal, and relief operations. The United States wanted the ITO to preside and disliked such interventionism.

36. Wilcox to Clayton, November 3, 1946, box 2423, 560.AL/11-346, NA; *FRUS, 1946*, 1:1365.

37. R. N. Gardner, *Sterling-Dollar*, 285. See also minutes of ECEFP meeting, December 27, 1946, box 14, Edminister Papers, HSTL.

38. Trade Negotiations Committee, Preparatory Committee for the Trade and Employment Conference, December 12, 1946, FO 371 52990, UE6067/38/53, BPRO. See also Canada, *Parliamentary Debates*, November 12, 1946, 6; Gallman to Byrnes, November 12, 1946, box 2423, 560.AL/11-1246, NA; and "Targets: The Balance of Payments," *New Statesman and Nation* 32:817 (October 19, 1946): 277.

39. Great Britain, *Parliamentary Debates*, November 12, 1946, 21–22. Interest groups in London Chamber of Commerce, NGEMG minutes, September 12, 1946, MS 16613, vol. 2, Guildhall Library.

40. Department of External Affairs, General Report, January 1947, 711/1/3/2, A1838/1, AA. See also Coombs to John Dedman, November 17, 1946, in Hudson and Way, *Documents on Australian Foreign Policy*, 10:371–74.

41. Recent Statements on U.S. Trade Program, October 15–November 27, 1946, box 48, OPOS. See also Hume Wrong to Secretary of State for External Affairs, November 19, 1946, RG 19, vol. 568, 152–17 ITO General, NAC.

CHAPTER 5

1. *FRUS, 1946*, 1:1349. The list included at least one item from 450 of the 503 paragraphs in the dutiable sections of the Tariff Act of 1930 and 150 of 211 paragraphs on the free list. See also Winthrop Brown OH, HSTL, 1–13, 19, and Dryden, *Trade Warriors*, 16.

2. *FRUS, 1946*, 1:1350–51. See also Acheson to Byrnes, November 7, 1946, box 2423, 560.AL/11-746, NA.

3. *PPP, 1946*, 475; Paterson, "The Economic Cold War," 73–105.

4. Reston, "The Real Test Is the Economic Peace," *New York Times Magazine*, February 9, 1947, box 157, in Clifford Papers, PSF, HSTL. See also Pollard, *Economic Security*, 123–40; Joseph Coppock, "U.S. Foreign Economic Policy," December 11, 1946, box 1, Coppock Papers, HSTL; and Herbert Feis, "The Conflict over Trade Ideologies," *Foreign Affairs* 25 (January 1947): 226–27.

5. Organizational Information Projects, December 11, 1946, and Recent Statements on U.S. Trade Program, October 15–November 27, 1946, box 48, OPOS; Committee for Economic Development, Handbook on International Trade, box 234, Harriman Papers, LC.

6. Statements of Congressional Leaders Who Have Spoken on Foreign Trade Issues since the November Election, January 13, 1947, box 48, OPOS (Tydings). See also Marshall to Knutson, February 28, 1947, box 1, Reed Papers, Ithaca.

7. Minutes of ECEFP meetings, March 14, 26, 1947, box 57, ECEFP-R; Report on informal hearings, [March 1947], box 22, ITF. Business, professional, and farm groups sent 109 witnesses; civic clubs, 41; and labor, consumer, religious, and veterans groups, 35. Mayors, educators, students, and port authority representatives also appeared. Hearings took place in Boston, Chicago, Denver, New Orleans, New York, San Francisco, and Washington, D.C.

8. *RTAA-House*, 1947, Clayton, 4; Wilcox speech, February 17, 1947, *DSB*, February 16, 1947, 288–93.

9. *PPP, 1947*, 167–72.

10. See also Recent Statements on U.S. Trade Program, October 15–November 27, 1946, box 48, OPOS; Bill Davidson, "The Two Mr. Vandenbergs," *Collier's*, June 19, 1948, 15; Boylan, *New Deal Coalition*; and Jones, *Fifteen Weeks*, 90.

11. Weekly Summary Report of January 6, 1947, box 23, ITF.

12. Recent Statements on U.S. Trade Program, October 15–November 27, 1946, box 48, OPOS; Leffler, *A Preponderance of Power*, 141 (Wherry). See also *Congressional Record–Senate*, January 27, 1947, Morse, 607–9.

13. Statements of Congressional Leaders Who Have Spoken on Foreign Trade Issues since the November Election, January 13, 1947, box 48, OPOS. See also *Congressional Record–House*, January 20, 1947, Jenkins, 477.

14. Butler to Clayton, December 19, 1946, *DSB*, January 26, 1947, 161–63.

15. T. R. Wilson to George Bell, April 23, 1947, box 354, OIT (CRI hearings); Selwyn Sharbrough [shrimper] to Senator Tom Connally, April 15, 1947, box 172, 2187 (fish); Harvey J. Lewis [union] to George Marshall, February 20, 1947, box 172, Connally Papers, LC; T. F. Sandoz [packer] to Knutson, March 18, 1947, box 1, Reed Papers, Ithaca; Gloucester Fisheries Association, "Shall We Allow America's Oldest Industry to Perish?," box 45, CRI, NA.

16. Jones, *Fifteen Weeks*, 98; Kelly, *Studies*, 126–27; "Spring Flower," *Time*, February 3, 1947, 19.

17. "Success Story," *Newsweek*, February 17, 1947, 35; *CQ-Almanac* 3 (1947): 114. Millikin

had opposed Bretton Woods and the British loan but backed the United Nations Relief and Rehabilitation Administration, Export-Import Bank lending authority, and United Nations. See also Acheson, *Present at the Creation*, 96.

18. Vandenberg to Sinclair Weeks, January 3, 1947, reel 4, Vandenberg Papers, Ann Arbor. See also Kelly, *Studies*, 124–26.

19. Kelly, *Studies*, 127. See also "Tariff Compromise," *Business Week*, March 8, 1947, 18; *PPP, 1947*, 151.

20. Weekly Summary Report of February 10, 1947, box 23, ITF (Butler); *RTAA-House*, 1947 (Knutson). See also "G.O.P. Saboteurs," *Nation*, February 15, 1947, 171–72.

21. Thompson-McCausland to R. W. B. Clarke, February 27, 1947, OV170/1, Bank of England. See also "The Vandenberg Tariff," *Economist* 152:5403 (March 15, 1947): 377.

22. Conversation at British Embassy, February 5, 1947, box 4, POF; U.S. Opinion on Foreign Trade Trends, January 18, 1946–February 18, 1947, box 48, OPOS (Stassen). See also John Magowan to James Helmore, February 21, 1947, FO 371 62286, UE1247/37/53, BPRO.

23. Willard Thorp OH, 93, HSTL. See also Position of U.S. Newspapers on the U.S. Foreign Trade Program, January 1–April 30, May 23, 1947, and An Estimate of the Public Opinion Situation, April 2, 1947 (polls), box 48, OPOS (polls). This survey found Alabama, Arkansas, Georgia, Louisiana, Maryland, Mississippi, New Mexico, North Carolina, South Carolina, Tennessee, and Virginia to be safe free trade states. Relatively safe were Arizona, Florida, Kentucky, New Hampshire, Oklahoma, Rhode Island, Texas, and Vermont, while somewhat critical were Delaware, Idaho, Oregon, Utah, and West Virginia. Manufacturing and farming made California, Colorado, Connecticut, Illinois, Indiana, Iowa, Kansas, Maine, Massachusetts, Michigan, Minnesota, Montana, New Jersey, New York, Ohio, Pennsylvania, Washington, and Wisconsin critical. Hopelessly opposed on principle were Nebraska, Nevada, North Dakota, South Daktoa, and Wyoming. See also *Congressional Record—Appendix*, Association of Southern Commissioners of Agriculture, January 6, 1947, A11–16.

24. *RTAA-House*, 1947, 455, 457; *Congressional Record–House*, February 3, 1947, 773–74.

25. *RTAA-House*, 1947, Ralph Baerman, 1684, and Mason, 462–63; *Congressional Record–House*, May 21, 1947, Reed, 5630–31.

26. Weekly Summary Report of February 24, 1947, box 23, ITF; Brown OH, HSTL, 45–46; U.S. Senate Committee on Finance, Hearings, *International Trade Organization* (hereafter cited as *ITO Hearings*).

27. U.S. Tariff Commission, *Operation . . . II*, 9–11; *CQ-Almanac* 4 (1948): 190.

28. Wilcox to Clayton, December 29, 1947, box 144, ITF; Conversation with Congressmen Fulton and Javits, March 12, 1948, box 15, U.S. Department of State, Clayton-Thorp, HSTL.

29. Citizen's Committee for Reciprocal World Trade (CCRWT), press release, March 25, 1948, box 31, Charles P. Taft Papers, LC; *PPP, 1948*, 230, 237. Led by General Electric's Gerard Swope and Alger Hiss of the Carnegie Endowment for Peace, the CCRWT included 275 business, farm, labor, veteran, and public affairs groups in 67 cities from 32 states. See also D. E. Bell memorandum for Charles Murphy, April 27, 1948, box 79, Elsey Papers, HSTL; *RTAA-House*, 1948, Marshall, 237–50, and Clayton, 415–75; "Freer Trade Seen Lasting Foundation for Peace," *Journal of Commerce*, April 8, 1948, box 6, ITF; Survey 156 DU-1, May 25, 1948, NORC (polls).

30. *CQ-Almanac* 4 (1948): Doughton, 191; *Congressional Record–Senate*, June 14, 1948, George, 8044. See also U.S. House Committee on Ways and Means, Views of the Minority, *House Report, Volume 4*, 5–10.

31. *Congressional Record–House*, May 26, 1948, Halleck, 6497–98. See also Daily Summary of Opinion Developments, May 11, 1948, box 3, OPOS, and *Congressional Record–House*, May 26, 1948, 6493–96, 6502–4.

32. *Congressional Record–House*, May 26, 1948, Jenkins, 6519–20, and Jerry Vorys (R-Ohio), 6520.

33. Memorandum on Bates, April 17, 1948, box 899, POF; Daily Summary of Opinion Developments, April 19, 1948, box 3, OPOS (satellites); Pollard, *Economic Security*, 161–63.

34. Vandenberg to Mrs. Don Connor, December 16, 1947, reel 4, Vandenberg Papers, Ann Arbor. See also *Congressional Record–Senate*, June 14, 1948, Millikin, 8032–40, and Vandenberg to Clayton, April 22, June 9, 1948, in ibid.

35. Murans, "Reciprocal Trade," 75; *Congressional Record—Appendix*, 94:10, March 30, 1948, Reed, A2007, and 94:11, May 20, 1948, A3179.

36. *CQ-Almanac* 4 (1948): 191–92.

37. *PPP, 1948*, 385. See also *Congressional Record–House*, May 26, 1948, Keating, 6535; and Daily Summary of Opinion Developments, June 15–17, 28, 1948, box 3, OPOS.

38. *PPP, 1948*, 700; Bell OH, 121–22, HSTL (North Dakota). See also *PPP, 1948*, 407, 504, 592–95, 748.

39. Public Discussion of Foreign Trade Plans of the Republican and Democratic Platforms, August 9, 1948, box 48, OPOS; Divine, *Foreign Policy*, 188–258.

CHAPTER 6

1. "Freer Trade vs. Control," *Fortune*, February 1947, 2.

2. Troutman to Marshall, April 18, 1947, box 2430, 560.AL/4-1747, NA (Clayton). See also "Gaston at Geneva," *Time*, April 28, 1947, 27; Cullather, *Illusions*, 35–41; and Memorandum on Inconsistencies between the U.S.–Philippines Agreement on Trade and the Proposed ITO Charter, box 15, ITF.

3. *FRUS, 1947*, 1:913–14.

4. Ibid., 911–13; Office memorandum, February 3, 1947, box 2427, 560.AL/2-347, NA.

5. D. C. Bliss, Progress of the Tariff Negotiations, May 24, 1947, and U.S. Imports and Proposed Trade Agreement Concessions, March 28, 1947, box 138, ITF.

6. Pollard, *Economic Security*, 60–80.

7. "The Power of the Debtor," *New Statesman and Nation* 33:838 (March 29, 1947): 207; "The Geneva Marathon," *Banker* 82 (May 1947): 89; Henry Drummond-Wolf, "What It Is About," *National Review* 128:772 (June 1947): 450–61.

8. "Trade Targets," *Spectator*, March 28, 1947, 324–25. See also "Let's Trade," *Life*, April 28, 1947, 34, and William Dunk memorandum, April 10, 1947, 711/1/3/2, A1838/1, AA.

9. Memorandum by president of Board of Trade, January 13, 1947, PREM 8 490, BPRO.

10. Cabinet Conclusion, February 19, 1947, RG 2, ser. A5a, vol. 2639–41, reel T 2365, BPRO; King diary, April 23, 1947, MG 26, J13, NAC; Wilgress to Secretary of State for Ex-

ternal Affairs, April 28, 1947, vol. 5798, 266(s), NAC. See also General Statement concerning the Canadian Delegation, box 111, ITF.

11. Conversation with Macarthy, December 5, 1946, box 201, ITF. See also Notes of Executive Meeting, April 11, 1947, bundle 2 pt. 2, CP 855/1/1; Memorandum Submitted by Australian Delegation, June 17, 1947, 199, A9913/1, AA; Dominions Office to Australia, April 3, 1947, BT 11 3664, BPRO; Bliss, Progress of Negotiations, May 24, 1947, box 138, ITF; Australia, *Parliamentary Debates* 190 (March 26, 1947), Menzies, 37–38, and Fadden, 41–42; Statement by the Prime Minister, January 20, 1947, ER47/1/21 pt. 1, A1068/1, AA; "Geneva Talks Concern Manufacturers," *Argus*, May 28, 1947, 26; J. N. Bailey and J. J. Murdoch [Dried Fruits Association] to J. J. Clark, March 15, 1947, bundle 1 pt. 1, CP 855/1/1, AA.

12. Wilson to Coombs, April 3, 1947, 262 pt. 2, A9913/1, AA; Australian Delegation, Second Preparatory Conference, Summary 4, April 11, 1947, ER47/1/22, 1068/7, AA.

13. Conversation with Helmore, May 8, 1947, and Bliss, Progress of Negotiations, May 24, 1947, box 138, ITF.

14. U.S. delegation meeting, April 30, 1947, box 133, U.S. Delegation to Clayton, May 15, 1947, box 10, ITF; Conversation on Cuban preferences, February 21, 1947, box 17, ITF.

15. U.S. delegation meetings, April 23, 30, May 7, 14, 1947, box 133, ITF; Conversation with Helmore, May 8, 1947, box 138, ITF.

16. Wilson to Wilcox, May 21, 1947, box 138, ITF; *FRUS, 1947*, 1:938–40.

17. Bliss, Progress of Negotiations, May 24, 1947, box 138, ITF.

18. U.S. Tariff Commission, *War Changes*, 1–16; Hussain, *Politics of Compensation*, 10–26; "More Exports to U.S.," *Sydney Morning Herald*, April 4, 1947, 6; McColl, *Australian Balance of Payments*, 68–80.

19. Robert Ashton minute, February 4, 1943, FO 371 35489, U409/39/71, BPRO; Matusow, *Farm Policies*, 93–94; 1945 Platform of the NWGA, January 29–31, 1945, box 62, O'Mahoney Papers, Boulder; U.S. Senate Special Committee, *Investigation of the Production, Transportation, and Marketing of Wool* (hereafter cited as *Wool Hearings*), 1945, O'Mahoney, 910–13; Conversation with Sylvan Stroock [woolens], September 7, 1945, 611.4117/9-745, box 2724, NA.

20. *Wool Hearings*, 1945, Mary Thomas Peavey, 1390–91. See also 1946 Platform of the NWGA, January 28, 1946 (box 62), and Byrnes to Barrett, February 11, 1946 (box 9), WWGA; *Bulletin of the NAWM*, vol. 66, 1946, p. 411.

21. An Effective Wool Program, March 11, 1946, box 157, O'Mahoney Papers, Boulder. See also Hussain, *Politics of Compensation*, 29–35; O'Mahoney to Truman, January 5, 1946, box 157, O'Mahoney Papers; Report and Recommendations of Conference of Representatives of the Commonwealth, April 16–May 28, 1945, DO 35 1224/WT853/18, BPRO.

22. ECEFP meeting, May 31, 1946, box 7, Edminister Papers, HSTL; James Evans, "American Wool Import Policy," *DSB*, November 3, 1946, 789; Report of first meeting of Wool Study Group, April 8, 1947, FO 371 62873, UE2527/1497/71, BPRO. America, Argentina, Belgium, Britain, Canada, China, France, India, Italy, the southern dominions, and Uruguay comprised the Wool Study Group.

23. Resolutions adopted by the Conference on Wool, January 11, 1947, box 62, O'Mahoney Papers, Boulder. See also Ackerman to Hunt, December 24, 1946, and NAWM brief for the American Wool Textile Industry to the CRI, December 21, 1946, ibid.

24. *CQ-Almanac* 3 (1947): 176–77; R. J. Keltie, Explanation of Parity and Comparable Price, March 26, 1947, box 163, BWTA; NWTA and Boston WTA letter, April 1, 1947, box 37, HCL; J. M. Jones [NWGA] to officers, April 8, 1947, box 40, O'Mahoney Papers, Boulder.

25. *CQ-Almanac* 3 (1947): 176–77; Matusow, *Farm Policies*, 96; Keith Hutchison, "Speak Up, Consumers!," *Nation*, June 7, 1947), 688.

26. Acheson memorandum for the President, April 16, 1947, box 1, RES. See also O'Mahoney to Reuel Walton, July 10, 1947, box 61, O'Mahoney Papers, Boulder.

27. Robert Stevens minute, April 22, 1947, FO 371 62291, UE2810/37/53, BPRO. See also J. W. Allen to Prime Minister, April 10, 1947, H325/10/2, A461/7, AA; Hussain, *Politics of Compensation*, 57–60; Department of Commerce and Agriculture, A Report on U.S. First Offers to Australia on Tariff Concessions, July 9, 1947, 43211 pt. 3, A9790/1, AA.

28. Werner Levi, "U.S.-Australian Relations Today," *Far Eastern Survey* 16:1 (January 15, 1947): 1–5; Gordon Greenwood, "The Australian Political Scene," *Pacific Affairs* 20:3 (September 1947): 283–87; Edwards, *Prime Ministers*, 140–85; Tennant, *Evatt*; Australian Request on U.S.A. for Reduction in Import Duties on Wool, May 3, 1947, box 108, ITF.

29. Conversation with Coombs and Macarthy, April 24, 1947, box 202, ITF; Coombs to Clayton, April 26, May 3, 1947, 43211 pt. 3, A9790/1, AA.

30. Conversation with Coombs and Macarthy, April 24, 1947, box 202, ITF; Coombs, "Keynesian Crusade," 30.

31. Foreign Office to U.K. delegation, May 8, 1947, BT 11 3649, BPRO; Grant [Queensland Merino Stud Sheep Breeders Association] to Prime Minister, May 24, 1947, 20/2/8, AA1974/156/1, AA; Australian Chambers of Manufacturers, Canberra Letter, June 4, 1947, box 20, M1455/1, AA; J. E. Holloway to Clayton, May 2, 1947, and Nash to Clayton, May 5, 1947, box 202, ITF.

32. Wilgress to Secretary of State for External Affairs, April 28, 1947, vol. 5798, 266(s), NAC; R. B. Stevens to U.K. delegation, Geneva, May 5, 1947, and Stevens minute, May 2, 1947, FO 371 62294, UE3347/37/53, BPRO.

33. *FRUS, 1947*, 1:920–22; Nitze to Clayton and Wilcox, May 2, 1947, box 2430, 560.AL/4-2847, NA; Brown memorandum for the President, May 16, 1947, box 108, ITF; "Black Sheep," *New Republic*, June 2, 1947, 8.

34. Dobney, *Selected Papers*, 204–5. See also *CQ-Almanac* 3 (1947): 177–79, and Helmore to Wilcox, June 20, 1947, BT 11 3649, BPRO.

35. Department of External Affairs to Australian Delegation, May 29, 1947, 20/2/8, AA1974/156/1, AA (Chifley). See also Wilcox to Clayton and Nitze, June 20, 1947, box 134, ITF; House of Representatives, Question without Notice, May 14, 1947, H325/10/2, A461/7, AA; J. P. Abbott [Country Party, New South Wales] to Coombs, June 12, 1947, bundle 1 pt. 1, CP855/1/1, AA; *New York Herald Tribune*, May 27, 1947, ER47/1/21 Pt 1, A1068/1, AA; and Richard Boyce, Local Reactions to Proposed American Wool Tax, June 3, 1947, box 202, ITF.

36. Marshall to Senator George Aiken (R-Vt.), June 4, 1947, box 1, RES. See also Wilson to O'Mahoney, May 20, 1947, and Edward O'Neal [AFBF] to O'Mahoney, June 18, 1947, box 40, O'Mahoney Papers, Boulder; Jones to Carter and Tubby, June 6, 1947 (560.Al/6-647), June 23, 1947 (560.AL/6-2347), box 2432, NA; and Hussain, *Politics of Compensation*, 127–37.

37. *CQ-Almanac* 3 (1947): 180–81.

38. *PPP, 1947*, 309–10; Dobney, *Selected Papers*, 215. See also Vandenberg to O'Neal, June 20, 1947, reel 4, Vandenberg Papers, Ann Arbor; *CQ-Almanac* 3 (1947): 181; and U.S. delegation meeting, July 2, 1947, box 133, ITF.

39. Hussain, *Politics of Compensation*, 110–11; Dedman press conference, July 4, 1947, box 7, 2/305/226, MP 98/1, AAV; Chifley message, July 1947, MS 987/12, NLA.

40. *FRUS, 1947*, 1:973. See also Marshall to Truman, July 30, 1947, box 51, WHCF, and Wood to Lovett, July 28, 1947, box 108, ITF.

41. Australian Delegation to Department of External Affairs, August 15, 1947 (43211 pt. 3, A9790/1), Press release, August 14, 1947 (CP 855/1/1, bundle 2 pt. 1, CP 855), and Chifley to Dedman, August 12, 1947 (20/2/8, AA1974/156/1), AA.

42. Dedman to Chifley, August 7, 1947, 43211 pt. 3, A9790/1, AA (Clayton). See also Dedman to Chifley, August 14, 1947, ibid., and Conversation with South African officials, August 11, 1947, box 202, ITF.

43. U.S. Tariff Commission, *War Changes*, 8; "Wool and Meat Spokesmen Welcome Tariff Cuts under Geneva Agreements," *Sydney Morning Herald*, November 19, 1947, 3; Wilson to Reed, October 15, 1947, box 1, Reed Papers, Ithaca; *Bulletin of the NAWM*, vol. 67, 1947, pp. 47–54, 342–46; Conversation with O'Mahoney, August 25, 1947, reel 3, Matthews-Hickerson File, NA.

CHAPTER 7

1. President of Board of Trade, Trade Negotiations at Geneva, July 21, 1947, FO 371 62308, UE6502/37/53, BPRO; Conversation between U.S. and U.K. delegations, July 12, 1947, box 138, ITF; *FRUS, 1947*, 1:954–55; Comparison of U.S. Offers and U.K. Offers, box 138, ITF; J. P. Summerscale memorandum, August 1, 1947, CO 852 701/1, BPRO.

2. U.S. delegation meeting, July 18, 1947, box 133, ITF.

3. Conversation between U.S. and U.K. delegations, July 14, 1947, box 138, ITF.

4. Crowe minute, July 22, 1947, FO 371 62305, UE6066/37/53, BPRO. See also Memorandum by president of Board of Trade, July 22, 1947, FO 371 62309, UE6706/37/53, BPRO.

5. Pimlott, *Diary of Hugh Dalton*, 485. See also Dobson, *Politics*, 105–21; Burr, "The Truman Administration," 54–59; Milward, *Reconstruction*, 214–55; Hogan, *Marshall Plan*, 46–95, 118–28; Howson, *British Monetary Policy*, 154–76; Morgan, *Labour*, 330–58; Dalton, *High Tide*, 93–286, 486–94; Attlee broadcast, August 10, 1947, folder 107, Attlee Papers, Bodleian Library; and Dalton broadcast, August 20, 1947, Dalton III, 9/3, Dalton Papers, LSE.

6. *FRUS, 1947*, 1:969–70. See also Bevin discussion with Ambassador Douglas, August 9, 1947, FO 800 514, BPRO; Cohen OH, HSTL; and "Articles Seven to Ten," *Economist* 153:5424 (August 9, 1947): 228–30.

7. Wilcox to Clayton, August 6, 1947, box 138, ITF.

8. Conversation between U.S. and British officials, August 20, 1947, box 138, ITF.

9. *FRUS, 1947*, 1:977–79.

10. Proposed draft of letter, August 28, 1947, box 138, ITF; Wilgress to Secretary of State

for External Affairs, August 25, 1947, vol. 3845, 9100-L-2-40, pt. 1, NAC; Nitze to Lovett, August 25, 1947, box 2434, 560.AL/8-2547, NA.

11. *FRUS, 1947,* 1:980–82.

12. Memorandum by president of Board of Trade, August 27, 1947, FO 371 62314, UE8189/37/53, BPRO.

13. Ibid.

14. U.K. delegation to Foreign Office, August 28, 1947 (FO 371 62313, UE8012/37/53), August 30, 1947 (FO 371 62314, UE8059/37/53), September 8, 1947 (FO 371 62315, UE8354/37/53), BPRO.

15. F. W. Marten minute, September 9, 1947, FO 371 62314, UE8314/37/53, BPRO (Attlee). See also C. T. Crowe minute, August 29, 1947, and Roger Makins minutes, August 30, September 1, 1947, FO 371 62314, UE8189/37/53, BPRO.

16. *FRUS, 1947,* 1:983–93.

17. Ibid.

18. Memorandum for Cripps, September 15, 1947, box 83, ITF; Fossedal, *Our Finest Hour,* 251.

19. Australian Delegation to Department of External Affairs, September 16, 1947, 43211 pt. 4, A9790/1, AA; Wilgress to Secretary of State for External Affairs, September 16, 1947, vol. 5798, 266(s), NAC.

20. Moscow Embassy to Foreign Office, September 17, 1947, and C. T. Crowe minutes, September 18, 1947 (both in FO 371 62317, UE8877/37/53), September 20, 1947 (FO 371 62317, UE8997/37/53), BPRO.

21. Douglas to Secretary of State, September 18, 1947, box 2438, 560.AL/9-1847, NA (Cripps). See also U.K. delegation to Board of Trade, September 18, 1947, FO 371 62317, UE9972/37/53, BPRO.

22. Conversation between U.S. and U.K. delegations, September 19, 1947, box 83, ITF. See also Colonial Office memorandum, September 8, 1947, BT 11 3660, BPRO.

23. Brown to Wilcox, September 24, 1947, box 286, ITF; Note by president of Board of Trade, September 22, 1947, FO 371 62317, UE8999/37/53, BPRO; Australian Delegation, Second Session of Preparatory Conference, September 26, 1947, ER47/1/22, A1068/7, AA.

24. Brown to Wilcox, September 24, 1947, box 286, ITF; Ronald Russell [Empire Economic Union] report from Geneva, FO 371 62310, UE6945/37/53, BPRO. See also *FRUS, 1947,* 1:995–96, and Empire Industries Association and British Empire League, *Monthly Bulletin,* vol. 78, October 1947, MSS 221/4/2/2/2, MRC.

25. Brown to Wilcox, September 24, 1947, box 286, ITF; Coombs to Chifley, September 25, 1947, 43211 pt. 4, A9790/1, AA; Attlee to Mackenzie King, August 26, 1947, and King to Attlee, September 24, 1947, vol. 5798, 266(s), NAC; Cuff and Granatstein, *American Dollars,* 64–82. In October the United States and Canada debated a customs union to cut tariffs beyond the GATT results. But Ottawa balked at abandoning the empire. A North American free trade zone was established in 1988.

26. Brown to Wilcox, September 24, 1947, box 286, ITF (Robertson). See also telegram from Wilgress, September 23, 1947, vol. 5798, 266(s), NAC.

27. Brown to Wilcox, September 24, 1947, box 286, ITF.

28. *FRUS, 1947,* 1:996–98. See also Brown OH, 27, HSTL.

29. *FRUS, 1947*, 1:999–1000; Memorandum by president of Board of Trade, September 24, 1947, PREM 8 490, BPRO.

30. Bevin to Inverchapel, September 30, 1947, FO 371 62318, UE9151/37/53, BPRO. See also Foreign Office to Inverchapel, nos. 9916, 9917, September 26, 1947, FO 371 62318, UE9040, BPRO, and *FRUS, 1947*, 1:1003–4.

31. *FRUS, 1947*, 1:1004–5. See also U.K. delegation to Foreign Office, September 29, 1947, FO 371 62318, UE9071/37/53, and Minute of meeting with Louis St. Laurent, September 30, 1947, vol. 5798, 266(s), NAC.

32. Brown to Wilcox, September 30, 1947, box 286, ITF.

33. Helmore to Foreign Office, October 2, 1947, FO 371 62319, UE9220/37/53, BPRO. See also Wilgress to John Deutsch, October 2, 1947, vol. 5798, 266(s), NAC, and U.K. Offers on Preferences, October 6, 1947, BT 11 3650, BPRO.

34. *FRUS, 1947*, 1:1006–7. See also Minutes of meeting between Coombs and Helmore, October 10, 1947, BT 11 3665, BPRO.

35. High Commissioner for Canada in Great Britain [LePan] to Secretary of State for External Affairs, October 8, 1947, and Wrong to Robertson, October 6, 1947, vol. 5798, 266(s), NAC.

36. Hall-Patch minute, October 7, 1947, FO 371 62321, UE9512/37/53, BPRO. See also Harold Wilson to Prime Minister, October 7, 1947, PREM 8 490, BPRO.

37. Memorandum by president of Board of Trade, October 8, 1947, FO 371 62320, UE9491/37/53, BPRO.

38. Chargé d'Affaires Stone to Pearson, October 10, 1947, vol. 5798, 266(s), NAC (Wilcox). See also *FRUS, 1947*, 1009–10, and Cabinet 79th Conclusions, October 9, 1947 (FO 371 62320, UE9591/37/53), Inverchapel to Foreign Office, October 10, 1947 (FO 371 62321, UE9531/37/53), and U.K. delegation to Foreign Office, October 11, 1947 (FO 371 62321, UE9564/37/53), BPRO.

39. Coombs to Department of External Affairs, October 11, 1947, 43211 pt. 4, A9790/1, AA; Minutes of Australia-U.S. Negotiations, October 2, 1947, and supplement, October 5, 1947, box 198, ITF; Australian Delegation to Department of External Affairs, October 11, 1947, folder Conflict of Ottawa Agreement and GATT, SP 182/1, AANSW; Draft articles on lamb and mutton, beef and veal, and butter, November 17, 1947, 14/1/3, A1422/13, AA.

40. U.K. delegation to Foreign Office, October 12, 1947, FO 371 62321, UE9665/37/53, BPRO. See also Brown to Wilcox, October 11, 1947, box 2438, 560.AL/10-1147, NA, and *FRUS, 1947*, 1:1011–13.

41. Makins to Bevin and Bevin to Prime Minister, October 14, 1947, FO 800 514, BPRO.

42. Brown to Wilcox, October 13, 1947, box 286, ITF.

43. U.S. Tariff Commission, *Operation . . . II*, 19 (GATT); Department of State, *Analysis of General Agreement*, 1–3; Jackson, *World Trade*. GATT was divided into three parts. The first contained the tariff schedules. The second reproduced the commercial policy provisions of the draft charter (which would supersede GATT). The third dealt with procedural matters and general exceptions.

44. Brown to the President, October 17, 1947, box 1, Wilcox Papers, Philadelphia; *PPP, 1947*, 480.

45. Brown to the President, Annexes A and C, October 17, 1947, box 1, Wilcox Papers, Philadelphia; Department of State, *Analysis of General Agreement*, 133–94; U.S. Tariff Commission, *Operation . . . III*, 9–15. America cut tariffs valued at $11 million from the southern dominions, receiving $81 million in return. They gained because U.S. imports from these nations had risen more than exports to them. Wool tariff cuts also promised them great rewards.

46. Brown memorandum for the President, Annex C, October 17, 1947, George B. L. Arner [USDA] to the President, October 7, 1947, Gregg to the President, October 15, 1947, and Cuban trade agreement (Brossard on tomatoes and okra), box 1, Wilcox Papers, Philadelphia. During negotiations, Holland and Benelux won more concessions on Edam and Gouda cheese, to the dismay of the U.S. Department of Agriculture. The Tariff Commission objected to larger tariff cuts for Cuban tomatoes and okra and for French cotton and silk lace. Czech petroleum products, Canadian zinc-coated sheets and plates and electric batteries, Chilean storage batteries, and lumber for Benelux were the strategic items of concern to the War Department and the Department of the Navy.

47. Brown to the President, and Annex B, October 17, 1947, box 1, Wilcox Papers, Philadelphia. See also U.S. Tariff Commission, *Operation . . . IV*, 20–23.

48. Leddy OH, 53–63, HSTL; Meyer, *International Trade*, 126–28.

49. Foreign Office to U.K. delegation, October 20, 1947, FO 371 62325, UE10310/37/53, BPRO; Great Britain, *Parliamentary Debates* 446 (January 29, 1948), Wilson, 1318–31 (vote in Great Britain). See also Great Britain, *Parliamentary Debates* 443, October 23, 1947, Cripps, 265–96, and October 29, 1947, Harold Wilson, 872–74.

50. "Tariffs and Trade" and "Trade under the New Tariff," *Economist* 153:5439 (November 22, 1947): 827–28, 848. See also Douglas to Marshall, November 18, 1947, box 2442, 560.AL/11-1847, NA.

51. Cabinet Agendum 1019F: GATT, October 24, 1947, vol. 22, CRS A2700/XM1, AA; Australia, *Parliamentary Debates* 196, February 26, 1948, Menzies, 10–14 (critics). See also "Success at Geneva," *Sydney Morning Herald*, November 1, 1947, 2.

52. "Tariff Pact," *Evening Post*, October 30, 1947, EA 1 104/4/7 pt. 1, NZA; GATT, November 18, 1947, NASH 100/0028 GATT, NZA.

53. King diary, October 20, 1947, J13, NAC; Canada, *Parliamentary Debates* I, 20th Parl., 4th sess., John Bracken, 104–14 (Conservatives). See also Prime Minister's Office, press release, December 29, 1947 (reel H-1522), and Abbott address, November 17, 1947 (reel H-1523), vol. 334, MG 26 J4, NAC.

54. Gentlemen's Agreement, October 10, 1947, DO35/3730, BPRO.

55. Clayton OH, 182, Clayton Papers, Houston; "Freer Trade for the Free World," *Newsweek*, October 27, 1947, 24; King diary, October 16, 1947, J13, NAC.

56. Public Reaction to GATT, October 31–November 13, 1947, box 135, OPOS. See also Wilcox to Editor of *Time*, November 14, 1947, box 2441, 560.AL/11-1447, NA, and Monthly Survey of American Opinion, August, 1947, box 11, OPOS.

57. Woll to the President, December 9, 1947, box 899, POF. See also Monthly Survey of

American Opinion, November 1947 (box 11) and Public Reaction to GATT, November 17–December 3, 1947 (box 47), OPOS.

58. Public Reaction to GATT, November 17–December 3, 1947, box 47, OPOS. See also *Congressional Record–House*, December 16, 1947, Knutson, 11482, and November 20, 1947, Robertson, 10673–75; and Conversation between Ways and Means Republicans and Brown, November 13, 1947, box 2441, 560.AL/11-1347, NA.

59. Lovett to Arthur Besse [NAWM], December 9, 1947, *DSB*, December 21, 1947, 1220–21. See also Wright Patman's Weekly Letter, October 2, November 13, 1947, box 1612, Patman Papers, LBJL; and Conversation between Ways and Means Democrats and Brown, November 14, 1947, box 2441, 560.AL/11-1447, NA.

CHAPTER 8

1. R. Glenday speech, January 21, 1947, MSS 200/F/3/D3/3/8, MRC. See also Kennedy, *The Rise and Fall*, 368–69; Orde, *The Eclipse*.

2. U.S. delegation meeting, June 4, 1947, box 133, ITF (Belgium-Luxembourg). See also U.S. delegation to Clayton, May 15, 1947, box 10, ITF, and Havlik OH, HSTL.

3. Subcommittee report on Chapter IV, August 11, 1947, box 13, 2/305/445, MP 98/1, AAV; Parker to Helmore, May 27, 1947, FO 371 62298, UE4077/37/53, BPRO; Thompson-McCausland to R. W. B. Clarke [Treasury], June 18, 1947, OV 170/2, Bank of England; U.S. delegation meeting, July 16, 1947, box 133, ITF; Brown, *Restoration of World Trade*, 99–102; United Nations, *Report of the Second . . . Preparatory Committee*, 13.

4. Wilcox press conference, October 1, 1947, box 1, Wilcox Papers, Philadelphia.

5. New Zealand to Dominions Office, June 19, 1947, FO 371 62302, UE4944/37/53, BPRO (Nash). See also 7th meeting of General Subjects Committee, British Commonwealth Talks, May 6, 1947, FO 371 62296, UE3692/37/53, BPRO.

6. Carl Corse to William Armstrong, March 6, 1947, box 2428, 560.AL/3-647, NA; Wilcox, *A Charter*, 128; U.S. delegation meeting, July 2, 1947, box 133, ITF.

7. Helmore to Board of Trade, August 19, 1947, FO 371 62313, UE7755/37/53, BPRO; Ernest Sturc to Camille Gutt, August 12, 1947, I 231, IMF. See also John Deutsch to W. C. Clark, May 30, 1947, vol. 3846, 9100-M-3-40 pt. 1, NAC; Conversation between British and American officials, July 31, 1947, box 138, ITF.

8. Clayton to Lovett, July 30, 1947, box 15, ITF; R. N. Gardner, *Sterling-Dollar*, 363.

9. Swann, *Hollywood*, 85.

10. Ibid., 8–9, 81–84. See also R. J. Shackle, American Films, February 7, 1946, and Don Bliss to Winthrop Brown, July 4, 1947, box 198, ITF. Such quotas were not limited to Britain, nor was economics their sole motivation. Czechoslovakia reserved 60 percent of screen time for Russian movies. And 90 percent of India's movies were produced at home, revealing cultural tastes.

11. Bliss to Brown, February 26, 1947, box 198, ITF.

12. Swann, *Hollywood*, 87–88; Dickinson, "The State," 75; Bliss to Brown, June 12, 1947, box 198, ITF; Board of Trade note on films, February 1947, and Films—The Johnston Offer, BT 11 3687, BPRO.

13. Bliss to Brown, June 10, 1947, box 198, ITF. See also U.K. delegation to Foreign Office, July 21, 1947, FO 371 62306, UE6269/37/53, BPRO.

14. Bliss, Motion Picture Transfer Problem in U.K., July 24, 1947, box 198, ITF; Note of 6th meeting between Wilson and TUC Economic Committee, January 14, 1948, MSS 292/520.9/2, TUC Records.

15. Swann, *Hollywood*, 90; Bliss to ambassador to Great Britain, June 25, 1947, box 198, ITF.

16. American Embassy to American Consul, Geneva, August 16, 1947, box 198, ITF. See also Bliss, Film Negotiations at Geneva, July 24, 1947, box 198, ITF, and Dickinson, "The State," 76.

17. Swann, *Hollywood*, 91, also 89–93. See also U.S. Embassy, London, to American Consul, Geneva, August 16, 1947, box 198, ITF; Board of Trade minute, August 31, 1947, FO 371 69014, UE7029/2400/53, BPRO; and Dickinson, "The State," 85–86.

18. Willoughby to Wilcox, August 22, 1947, box 198, ITF. See also Wilcox press conference, October 1, 1947, box 1, Wilcox Papers, Philadelphia, and Bliss to U.S. Consul, September 12, 1947, box 198, ITF.

19. U.K. Films Tax, February 10, 1948 (FO 371 69014, UE3802/2480/53), and Tom O'Brien [exhibitor] to Bevin, March 2, 1948 (FO 371 69014, UE3048/2400/53), BPRO.

20. O. L. Moreland to Inverchapel, February 20, 1948 (FO 371 69014, UE2400/2400/53), and Roberts minute, March 1, 1948 (FO 371 69014, UE2757/2400/53), BPRO; Swann, *Hollywood*, 99–100.

21. Memorandum of Agreement, March 11, 1948, FO 371 69014, UE3147/2400/53, BPRO; Swann, *Hollywood*, 100–102.

22. Wilson to Bevin, July 8, 1948, FO 371 69014, UE6181/2400/53, BPRO. See also Conversation with Bliss, Somervell, and Bartlett, August 12, 1948 (FO 371 69014, UE6714/2400/53), Aide-mémoire, August 12, 1948 (FO 371 69014, UE6773/2400/53), and Somervell to Makins, August 19, 1948 (FO 371 69014, UE6787/2400/53), BPRO; and Dickinson, "The State," 87.

23. Wilcox address, August 23, 1947, *DSB*, August 31, 1947, 425–26; Wilcox press conference, October 1, 1947, box 1, Wilcox Papers, Philadelphia. See also Clayton broadcast, September 6, 1947, box 2435, 560.AL/9-647, NA.

24. Wilcox address, October 21, 1947, *DSB*, November 2, 1947, 885.

25. Dedman statement on Geneva Negotiations, November 11, 1947, ER47/1/21 Pt 2, A1068/7, AA. See also Wilson in Fisher to Holmes, [November 1947], FO 371 62313, UE7755/37/53, BPRO; Thurston to Marshall, November 20, 1947, box 2441, 560.AL/10-2347, NA; and Caffery to Marshall, September 20, 1947, box 2438, 560.AL/9-1947, NA.

26. "Final Touches for ITO Charter," *Business Week*, November 15, 1947, 109. See also Jones to Aulette, September 29, 1947, box 2438, 560.AL/9-2947, NA, and U.S. Public Reaction to the Achievements of the Geneva Conference, August 15–September 5, 1947, box 136, ITF.

27. NAM Position on the Geneva Draft, October 29, 1947, box 20, NAM-A. See also Wilcox to John Leddy, January 22, 1947, box 4, ITF.

28. U.S. Public Reaction to the Achievements of the Geneva Conference, August 15–September 5, 1947, box 136, ITF; Butler to Marshall, December 15, 1947, box 1453, RG 16, NA.

29. Wilcox press conference, October 1, 1947, box 1, Wilcox Papers, Philadelphia; Willis Armstrong to Brown, November 7, 1947, box 149, ITF.

30. Canadian chargé d'affaires, Moscow, to Secretary of State for External Affairs, May 28, 1947, vol. 3845, 9100-L-40, pt. 1, NAC; U.S. delegation meeting, May 21, 1947 (box 133), and E. Varga, "The Geneva Trade Talks," *New Times*, published by *Trud*, May 16, 1947 (box 13), ITF.

31. U.S. delegation meeting, July 9, 1947, box 133, ITF; Coombs to Chifley, February 11, 1947, bundle 1 pt. 1, CP 855/1/1, AA.

32. Clayton broadcast, December 8, 1947, *DSB*, December 21, 1947, 1213. See also Truman address, October 24, 1947, *DSB*, November 2, 1947, 853–55.

33. Conversation between American and British officials, July 12, 1947 (box 16), and ECEFP Working Group on ITO, "The European Recovery Program and the ITO," October 3, 1947 (box 15), ITF; Thorp OH, HSTL, 98–99.

34. Clayton speech, February 2, 1948, box 20, Clayton Papers, Houston.

35. F. K. Roberts to Bevin, March 31, 1948, FO 371 68902, UE3550/54/53, BPRO.

36. United Nations, *Conference on Trade and Employment*, 3d–9th Plenary Meetings, November 26–December 1, 1947; ECEFP meeting, November 7, 1947, box 57, ECEFP-R; Clayton to Marshall, December 26, 1947, box 2444, 560.AL/12-2647, NA.

37. "Blackmail at Havana," *Trud*, December 28, 1947, box 13, ITF. See also Mallory to Marshall, December 26, 1947, box 2444, 560.AL/12-2647, NA.

38. Schaetzel, "Analysis of Latin American Proposals," March 30, 1948, box 144, ITF. See also Brown, *Restoration of World Trade*, 137–58.

39. United Nations, *Conference on Trade and Employment*, 3d Plenary Meeting, November 26, 1947 (Bateta). See also Schaetzel, "Analysis of Latin American Proposals," March 30, 1948, and Wilcox to Brown, November 25, 1947, box 144, ITF.

40. Dispatch 11 from American Embassy, Canberra, January 17, 1948, box 2445, 560.AL/1-2248, NA. See also U.K. delegation to Foreign Office, November 27, 1947, FO 371 62761, UE11633/11519/53, BPRO, and United Nations, *Conference on Trade and Employment*, 3d, 6th, and 7th Plenary Meetings, November 26–29, 1947.

41. Reaction by Various European Countries to the Geneva Charter, box 6, ITF. See also Crowe minute, December 29, 1947 (FO 371 62764, UE12511/11519/53), and Memorandum by president of Board of Trade, December 29, 1947 (FO 371 68873, UE69/11/53), BPRO; and Brown, *Restoration of World Trade*, 153–58.

42. Wilcox to Brown, November 25, 1947, box 144, ITF.

43. Wilcox, *A Charter*, 48; Brown, *Restoration of World Trade*, 156–58.

44. R. N. Gardner, *Sterling-Dollar*, 366. See also Wilcox, "Outcome of United Nations Conference on Trade and Employment," March 18, 1948, and attached Memorandum for Abbink from Seymour Rubin, box 6, ITF; Conversation between Clayton and Antonio Parha and Augusto Dillon of Ecuador, January 6, 1948, box 6, ITF; Brown, *Restoration of World Trade*, 155–58.

45. Mallory for Wilcox to Marshall, December 27, 1947, box 2444, 560.AL/12-2747, NA. See also Brown to Clayton, December 30, 1947, box 144, ITF.

46. Lester Schockner to Undersecretary of the Army, February 8, 1948, 560.AL/2-848, NA; Norweb to Marshall, February 9, 1948, 560.AL/2-948, box 2445, NA.

47. Harold Neff memorandum, October 23, 1947, box 84, ITF; W. J. Sebald to Marshall, December 5, 1947, box 2443, 560.AL/12-547, NA.

48. Neff memorandum, October 23, 1947, box 84; Wayne Jackson to Brown, January 27, 1948, box 11, ITF; Inverchapel to Foreign Office, January 30, 1948, FO 371 68878, UE1326/11/53, BPRO; Clayton to Lovett, February 16, 1948, box 2446, 560.AL/2-1548, NA.

49. Royall to Marshall, February 24, 1947, box 2428, 560.AL/2-2447, NA; Schockner memorandum of conversation with State Department representatives, January 26, 1948, box 11, ITF.

50. Charles Saltmann to Nitze, March 30, 1948, box 11, ITF.

51. Brown, *Restoration of World Trade*, 147–49.

52. H. J. B. Lintott minute, February 9, 1948, BT 11 3800, BPRO. See also Brown, *Restoration of World Trade*, 150–52; Foreign Office to U.K. delegation, February 14, 1948 (FO 371 68880, UE1728/11/53), and U.K. delegation to Foreign Office, February 18, 1948 (FO 371 68883, UE2256/11/53), BPRO.

53. Geoffrey Parker minute, March 17, 1948, FO 371 68883, UE2315/11/53, BPRO. See also Foreign Office to U.K. delegation, February 25, 1948 (FO 371 68883, UE2401/11/53), and U.K. delegation to Foreign Office, March 12, 1948 (FO 371 68886, UE3059/11/53).

54. R. N. Gardner, *Sterling-Dollar*, 364. See also Wilcox, *A Charter*, and Thompson-McCausland to E. Rowe-Dutton, November 11, 1947, OV170/2, Bank of England.

55. Seymour Rubin, "Analysis of Articles 13–24," box 6, ITF. See also Conversations with Pierre Siraud, March 2, 4, 1948, box 15, U.S. Department of State, Clayton-Thorp, HSTL, and Conversation with Anthony Percival, March 12, 1948, box 15, ITF.

56. Coppock to Brown, December 30, 1947, box 144, ITF.

57. Wilcox to Brown, February 25, 1948, ibid. See also Wilcox, "Outcome of United Nations Conference," March 18, 1948, box 6, ITF.

58. Wilcox and Terrill meeting with Non-Governmental Advisers on ITO, box 1, ITF.

59. Wilcox, *A Charter*, 49; *PPP, 1948*, 190. See also Initial U.S. Public Reaction to the Signing of the ITO Charter, March 24–April 1, 1948, box 9, ITF, and Brown, *Restoration of World Trade*, 158–60, chap. 7.

60. Wilcox's book, *A Charter for World Trade*, appeared in 1949. See also press releases, September 20, 22, 1948, *DSB*, October 3, 1948, 444–45.

CHAPTER 9

1. Conference-Comics II, Christmas, 1947, box 57, ITF.

2. "Results of the Havana Conference," *Vneshnyaya Torgovlya* 18 (June 1948); Arutiunian speech to ECOSOC, August 11, 1948, box 13, ITF; Wilgress, Report of the Canadian Delegation, July 13, 1948, vol. 3847, 9100-S-40 file pocket, NAC; Mr. Holland's Speech on GATT, June 24, 1948, NASH 80/0689-1418, NZA; Draft Cabinet Agendum, April 19, 1948, 2/305/364, MP 98/1, AAV; R. N. Gardner, *Sterling-Dollar*, 369–71.

3. Remarks before Lincoln Club, February 11, 1950, book 3, Millikin Collection, Boulder. See also *RTAA-House*, 1948, 132; American Tariff League resolution, October 27, 1948,

box 3, ITF; *Congressional Record–Senate*, May 1, 1950, Malone, 6060–64; Elvin Kilheffer, "ITO—Illusion or Reality?," *Annals of the American Academy of Political and Social Science* 264 (July 1949): 79–80.

4. U.S. Senate, *International Wheat Agreement*, 55. See also *CQ-Almanac* 5 (1949): 370, OPOS. The Democrats ratified the wheat agreement in 1949 after retaking Congress. See also Kelly, *Studies*, 202–5; Hamby, *Beyond the New Deal*, 303–5; Matusow, *Farm Policies*, 170–221.

5. Serge Benson, Glossary of ITO Charter, box 1, Reed Papers, Ithaca; *Congressional Record–Senate*, May 1, 1950, Bridges, 6064.

6. *PPP, 1950*, 404.

7. Statements by Business Spokesmen on ITO, box 3, ITF. See also NAM Resolution, March 30, 1949, box 20, NAM-A; Robert Loree [NFTC] to Acheson, January 21, 1949, box 2461, 560.AL/1-2149, NA; and "The Chamber and the Charter," September 1949, box 6, ITF.

8. Monthly Survey of American Opinion, March, April 1949, box 12, OPOS.

9. *Commercial and Financial Chronicle*, September 30, 1948, box 3, ITF. See also NFTC Fifth Summary Report on the Charter, March 19, 1948, box 9, ITF.

10. Meeting with Non-Governmental Advisors on ITO, [1948], box 1, ITF. See also Charles Carroll [General Motors], *New York Journal of Commerce*, November 8, 1948, box 3, ITF, and William Harrison [NFTC] to Clayton, March 7, 1949, box 22, Clayton Papers, Houston.

11. Wohl, "Now We've Bought It, What Is It?," *Barron's*, April 19, 1948, 30. See also *Wall Street Journal*, August 9, 1948.

12. Batt to Charles Taft, box 185, Charles P. Taft Papers, LC; Nitze address, October 25, 1948, *DSB*, November 7, 1948, 582.

13. Meeting with Non-Governmental Advisors on ITO, [1948], box 1, ITF. See also Briefing Book, "Consequences and Advantages to American Businessmen If ITO Is Not Adopted," [1948], box 6, ITF.

14. Griffith, "Forging America's Postwar Order," 87–88, also 63–84. See also Diebold, "End of the ITO," 13–19; Hamby, *Liberalism*, 62–67; and Vogel, "Why Businessmen Distrust Their State."

15. Garet Garett, *American Affairs* [NICB]; Kilheffer address, September 22, 1948, box 3, ITF.

16. NAM resolution, November 1948, box 3, ITF. See also Brown to Acheson, February 19, 1949, box 2461, 560.AL/1-2149, NA, and Report of Twentieth Century Fund's Committee on Cartels and Monopoly, May 31, 1948, box 3, ITF.

17. Cortney to Clayton, March 18, 1949, box 76, Clayton Papers, HSTL. Cortney was a Rumanian-born French engineer, educated in political science and economics at Columbia University, whose career in world trade dated back to 1922. He cofounded a European steel export firm and directed the Banque Transatlantique of Paris before joining Coty in 1940. In 1949 Cortney served on NAM's International Relations Committee, which had unanimously rejected the ITO. From 1957 to 1959 he was chairman of the U.S. Council of the International Chamber of Commerce.

18. Cortney to Taft, May 11, 1950, box 666, Robert A. Taft Papers, LC; Cortney to Acheson, January 11, 1950 (box 1423, 394.ITO/1-1150), April 4, 1950 (box 1424, 394.ITO/4-450), NA.

19. Cortney to Clayton, March 3, 1949 (box 22), February 8, 1949 (box 21), Clayton Papers, Houston; and March 18, 1949, box 76, Clayton Papers, HSTL.

20. Cortney to Clayton, March 18, 1949, box 76, Clayton Papers, HSTL. See also Cortney, *Economic Munich*, x-35, Part III; U.S. Senate Committee on Finance, Hearings, *International Trade Organization* (hereafter cited as *ITO Hearings*), Cortney, 777.

21. William Gray to Clayton, March 7, 1949, box 22, Clayton Papers, Houston; Melvin Fox to Charles Weaver, September 12, 1949, box 76, Clayton Papers, HSTL.

22. U.S. Council of the ICC, "The Havana Charter," May 9, 1950, box 10, ITF.

23. Conversation with Baruch, September 18, 1948, box 2455, 560.AL/9-1848, NA.

24. Lovett to the President, May 21, 1948; George Elsey to Clark Clifford, May 26, 1948, box 7, Clifford Files, HSTL; Conversation with David Bell, June 3, 1948, box 2454, 560.AL/6-3488, NA; William Baldwin [Citizen's Committee for Reciprocal World Trade] to Clayton, December 28, 1948, box 76, Clayton Papers, HSTL.

25. Conversation with Vandenberg and Bohlen, January 25, 1949, box 2461, 560.AL/1-2549, NA; E. A. Gross to Acheson, March 25, 1949, box 2463, 560.AL/3-2549, NA; Big Four Discussion on Legislative Program, March 28, 1949, box 64, Acheson Papers, HSTL; Brown to the President, April 25, 1949, box 59, RES.

26. Stinebower OH, HSTL, 37–38.

27. Daily Summary of Opinion Developments, January 31, 1949, box 3, OPOS. See also Roster of the Committee, May 4, 1949, box 185, Charles P. Taft Papers, LC, and Committee for the ITO Statement of Objectives, May 1949, box 6, ITF.

28. Wilcox, "The Promise of the World Trade Charter," *Foreign Affairs* 27 (April 1949): 486–96. See also Clayton on comments of Henry Bristol, April 13, 1949 (box 22), Clayton to Arthur Krock, February 26, 1949 (box 21), and Clayton to Cortney, April 4, 30, 1949 (box 22), Clayton Papers, Houston.

29. "Cortney's Approach to the ITO," box 76, Clayton Papers, HSTL. See also Clayton review, *Economic Munich*, ibid.

30. Batt to Clayton, June 17, 1949, and Fox to Weaver, September 12, 1949, box 76, Clayton Papers, HSTL.

31. Fox to Weaver, September 12, 1949, box 76, Clayton Papers, HSTL.

32. Acheson address, May 3, 1949, *DSB*, May 15, 1949, 623–27. See also *PPP, 1949*, 233–35.

33. Acheson to Paul Hoffman, February 20, 1950, box 1424, 394.ITO/2-2050, NA; Armstrong OH and Becker OH, HSTL.

34. Memorandum to John Leddy, October 27, 1949; Conversation with Javits, Kirlin, and Brown, January 12, 1950, box 12, ITF.

35. Raymond Vernon OH, 25, HSTL. See also conversation with Francis Wilcox, Thorsten Kalijarvi, and State Department staff, December 14, 1949, box 2, ASSCR; and Acheson, *Present at the Creation*, 362–70.

36. Conversations between Hal Holmes (R-Wash.) and Brown, January 27, 1950, and be-

tween Springer and Brown, February 2, 1950 (box 1423, 394.ITO/2-2750), and between Clayton and Brown, February 13, 1950 (box 1424, 394.ITO/2-1350), NA; Acheson notes on Meeting with the President, February 9, 1950, box 9, RES.

37. *ITO Hearings*, NFTC, 177–269.

38. Conversation, February 15, 1950, box 1424, 394.ITO/2-1550, NA; Cortney, *Economic Munich*, 81.

39. *ITO Hearings*, Acheson, 14–15, Johnson to John Kee, February 28, 1950, 477.

40. *ITO Hearings*, Acheson, 10, and Javits, 143. See also Fairbanks to Kee, March 27, 1950, box 87:6, Douglas Collection; Literature favoring ITO, box 11, ITF.

41. *PPP, 1950*, 239–40; Acheson to the President, February 16, 1950, box 3, RES. See also ECA report on sales of European products in the Western Hemisphere, December 7, 1949, box 24, Gray Files, HSTL; Report to the President on Foreign Economic Policies, November 10, 1950, box 9, NACIM (ITO, p. 16). See also Charles D. Jackson, "Total Business Diplomacy," *Vital Speeches of the Day* 16:14 (May 1, 1950): 424, and "Customs: Barrier to Trade," *Business Week*, October 8, 1949, 105–6. Customs procedures amounted to invisible, and onerous, barriers. For example, a tourist sent home a Persian rug worth $100 but learned that he was liable for $710 worth of fines and duties. His fringed rug was classified as lace and carried a 90 percent ad valorem duty instead of the normal 30 percent placed on carpets. If he tried to throw the rug away at customs, he would still owe $150.

42. *ITO Hearings*, Batt, 123, and Johnston, 718. See also Public Attitudes Relating to Foreign Economic Issues, July 31, 1951, box 14, Gray Files, HSTL.

43. Conversation with British officials, December 13, 1949, box 2460, 560.AL/12-1348, NA; in Conversation with Murray [Canadian Embassy], January 10, 1950, box 12, ITF, and January 31, 1950, box 1423, 394.ITO/1-3150, NA; U.S. Mission to the United Nations, memorandum of conversation, October 5, 1949, box 55, ITF.

44. Public Attitudes Relating to Foreign Economic Issues, July 31, 1951, box 14, Gray Files, HSTL.

45. Acheson to the President, May 3, 1950, box 2, ASSCR.

46. Acheson to the President, April 26, 1950, box 1424, 394.ITO/4-2650, NA; Brown to McFall, Republican Strategy in Senate on ITO, May 2, 1950, box 12, ITF; McFall to Thorp, May 2, 1950, box 1424, box 59, 394.ITO/5-250, NA.

47. James Webb memorandum, May 10, 1950, box 1428, 394.31/5-1050, NA; Connally to Clayton, May 31, 1950, box 24, Clayton Papers, Houston.

48. George Elsey to Stephen Spingarn, May 27, 1950, box 20, Spingarn Papers, HSTL; McFall to Webb, May 25, 1950, box 1424, 394.ITO/5-2550, NA; Batt to Clayton, May 23, 1950, box 24, Clayton Papers, Houston. Congressmen Matthew Neely (D-W.Va.) and Tom Steed (D-Tex.) held hearings on the unemployment-imports link.

49. Kee to the President, August 10, 1950, box 20, Spingarn Papers, HSTL. See also Truman to Kee, August 14, 1950, ibid., and Leddy to Eric Wyndham White, August 11, 1950, box 1424, 394.ITO/8-1150, NA.

50. Acheson to the President, November 20, 1950, box 4, RES.

51. Ibid. See also Conversation with William Swingle [NFTC], September 27, 1950, box 1431, 394.31/9-2750, NA. Acheson noted that ITO's employment provisions were carried out by ECOSOC, whereas Point Four, bilateral agreements, and certain GATT clauses took

care of development. Chapters on commodity agreements, cartels, and organization could be added to GATT.

52. Secretary of State's notes, November 21, 1950, box 9, RES; McFall to Acheson, November 24, 1950, box 2, ASSCR; O'Gara to Byroade, December 6, 1950, box 1424, 394.ITO/12-650, NA.

53. Conversation with Holmes, November 28, 1950, box 165, ITF. See also Brown to Thorp, November 7, 1950, ibid.

54. U.S. Department of State to Margaret Potter, January 2, 1951, box 1434, 394.31/1-251, NA.

CHAPTER 10

1. *PPP, 1949*, 27. See also Lovett to the President, December 27, 1948, box 899, POF; *RTAA-House Report*, 1948, 2–9.

2. U.S. Senate Committee on Foreign Relations, *European Recovery*, 417–22. See also *Congressional Record–Senate*, September 15, 1949, 12883–94; Public Discussion Concerning Effects of Increased Foreign Competition on the U.S. Economy, April 19, 1949, box 48, OPOS; *RTAA-Senate*, Minority Views, 1–7; *RTAA-Senate*, 1949, Malone, 869–78, and Robert Taft, 1084–85; and *Congressional Record–Senate*, August 1, 1949, Millikin, 10466.

3. Daily Summary of Opinion Developments, May 10, 1949, box 3, OPOS. See also *RTAA-House*, 1949, 60–61, 119, 390.

4. *Congressional Record–Senate*, September 14, 1949, 12844.

5. *PPP, 1949*, 356, 359; Murans, "Reciprocal Trade," 94–96.

6. *Congressional Record—Appendix*, vol. 95, pt. 15, August 4, 1949, Reed, A5124–25.

7. *RTAA-Senate*, 1949, Millikin, 175–76, and Cenerazzo, 517–18.

8. Lucas statements, May 10, 1949, box 33, Lucas Papers, Springfield; *Congressional Record–House*, February 8, 1949, Boggs, 1020. See also Paul Hoffman to CED, May 11, 1949, box 102, Flanders Papers, Syracuse.

9. *PPP, 1949*, 447–48, 450–51.

10. *RTAA-House*, 1949, Forrestal to Doughton, 387; Harris, 760; also National Farmers Union, 70; National Women's Trade Union League, 81; Brotherhood of Railway Clerks, 747–48.

11. *Congressional Record–Senate*, September 7, 1949, Robertson, 12623.

12. Daily Summary of Opinion Developments, January 31, 1949, box 3, OPOS. See also Paterson, "Economic Cold War," 44; *RTAA-House*, 1949, 183–84, 666–67.

13. *CQ-Almanac* 7 (1951): 785 (Millikin). See also *CQ-Almanac* 5 (1949): 364–69, 425, 430, and Murans, "Reciprocal Trade," 98–112. House Republicans voted 84–63 for the RTAA; Democrats voted 234–6. The Senate GOP opposed it 18–15, but the Democrats tallied 47–1 in favor.

14. "Tariff Perils," *Economist* 157:5536 (October 1, 1949): 721; *PPP, 1949*, 486–87.

15. U.S. Tariff Commission, *Third Report*, 43–45. Eventually, ten nations—Denmark, the Dominican Republic, Finland, Greece, Haiti, Italy, Liberia, Nicaragua, Sweden, and Uruguay —acceded.

16. U.S. Tariff Commission, *Third Report*, 24–25, 32–34; Willoughby to Corse, April 29, May 19, 1949, box 160, ITF; Report of the U.S. Delegation, September 1949, box 215, ITF.

17. *FRUS, 1949*, 1:678. See also L. P. Thompson-McCausland memorandum, May 9, 1949, ADM14/25, Bank of England; U.S. Tariff Commission, *Third Report*, 34–36.

18. *FRUS, 1949*, 1:651–53, 682–86, 693, 709–14n, 717–18; Milward and Brennan, *Britain's Place*.

19. U.S. Tariff Commission, *Third Report*, 36–38; Report of U.S. Delegation, September 1949, box 215, ITF; Milward, *Reconstruction*, 311.

20. U.S. Tariff Commission, *Third Report*, 38–40; *FRUS, 1949*, 1:661–63.

21. Association of British Chambers of Commerce meeting, December 1, 1948, MS 14487, vol. 5, Guildhall Library; U.S.-Commonwealth meeting, November 1, 1948, 602/2 pt. 1, A9793/3, AA; Milward, *Reconstruction*, 114–16; David Bane to William Sebald, December 1, 1948, box 2460, 560.AL/12-148, NA; Lowe, *Origins*, 75–76.

22. *FRUS, 1949*, 1:666–67.

23. Ibid., 656–57; Pollard, *Economic Security*, 178–87; Borden, *Pacific Alliance*, 61–102; Schaller, *American Occupation*.

24. *FRUS, 1949*, 1:663–66; G. Kimber to Prime Minister's Department, March 22, 1949, 602/2 pt. 1, A9793/3, AA.

25. Conversation between U.S. and Canadian officials, March 5, 1949, and Willoughby to Corse, May 3, 1949, box 160, ITF. See also *FRUS, 1949*, 1:670–704, and Acheson to U.S. delegation, August 23, 1949, box 2468, 560.AL/8-2249, NA.

26. Report of U.S. Delegation, September 1949, box 215, ITF. See also *FRUS, 1949*, 1:704–9.

27. Political Adviser for Germany, "MFN Treatment of Germany," January 3, 1949, box 2464, 560.AL/1-2149, NA.

28. Willoughby to David Stowe, February 10, 1949, and Webb to the President, February 23, 1949, box 52, POF; Jones to Willoughby, August 9, 1949, box 2468, 560.AL/8-949, NA; *FRUS, 1949*, 1:723, 726; U.S. Tariff Commission, *Third Report*, 41–47.

29. Corse to the President, April 6, 1949, box 2464, 560.AL/4-749, NA; "Next Round in Tariff Bargaining," *Economist* 156:5513 (April 23, 1949): 757.

30. Thorp to Willoughby, March 21, 1949, box 213, ITF; "Commonwealth Countries Regain Prewar Share of World Trade," *Foreign Trade* 6:153 (December 3, 1949): 1026–27.

31. Frances L. Hall, "Britain's Trade Making Noteworthy Gains—'Dollar Problem' Persists," *Foreign Commerce Weekly*, April 18, 1949, 3–9, 46; Memorandum by John Heinz, August 16, 1949, box 70, Clayton Papers, HSTL; Howson, *British Monetary Policy*, 211–48.

32. *FRUS, 1949*, 4:419; Chifley speech, June 12, 1949, Chifley folder, Evatt Papers, Australia; London Financial Discussions, July 7, 1949, MS 987/14/2, NLA; Hogan, *Marshall Plan*, 223–29.

33. P. M. Williams, *Gaitskell*, 115; Foreign Office to Washington Embassy, July 17, 1949, FO 371 78075, UR257/258/98, BPRO.

34. Hogan, *Marshall Plan*, 231–34, 277–78; George Ball, "Proposal for Study Group on Economic Policy," December 9, 1949, vol. 35 1949/50, CFR-R; Harris, *Attlee*, 436–37; Alzada Comstock, "British Commonwealth in Crisis," *Forum* 112:5 (November 1949):

263–66; "Surplus of Dollars Rolling Up Abroad," *U.S. News and World Report*, November 17, 1950, 20–21; "Korea and the Dollar Gap," *Business Week*, August 19, 1950, 100; "U.S. Strikes a New Trade Balance," *Business Week*, December 9, 1950, 101–3.

35. Leddy to Thorp and Nitze, August 25, 1949, box 277, ITF.

36. Willoughby to the President, October 6, 1949, box 52, WHCF; "Concessions Granted from Negotiations at Annecy," *DSB*, October 17, 1949, 596–98.

37. Supplement to the Confidential Report, box 215, ITF; U.S. Department of State, *Analysis*, Annecy, 21–123.

38. Willoughby to Acheson, July 18, 1949 (box 2467, 560.AL/7-1549), August 3, 1949 (box 2468, 560.AL/8-349), NA; Corse to the President, August 17, 1949, box 2468, 560.AL/8-1748, NA; Webb meeting with the President, September 19, 1949, and Webb to Acheson, October 10, 1949, box 8, RES; Lawrence Mehren [Arizona Citrus Growers] to Hayden, March 9, 1949, Mehren to Hayden, October 12, 1949, Truman to Hayden, November 19, 1949, Steelman to Hayden, January 25, 1950, and Hayden to Secretary of Agriculture, March 25, 1950 (all in box 42:3), and California Fruit Growers Exchange and Exchange Lemon Products Company before CRI, June 9, 1950 (box 89:8), Hayden Papers, Tempe; McFall to Helen Gahagan Douglas, May 15, 1950, box 73:1, Douglas Collection. Truman did ask Italy to space its shipments so that lemons would not arrive in such large volume.

39. U.S. Tariff Commission, *Third Report*, 7–11. Peril points were breached on red onions, wool felt hat bodies, paperboard, alpargata, surgical instruments, blue-mold cheese, figs, and cellulose sponges.

40. Public Reaction to the Annecy Trade Agreement Announcement, October 24, 1949, box 47, OPOS. See also Jones to Willoughby, August 18, 1949, box 2468, 560.AL/8-1849, NA.

41. Wilgress speech, August 24, 1949, box 215, ITF. See also Public Reaction to Annecy, October 24, 1949, box 47, OPOS, and *FRUS, 1949*, 1:724–25.

42. *FRUS, 1949*, 1:725; Willoughby, "The Annecy Conference on Tariffs and Trade," *DSB*, November 21, 1949, 778; Interim Committee of the ITO, "The Attack On Trade Barriers," August 1949, box 211, ITF.

43. Corse to the President, September 21, 1949, box 2469, 560.AL/9-2249, NA. See also U.S. Tariff Commission, *Third Report*, 11–13.

CHAPTER 11

1. U.S. Tariff Commission, *Fourth Report*, 8–9, 48; "Tariff Slashes," *Business Week*, May 26, 1951, 115–16; *FRUS, 1950*, 1:1319–72; P. D. Allen to U.S. Delegation, February 27, 1951, box 216, ITF.

2. U.S. Tariff Commission, *Fourth Report*, 79–91; *FRUS, 1950*, 1:694–779.

3. Acting High Commissioner for Canada to Secretary of State for External Affairs, September 22, 1950, vol. 3845, 9100-D-40, NAC. See also Recommendations of the Committee on Trade Agreements, March 31, 1950, and William Beale to Corse, October 1950, box 219, ITF; U.S. Tariff Commission, *Fourth Report*, 49–52; and Association of British Cham-

bers of Commerce, Overseas Committee minutes, October 4, 1950, MS 14487, vol. 5, Guildhall Library.

4. Eckes, *Opening America's Market*, 163. See also notes of meeting between U.K. and U.S. officials, January 25, 1950, box 1426, 394.31/2-350, NA; *FRUS, 1950*, 1:791–93; Brown to Leddy, November 18, 1950, box 165, ITF; Joseph Todd to U.S. Department of State, August 4, 1950, and Annexes A and B, box 1429, 394.31/8-450, NA; and Robert Nowell minute, January 1, 1951, BT 64/594, BPRO.

5. *FRUS, 1950*, 1:800, 802–3, 805–6; Conversation with USDA Secretary Brannan, March 31, 1950, box 1427, 394.31/3-3150, NA.

6. Holmes to Reginald Franklin, January 2, 1951, BT 64/594, BPRO. See also Consultative Committee for Industry, October 19, 1950, MSS 292/522/1/1, MRC, and Trade Negotiations Committee minutes, March 21, 1951, BT 64/695, BPRO.

7. *FRUS, 1950*, 1:1253–54. See also Walter Gifford to Herbert Morrison, March 19, 1951, FO 371/91903, UEE 5/25, BPRO, and Thorp to Batt, British Stake in GATT, box 2, BCNEA.

8. Conversation with Holmes, March 23, 1951, box 6, BCNEA. See also Roger Makins, Anglo-American Trade Negotiations, March 9, 1951, FO 371/91903, UEE 5/23, BPRO.

9. *FRUS, 1950*, 1:1285–1316; White Paper, Report on the Torquay Tariff Negotiations, April 21, 1951, BT 64/595, BPRO.

10. *FRUS, 1950*, 1:1253–56, 1259, 1311–13, 1317.

11. "Goodbye to All GATT," *Economist* 160:5617 (April 21, 1951): 901–2. See also Molesworth to Department of State, May 16, 1951, box 1435, 394.31/5-1651, NA; Eckes, *Opening America's Market*, 163; and Roger Makins, Anglo-American Tariff Negotiations, March 27, 1951, FO 371/91903, UEE 5/31, BPRO.

12. Willoughby to Department of State, May 9, 1951, box 216, ITF; *FRUS, 1950*, 1:788–90; Jackson, *World Trade*, 50–51.

13. "Conclusion of the Torquay Tariff Conference," *DSB*, April 30, 1951, 702. See also Corse to Leddy, April 9, 1951, box 219, ITF; Steelman to the President, May 2, 1951, box 57, WHCF; London Chamber of Commerce, memorandum of reply to questionnaire, May 6, 1952, MS 16661, vol. 4, Guildhall Library; Draft communiqué and minutes, Commonwealth Economic Conference, December 10, 1952, CAB 133, BPRO; and Eckes, *Opening America's Market*, 180–83.

14. "U.S. Opposes Postponement of Torquay Tariff Negotiations," *DSB*, September 18, 1950, 475; Acheson to Green, August 28, 1950, box 1429, 394.31/8-1150, NA. See also Green to Acheson, August 11, 1950, box 1429, 394.31/8-1150, NA; Conversation with Doughton, August 23, 1950, box 1430, 394.31/8-2350, NA; and Battle to Acheson, September 1, 1950, box 65, Acheson Papers, HSTL.

15. U.S. Tariff Commission, *Fourth Report*, 143–45; *FRUS, 1950*, 1:1522–72; Eckes, *Opening America's Market*, 228; "Mounting U.S. Trade Barriers Pose New Dilemma to Europe," *Newsweek*, May 26, 1952, 75. Truman upheld a recommendation not to restrict spring clothespins from Mexico.

16. *DSB*, August 20, 1951 (pp. 290–92), October 15, 1951 (pp. 621–24), and December 17, 1951 (p. 977). See also Funigiello, *American-Soviet Trade*.

17. U.S. Tariff Commission, *Fourth Report*, 146–47; *FRUS, 1950*, 1:1460–78; *FRUS, 1951*, 1:1424–78; Brown to Truman Nold [National Apple Institute], April 11, 1951, box 288, ITF.

18. Brown, "The Trade Agreements Act: Its Performance and Its Possibilities," box 17, Gray Files, HSTL.

19. Richard Neustadt to Charles Murphy, October 20, 1950, box 6, Neustadt Files, and Neustadt to Murphy, December 30, 1950, box 22, Murphy Papers, HSTL.

20. Protectionists in *RTAA-House, 1951*, 200–217, 300–302, 356–57; *RTAA-Senate, 1951*, 48–49, 191–92, 765–823; *Congressional Record–House*, January 31, 1951 (pp. 796–838), February 7, 1951 (pp. 1037–81); *Congressional Record–Senate*, April 25, 1951 (pp. 4322–42), May 17, 1951 (pp. 5430–31), May 22, 1951 (pp. 5555–87).

21. *CQ-Almanac* 7 (1951): 215–19; U.S. Tariff Commission, *Fourth Report*, 27–33; Department of State to Senator George, August 1, 1950, box 20, Spingarn Papers, HSTL.

22. Marjorie Belcher to the President, April 12, 1951, box 901, POF; *CQ-Almanac* 14 (1958): 177–82; Kelly, *Studies*, 132–38; Leffler, *A Preponderance of Power*, 446–47.

23. Johnson to March E. Oliver, May 31, 1951, box 236, Johnson Senate Political Files, LBJL; *Congressional Record–House*, June 25, 1952, Kennedy, 8085.

24. *PPP, 1951*, 340; Clayton address, "World Trade," box 24, Clayton Papers, Houston; Rosamond and Bradford Bachrach to Leverett Saltonstall (D-Mass.), March 12, 1951, box 82d Cong., Re-Sa 1951–52, Saltonstall Papers, Boston.

25. "1952: Will Barriers Go Up Again?," *Business Week*, May 10, 1952, 148–51. Congress considered thirteen import bills.

26. *PPP, 1952*, 1108. See also "Blast at U.S.," *Newsweek*, November 10, 1952, 54.

27. Acheson press conference, *DSB*, May 12, 1952, 737. See also Thompson-McCausland to the Governor, April 29, 1952, and Official Committee on Commercial Policy meeting, June 19, 1952, OV170/3, Bank of England; U.S. Tariff Commission, *Sixth Report*, 84–89.

28. "A Blow For Freedom," *Time*, August 25, 1952, 66.

29. "Applying Our Tariff Policy," *Business Week*, August 30, 1952, 100. See also *DSB*, August 25, 1952 (303–7), September 1, 1952 (337–38); Truman to Senator George, July 21, 1952, and D. A. Fitzgerald to Roger Jones, August 12, 1952, box 57, WHCF; and Eckes, *Opening America's Market*, 229–30.

30. "Buy Free World," *Time*, April 28, 1952, 21; David Cohn, "Junior, Drop That Japanese Toy!," *Atlantic Monthly*, December 1951, 45; Keith Hutchison, "High Tariffs vs. Foreign Policy," *Nation*, May 31, 1952, 522–24.

31. *PPP, 1952*, 475. See also PAB meeting, May 21, 1952, PAB; Editorial Comment, July 21, 1952, box 15, PAB; and Thorp to Acheson, July 11, 1952, box 3, ASSCR, NA.

32. Public Advisory Board, *A Trade and Tariff Policy*, 1. See also Eckes, *Opening America's Market*, 166. The Bell Report advised a simplified tariff act to lower duties and consolidate hundreds of tariffs into seven schedules. The president would also enter into trade negotiations without a time limit and with authority to cut tariffs, without specified limits, in return for concessions by other nations. Customs procedures would be simplified, tariffs and quotas on farm goods liberalized, and some on metals and minerals that were critical to defense eliminated. Excise taxes on oil imports would end, the cargo preference that required 50

percent of aid and loan goods be carried on domestic ships would be dropped, and the Buy American Act would be severely curtailed. Congress would be asked to take the steps necessary for U.S. membership in a trade organization to administer GATT. Meanwhile, to help domestic producers and workers hit by imports, assistance in the form of unemployment insurance, retraining, and conversion would be offered.

33. J. B. Martin, *Adlai Stevenson*, 734–35; Johnson, *Governor of Illinois*, 175–76, 193, and *"Let's Talk Sense,"* 66, 80–81, 154–55; Galambos and Chandler, *Papers of . . . Eisenhower*, 865–66, 1229; "Significance: The Nominees and Foreign Policy," *Newsweek*, August 25, 1952, 22.

34. Eisenhower, *Mandate for Change*, 195, 208; "Businessmen: New Soviet Pawns in the Cold War?," *Business Week*, April 26, 1952, 152–55; Frank Altschul, "America's New Economic Role," *Foreign Affairs* 31 (April 1953): 393–94.

35. Galambos and Chandler, *Papers of . . . Eisenhower*, 1504. See also Kaufman, *Trade and Aid*, 12–14; "Trade, Not Aid," *Business Week*, December 13, 1952, 172.

CONCLUSION

1. L. Withall to H. V. Evatt, January 8, 1954, folder GATT, Evatt Papers, Australia.

2. Jackson, *World Trade*, 51–52; Kaufman, *Trade and Aid*, 43–44, 74–75. The OTC would have administered GATT by an executive committee, assembly, and secretariat. Eisenhower withdrew it in the face of congressional opposition. Because Congress never ratified GATT, State Department conference funds underwrote delegation expenses.

3. Diebold, "Foreign Economic Policy," 248–49.

4. This conclusion follows the European "revisionist" school of thought, which posits that American hegemonic designs were blocked or revised by European nations after the war. For other cases, see Burnham, "Re-evaluating the Washington Loan Agreement," and Milward, *Reconstruction* (on the Marshall Plan).

5. Stein, "The Hegemon's Dilemma" (hegemonic behavior); Brusse, *Tariffs, Trade, and European Integration* (European integration); Yergin, *The Commanding Heights* (trade growth).

Bibliography

MANUSCRIPT SOURCES

Official Documents

Australia

Australian Archives, National Office, Canberra

CA 10: Department of Trade and Customs, Central Office

A1667: International Trade Relations Files

A9879: Papers Related to Postwar Economics, GATT

A9913: GATT, Commercial Policy, Trade Agreements Branch; Commercial Policy and Trade Relations Branch

CA 12: Prime Minister's Department

A461: Correspondence Files, Multiple No. Series

A9790: Correspondence Files, Single No. Series

A9793: Correspondence Files, Two No. Series

CA 18: Department of External Affairs (II), Central Office

1068: Correspondence Files, Multiple No. Series

A1838: Correspondence Files, Multiple No. Series

CA 64: Department of Trade (I), Central Office

AA1974/156: GATT Trade Negotiations and Agreements Files, Multiple No. System (20/2), 1947–61

CA 983: Bureau of Agriculture Economics

A1422/13: Correspondence Files, Multiple No. Series

CP 43/1: Department of Postwar Reconstruction, Central Office, General Correspondence, 1943–49

/907: British Trade Policy, 1941–46

/909: United States—General Trade Policy, 1941–47

CP 119: Papers of Dr. Herbert Cole Coombs

M448: Research Materials

CP 855: Papers of Dr. Herbert Cole Coombs

Bundle 1, Pt. 1: Documents Associated with the Second Session of the Preparatory Committee of the United Nations Conference on Trade and Employment, Geneva, 1947

Bundle 1, Pt. 2: H. C. Coombs Personal Papers, Documents Connected with
Havana Conference
Bundle 2, Pt. 1: H. C. Coombs Personal Papers
Bundle 2, Pt. 2: Notes of Meetings in April 1947
CRS A2700/XM1: Secretary to Cabinet/Cabinet Secretariat [I], Curtin, Forde and
Chifley Ministries—folders of cabinet minutes and agenda, 1941–49
Volume 22: Submission 1019F
Australian Archives, Melbourne, Victoria
MP 98/1/0: Records of the Department of Postwar Reconstruction, Division of
Secondary Industries and Division of Industrial Development: General
Administrative and Correspondence Files
Australian Archives, Sydney, New South Wales
SP 182: Papers of C. E. Morton
National Library of Australia, Canberra
MS 987: John Dedman Papers
Canada
National Archives of Canada, Ottawa
RG 2: Records of the Privy Council Office
A-5-a: Cabinet Conclusions, Agendas (microfilm)
RG 19: Records of the Department of Finance
ITO General: Central Registry File
RG 25: Records of the Department of External Affairs and International Trade
40 Series; S Series
MG 26: William Lyon Mackenzie King Papers
J2: Prime Minister's Office Correspondence
J4: Memoranda and Notes (microfilm)
J13: Diaries (transcripts-microfiche)
Great Britain
British Public Record Office, Kew, England
Records of the Board of Trade
BT 11: Commercial Department: Correspondence and Papers
BT 64: Industries and Manufactures Department: Correspondence and Papers
Records of the Cabinet Office
CAB 65: War Cabinet: Minutes
CAB 72: War Cabinet: Committee on Economic Policy
CAB 87: War Cabinet: Committee on Reconstruction Series
CAB 99: War Cabinet: Commonwealth and International Conferences
CAB 123: Lord President of the Council: Secretariat File
CAB 127: Sir Stafford Cripps Papers
CAB 133: International and Commonwealth Conferences
Records of the Colonial Office
CO 852: Colonies (General) Economic
Records of the Dominions Office and Commonwealth Relations Office
DO 35: Correspondence, Original

Records of the Foreign Office
    FO 371: Political Departments: General Correspondence
    FO 800: Ernest Bevin Papers
Records of the Prime Minister's Office
    PREM 4: Confidential Papers
    PREM 8: Correspondence and Papers, 1945–51
Records of the Treasury
    T 247 John Maynard Keynes Papers
New Zealand
  National Archives of New Zealand, Wellington
    Papers of Walter Nash
        NASH 70: ITO Papers and Correspondence
        NASH 80: International Trade Organization
        NASH 100: GATT and ITO—Comments and General
    External Affairs Department Registered Files
        EA Series 1 104: United Nations Conference on Trade and Employment,
            1946–47
United States
  Franklin D. Roosevelt Library, Hyde Park, New York
    Adolf A. Berle Papers
    Harry L. Hopkins Papers: Group 24
    Franklin D. Roosevelt Papers
        Official File
        President's Secretary's File
  Harry S. Truman Library, Independence, Missouri
    Dean Acheson Papers
    Willis C. Armstrong Oral History
    Clinton P. Anderson Papers
    Eben A. Ayers Papers
    Nathan M. Becker Oral History
    David E. Bell Oral History
    Thomas C. Blaisdell Papers
    Winthrop Brown Oral History
    William L. Clayton Papers
    Clark M. Clifford Files
    Clark M. Clifford Papers
        President's Speech File
    Sir Edgar Cohen Oral History
    Joseph D. Coppock Papers
    Lynn R. Edminister Papers
    George M. Elsey Papers
    Gray Gordon Files
    Hubert F. Havlik Oral History
    John Leddy Oral History

Charles S. Murphy Papers
Richard E. Neustadt Files
Stephen J. Spingarn Papers
Leroy Stinebower Oral History
Willard Thorp Oral History
Harry S. Truman Papers
   White House Central Files
   President's Confidential File
   President's Official File
   President's Secretary's File: Subject File: Conferences
   Senatorial Files
U.S. Department of State—Office Files of the Assistant Secretary for Economic
   Affairs and the Under Secretary for Economic Affairs, 1944–48 (Clayton-Thorp)
Raymond Vernon Oral History
Herbert Hoover Library, West Branch, Iowa
  Bourke B. Hickenlooper Papers: Foreign Relations Committee:
    Subject and Individual Files
  Herbert Hoover Post-Presidential Papers: Subject File
International Monetary Fund Archives, Washington, D.C.
  IMF: Central File: Category I (Other International Organizations)
Library of Congress, Washington, D.C.
  Clinton P. Anderson Papers
  Emanuel Celler Papers
  Tom Connally Papers
  Herbert Feis Papers
  W. Averell Harriman Papers
  Cordell Hull Papers (microfilm)
  League of Women Voters Records
  Francis Bowes Sayres Papers
  Charles P. Taft Papers
  Robert A. Taft Papers
Lyndon B. Johnson Library, Austin, Texas
  Lyndon B. Johnson Senate Political Files
  Wright G. Patman Papers
National Archives of the United States, College Park, Maryland
  RG 16: Records of the Office of the Secretary of Agriculture:
    General Correspondence
  RG 43: Records of International Conferences, Commissions, and Expositions
    International Trade Files—Lot 57D-284
  RG 46: Records of the U.S. Senate
    Bills and Resolutions File: Committee Records and Reports: Committee on
      Finance
  RG 56: General Records of the Department of the Treasury

Records of the National Advisory Council on International Monetary and
     Financial Policies: Subject Files
RG 59: General Records of the Department of State
   Central Decimal Files: 394-ITO, 394.31, 394.41, 560.AL
   Leo Pasvolsky Office Files
   Office of Public Opinion Studies
      Assistant Secretary of State for Congressional Relations, 1940–52:
         Lot 55D650
   Executive Secretariat: Dean Acheson
   Harley A. Notter File
   Office of British Commonwealth and Northern European Affairs, 1941–53:
         Lot 54D224
   Office of European Affairs: Matthews-Hickerson File
RG 151: Records of the Bureau of Foreign and Domestic Commerce
   Office of International Trade: Central Files
RG 233: Records of the U.S. House of Representatives: Committee Records: House
      Special Committee on Postwar Economic Policy and Planning
RG 353: Records of Interdepartmental and Intradepartmental Committees
   Secretary of State's Staff Committee, 1944–47
   Executive Committee on Economic Foreign Policy
RG 364: Records of the Office of the Special Representative for Trade Negotiations:
      Records of the Committee on Reciprocity Information
Washington National Records Center, Suitland, Maryland
   RG 469: Records of the U.S. Foreign Assistance Agencies, 1948–61: Executive
      Secretariat
   Records Relating to the Public Advisory Board, 1948–54

Private Collections

Australia
   University of Adelaide, Flinders, South Australia
      Herbert Vere Evatt Papers
Great Britain
   Bank of England, Archives Section, London
      ADM14, L. P. Thompson–McCausland Papers
      OV170, ITO and GATT Files
      OG1, Governor's Files
   British Library of Political and Economic Science, London School of Economics,
         London
      Hugh Dalton Papers: Diary; Papers, 1945–60
      James Meade Papers: Correspondence and Papers, 1940–49; Diaries
   Bodleian Library, Oxford University, Oxford
      Clement Attlee Papers
   Guildhall Library, London

MS 14487, Association of British Chambers of Commerce, Overseas Committee
   Minutes, 1921–64
MS 16613, London Chamber of Commerce, National General Export Merchants
   Group Minutes, 1940–64
MS 16661, London Chamber of Commerce, Import and Export Merchants Section
   Minutes, 1917–71
Modern Records Centre, University of Warwick, Coventry
  MSS 200, Federation of British Industries Records
  MSS 221, British Industries Association Records
  MSS 222, Archives of the Empire Industries Association
  MSS 292, Trade Union Congress Records
United States
  Ann Arbor, Michigan: Bentley Historical Library
    Arthur H. Vandenberg Papers
  Arkadelphia, Arkansas: Ouachita Baptist University
    John L. McClellan Collection
  Boston
    Boston University
      John W. McCormack Papers
    Massachusetts Historical Society
      Henry Cabot Lodge II Papers
      Leverett Saltonstall Papers
  Boulder: University of Colorado
    Joseph C. O'Mahoney Papers, James Patton Collection
    Eugene D. Millikin Collection
    National Farmers Union Papers
  Chapel Hill: University of North Carolina
  Charlottesville: University of Virginia
    Edward R. Stettinius Papers
  Chicago: National Opinion Research Center Records, University of Chicago
    NORC Studies for the U.S. Department of State, 1945–57
    Robert L. Doughton Papers
  Clemson, South Carolina: Clemson University
    James Byrnes Papers
  Des Moines: State Historical Society of Iowa
    Thomas E. Martin Papers
  Fayetteville: University of Arkansas
    J. William Fulbright Papers
  Hattiesburg: University of Southern Mississippi
    William M. Colmer Papers: Legislation Files: Special Committee on Postwar
      Economic Policy and Planning
  Houston, Texas: Rice University
    William L. Clayton Papers

Reminiscences of William Lockhart Clayton
Iowa City: University of Iowa
  Henry A. Wallace Papers
Ithaca, New York: Cornell University
  Daniel A. Reed Papers
Laramie: American Heritage Center, University of Wyoming
  Frank Barrett Papers
  National Wool Growers Association Papers
  Western Wool Growers Association Papers
Lexington, Virginia: George C. Marshall Research Library
  George C. Marshall Papers
New Haven, Connecticut: Yale University
  Dean G. Acheson Papers
New York, New York
  Council on Foreign Relations Archives
Norman, Oklahoma: Carl Albert Congressional Research Center
  Helen Gahagan Douglas Collection
  Robert S. Kerr Collection: Legislative File
  George B. Schwabe Collection
North Andover, Massachusetts: Museum of American Textile History
  Boston Wool Trade Association
Philadelphia: University of Pennsylvania
  Clair Wilcox Papers Relating to International Trade
Silver Spring, Maryland: George Meany Memorial Archives
  AFL, AFL-CIO Department of Legislation Files
  Minutes, Meetings of the Executive Council, AFL
Springfield: Illinois State Historical Library
  Scott W. Lucas Papers
Syracuse, New York: Syracuse University
  Ralph E. Flanders Papers
Tempe: Arizona State University
  Carl T. Hayden Papers
Washington, D.C.
  American Farm Bureau Federation
Williamsburg, Virginia: College of William and Mary
  A. Willis Robertson Papers
Wilmington, Delaware: Hagley Museum and Library
  Chamber of Commerce of the United States Records
  Vada Horsch Papers, NAM Archives
  National Association of Manufacturers Archives: Series I
  National Industrial Conference Board Archives

PUBLISHED OFFICIAL DOCUMENTS

Australia

Hudson, W. J., and Wendy Way. *Documents on Australian Foreign Policy, 1937–1949.* Vol. 9, January–June, 1946. Canberra: Australia Government Publishing Service, 1989.

Hudson, W. J., and Wendy Way. *Documents on Australian Foreign Policy, 1937–1949.* Vol. 10, July–December 1946. Canberra: Australia Government Publishing Service, 1993.

Parliamentary Debates, House of Commons Official Report, 1942–50.

Canada

Parliamentary Debates, House of Commons Official Report, 1946–50.

Great Britain

Parliamentary Debates, House of Commons Official Report, 1939–50.

United States

Congressional Quarterly-Almanac. Washington, D.C.: Congressional Quarterly, 1945–51.

Congressional Record, 1934–53.

Public Advisory Board for Mutual Security. *A Trade and Tariff Policy in the National Interest.* Washington, D.C.: GPO, 1953.

Public Papers and Addresses of Franklin D. Roosevelt, 1940 Volume: War—And Aid to Democracies. New York: Macmillan, 1941.

Public Papers of the Presidents: Harry S. Truman, 1946. Washington, D.C.: GPO, 1962.

Public Papers of the Presidents: Harry S. Truman, 1947. Washington, D.C.: GPO, 1963.

Public Papers of the Presidents: Harry S. Truman, 1948. Washington, D.C.: GPO, 1964.

Public Papers of the Presidents of the United States: Harry S. Truman, 1949. Washington, D.C.: GPO, 1964.

Public Papers of the Presidents: Harry S. Truman, 1950. Washington, D.C.: GPO, 1956.

Public Papers of the Presidents: Harry S. Truman, 1951. Washington, D.C.: GPO, 1965.

United Nations. *Report of the Second Session of the Preparatory Committee of the United Nations Conference on Trade and Employment.* New York: August 1947.

————. *United Nations Conference on Trade and Employment.* Summary Record of 3d–9th Plenary Meetings, November 26–December 1, 1947.

U.S. Department of Commerce. *Historical Statistics of the United States: Colonial Times to the 1970, Parts I and II.* Washington, D.C.: GPO, 1975.

U.S. Department of State. *Bulletin.* 1935–53.

————. *Foreign Relations of the United States.* Washington, D.C.: GPO, 1940–52.

————. Publication 2983, Commercial Policy Series 109. *Analysis of General Agreement on Tariffs and Trade.* Washington, D.C.: GPO, November 1947.

————. Publication 3651, Commercial Policy Series 120. *Analysis of Protocol of Accession and Schedules to the General Agreement on Tariffs and Trade.* Annecy, France, April–August 1949, Washington, D.C.: GPO, October 1949.

U.S. House Committee on Foreign Affairs. Hearings. *Membership and Participation by the United States in the International Trade Organization.* 81st Cong., 2d sess., 1950.

U.S. House Committee on Ways and Means. Hearings. *Extension of Reciprocal Trade Agreements Act.* 76th Cong., 3d sess., 1940.

———. Hearings. *Extension of Reciprocal Trade Agreements Act.* 78th Cong., 1st sess., 1943.

———. Hearings. *1945 Extension of the Reciprocal Trade Agreements Act.* 79th Cong., 1st sess., 1945.

———. Report. Minority Views. *Foreign Trade Agreements.* 79th Cong., 1st sess., 1945.

———. Report. *Foreign Trade Agreements.* 79th Cong., 1st sess., 1945.

———. *The Operation of the Trade Agreements Act and the Proposed International Trade Organization.* 80th Cong., 1st sess., 1947.

———. Views of the Minority Members on H.R. 6556. *House Report, Volume 4.* 80th Cong., 2d sess., 1948.

———. *Extension of the Reciprocal Trade Agreements Act.* Report 19, 81st Cong., 1st sess., 1949.

———. *1951 Extension of the Reciprocal Trade Agreements Act.* 82d Cong., 1st sess., 1951.

U.S. House of Representatives. *Trade Agreements Extension Act of 1949: Views of the Minority.* 81st Cong., 1st sess., 1949.

———. *The Post-War Foreign Economic Policy of the United States.* Report 541. 79th Cong., 1st sess., 1945.

U.S. House Special Committee on Postwar Economic Policy and Planning. *Economic Reconstruction in Europe.* 8th Report. 79th Cong., 1st sess., 1945.

U.S. House Subcommittee No. 2 of the Committee on Foreign Relations. Report by James G. Fulton and Jacob K. Javits. *The International Trade Organization.* 80th Cong., 2d sess., 1948.

U.S. House Subcommittee on Tariffs and Foreign Trade of the Committee on Ways and Means. *Operation of the Trade Agreements Program (Testimony).* 80th Cong., 2d sess., 1948.

U.S. Senate Committee on Finance. *Extension of Reciprocal Trade Agreements Act.* 76th Cong., 3d sess., 1940.

———. Hearings. *International Trade Organization.* 80th Cong., 1st sess., 1947.

———. *Extending Authority to Negotiate Trade Agreements.* 80th Cong., 2d sess., 1948.

———. Hearings. *Extension of Reciprocal Trade Agreements Act.* 81st Cong., 1st sess., 1949.

———. Report. Minority Views. *Trade Agreements Extension Act of 1949.* 81st Cong., 1st sess., 1949.

———. *Trade Agreements Extension Act of 1951.* 82d Cong., 1st sess., 1951.

U.S. Senate Committee on Foreign Relations. Hearings. *Extension of European Recovery.* 81st Cong., 1st sess., 1949.

U.S. Senate Special Committee to Investigate the Production, Transportation, and Marketing of Wool. *Investigation of the Production, Transportation, and Marketing of Wool.* 79th Cong., 1st sess., 1945.

U.S. Senate Subcommittee on Foreign Relations. *The International Wheat Agreement.* 80th Cong., 2d sess., 1948.

U.S. Tariff Commission. Report No. 160, 2d series. *Operation of the Trade Agreements Program, June 1934 to April 1948, Part I: Summary.* Washington, D.C.: GPO, 1948.

———. *Operation of the Trade Agreements Program, June 1934 to April 1948, Part II: History of the Trade Agreements Program.* Washington, D.C.: GPO, 1947.

————. *Operation of the Trade Agreements Program, June 1934 to April 1948, Part III: Trade Agreement Concessions Granted by the United States.* Washington, D.C.: GPO, 1949.

————. *Operation of the Trade Agreements Program, June 1934 to April 1948, Part IV: Trade Agreement Concessions Granted by the United States.* Washington, D.C.: GPO, 1949.

————. *Operation of the Trade Agreements Program, April 1948–March 1949: Second Report.* Washington, D.C.: GPO, 1950.

————. *Operation of the Trade Agreements Program, April 1949–June 1950: Third Report.* Washington, D.C.: GPO, 1951.

————. *Operation of the Trade Agreements Program, July 1950–June 1951: Fourth Report.* Washington, D.C.: GPO, 1952.

————. *Operation of the Trade Agreements Program, July 1952–June 1953: Sixth Report.* Washington, D.C.: GPO, 1954.

————. *War Changes in Industry Series: Report No. 29: Woolens and Worsteds.* Washington, D.C.: GPO, 1949.

NEWSPAPERS AND PERIODICALS

American Economic Review

American Exporter

American Mercury

American Political Science Review

Annals of the American Academy of Political and Social Science

Argus (Melbourne, Australia)

Atlantic

Banker

Barron's

British Trade Journal and Export World

Bulletin of the National Association of Wool Manufacturers

Business Week

Canadian Affairs

Canadian Forum

Christian Science Monitor

Collier's

Commercial and Financial Chronicle

Commonwealth and Empire Review

Denver Post

Economic Journal

Economist

Export Trade and Shipper

Far Eastern Survey

Forbes

Foreign Affairs

Foreign Commerce Weekly

Foreign Trade
Fortune
Forum
Freedom and Union
Harper's Magazine
International Affairs
International Labour Review
Life
Living Age
Manchester Guardian
Nation
National Review (London)
Nation's Business
New Republic
New Statesman and Nation
Newsweek
New York Times
Pacific Affairs
Political Science Quarterly
Rotarian
Round Table
Saturday Evening Post
Scope
Spectator
Sydney Morning Herald
Time
United States News
UN World
U.S. News and World Report
Vital Speeches of the Day, 1940–1952
Wall Street Journal
Washington Post

BOOKS

Aaronson, Susan. *Trade and the American Dream: A Social History of Postwar Trade Policy.* Lexington: University of Kentucky Press, 1996.

Acheson, Dean. *Present at the Creation: My Years in the State Department.* New York: Norton, 1969.

Almond, Gabriel A. *The American People and Foreign Policy.* New York: Praeger, 1965.

Attlee, Clement R. *As It Happened.* New York: Viking, 1954.

Bairoch, Paul. *Economics and World History: Myths and Paradoxes.* Chicago: University of Chicago Press, 1993.

Baldwin, Robert E. *The Political Economy of U.S. Import Policy*. Cambridge: MIT Press, 1985.

Barnes, John, and David Nicholson, eds. *The Empire at Bay: The Leo Amery Diaries, 1929–1945*. London: Hutchison, 1988.

Bauer, Raymond A., Ithiel de Sola Pool, and Lewis Anthony Dexter. *American Business and Public Policy: The Politics of Foreign Trade*. 2d ed. New York: Aldine, 1972.

Becker, William H., and Samuel F. Wells Jr., eds. *Economics and World Power: An Assessment of American Diplomacy since 1789*. New York: Columbia University Press, 1984.

Bell, Philip, and Roger Bell. *Implicated: The United States in Australia*. Melbourne: Oxford University Press, 1993.

Bhagwati, Jagdish. *Protectionism*. Cambridge: MIT Press, 1988.

Bidwell, Percy W. *Our Trade with Britain: Basis for a Reciprocal Tariff Agreement*. New York: Council on Foreign Relations, 1938.

Borden, William S. *The Pacific Alliance: United States Foreign Economic Policy and Japanese Trade Recovery, 1947–1955*. Madison: University of Wisconsin Press, 1984.

Bothwell, Robert. *Canada and the United States: The Politics of Partnership*. New York: Twayne, 1992.

Boylan, James. *The New Deal Coalition and the Election of 1946*. New York: Garland, 1981.

Brinkley, Douglas, and David R. Facey-Crowther. *The Atlantic Charter*. New York: St. Martin's Press, 1994.

Brown, William Adams, Jr. *The United States and the Restoration of World Trade*. Washington, D.C.: Brookings, 1950.

Brusse, Wendy Asbeek. *Tariffs, Trade, and European Integration, 1947–1957: From Study Group to Common Market*. New York: St. Martin's Press, 1997.

Buchanan, Patrick. *The Great Betrayal: How American Sovereignty and Social Justice Are Being Sacrificed to the Gods of the Global Economy*. New York: Little, Brown, 1998.

Bullock, Alan. *Ernest Bevin: Foreign Secretary, 1945–1951*. New York: Norton, 1983.

Cantril, Hadley, ed. *Public Opinion, 1935–1946*. Princeton: Princeton University Press, 1951.

Carnoy, Martin. *The State and Political Theory*. Princeton: Princeton University Press, 1984.

Chisholm, Ann, and Michael Davie. *Lord Beaverbrook: A Life*. New York: Knopf, 1993.

Committee for Economic Development. *The International Trade Organization and the Reconstruction of World Trade*. New York: CED, 1959.

Cortney, Philip. *The Economic Munich: The ITO Charter*. New York: Philosophical Library, 1949.

Crisp, L. F. *Ben Chifley: A Biography*. London: Longmans, 1960.

Cuff, R. D., and J. L. Granatstein. *American Dollars–Canadian Prosperity: Canadian-American Economic Relations, 1945–1950*. Toronto: Samuel-Stevens, 1978.

Cullather, Nick. *Illusions of Influence: The Political Economy of United States–Philippines Relations, 1942–1960*. Stanford: Stanford University Press, 1994.

Dallek, Robert. *Franklin D. Roosevelt and American Foreign Policy, 1932–1945*. Oxford: Oxford University Press, 1979.

Dalton, Hugh. *High Tide and After: Memoirs, 1945–1960*. London: Frederick Muller Ltd., 1962.

Dalunay, H. G., and Edward Hake Phillips, eds. *Speak, Mr. Speaker.* Bonham, Tex.: Sam Rayburn Foundation, 1978.

Darilek, Richard E. *A Loyal Opposition in Time of War: The Republican Party and the Politics of Foreign Policy from Pearl Harbor to Yalta.* Westport: Greenwood Press, 1976.

Dilks, David, ed. *The Diaries of Sir Alexander Cadogan, 1938–1975.* New York: G. P. Putnam's Sons, 1972.

Divine, Robert A. *Foreign Policy and U.S. Presidential Election, 1940–1948.* New York: New Viewpoints, 1974.

Dobney, Frederick J., ed. *Selected Papers of Will Clayton.* Baltimore: Johns Hopkins Press, 1971.

Dobson, Alan. *The Politics of the Anglo-American Economic Special Relationship, 1940–1987.* New York: St. Martin's Press, 1988.

———. *U.S. Wartime Aid to Britain, 1940–1946.* New York: St. Martin's Press, 1986.

Doenecke, Justus D. *Not to the Swift: The Old Isolationists in the Cold War Era.* Lewisburg: Bucknell University Press, 1979.

Drummond, Ian M. *British Economic Policy and the Empire, 1919–1939.* London: G. Allen, 1972.

Dryden, Steve. *Trade Warriors: USTR and the American Crusade for Free Trade.* New York: Oxford University Press, 1995.

Eckes, Alfred E., Jr. *Opening America's Market: U.S. Foreign Trade Policy since 1776.* Chapel Hill: University of North Carolina Press, 1995.

Edwards, P. G. *Prime Ministers and Diplomats: The Making of Australian Foreign Policy, 1901–1949.* Oxford: Oxford University Press, 1983.

Eisenhower, Dwight D. *Mandate for Change, 1953–1956.* Garden City: Doubleday, 1963.

Estorick, Eric. *Stafford Cripps: A Biography.* London: Heinemann, 1949.

Evans, Peter, Dietrich Rueschemeyer, and Theda Skocpol, eds. *Bringing the State Back In.* Cambridge: Cambridge University Press, 1985.

Fossedal, Gregory A. *Our Finest Hour: Will Clayton, the Marshall Plan, and the Triumph of Democracy.* Stanford: Hoover Institution Press, 1993.

Foster, H. Schuyler. *Activism Replaces Isolationism: U.S. Public Attitudes, 1940–1975.* Washington, D.C.: Foxhall Press, 1983.

Funigiello, Philip J. *American-Soviet Trade in the Cold War.* Chapel Hill: University of North Carolina Press, 1988.

Gaddis, John Lewis. *The United States and the Origins of the Cold War, 1941–1947.* New York: Columbia University Press, 1972.

Galambos, Louis, and Alfred D. Chandler. *The Papers of Dwight David Eisenhower, NATO, and the Campaign of 1952: XIII.* Baltimore: Johns Hopkins University Press, 1989.

Gardner, Lloyd C. *Economic Aspects of New Deal Diplomacy.* Madison: University of Wisconsin Press, 1964.

Gardner, Richard N. *Sterling-Dollar Diplomacy: The Origins and the Prospects of Our International Economic Order.* 2d ed. New York: McGraw-Hill Book Company, 1969.

Gilpin, Robert. *The Political Economy of International Relations.* Princeton: Princeton University Press, 1987.

Goldstein, Judith. *Ideas, Interests, and American Trade Policy.* Ithaca: Cornell University Press, 1993.

Hamby, Alonzo L. *Beyond the New Deal: Harry S. Truman and American Liberalism*. New York: Columbia University Press, 1973.

———. *Liberalism and Its Challengers: From F.D.R. to Bush*. 2d ed. New York: Oxford University Press, 1992.

Harper, John Lamberton. *American Visions of Europe: Franklin D. Roosevelt, George F. Kennan, and Dean G. Acheson*. Cambridge: Cambridge University Press, 1994.

Harris, Kenneth. *Attlee*. New York: Norton, 1982.

Hathaway, Robert. *Ambiguous Partnership: Britain and America, 1944–1947*. New York: Columbia University Press, 1981.

Havinden, Michael, and David Meredith. *Colonialism and Development: Britain and Its Tropical Colonies, 1850–1960*. London: Routledge, 1993.

Hawkins, Harry C. *Commercial Treaties and Agreements: Principles and Practice*. New York: Rinehart, 1951.

Hildebrand, Robert C. *Dumbarton Oaks: The Origins of the United Nations and the Search for Postwar Security*. Chapel Hill: University of North Carolina Press, 1990.

Hogan, Michael J. *The Marshall Plan: America, Britain, and the Reconstruction of Western Europe, 1947–1952*. Cambridge: Cambridge University Press, 1987.

Hoover, Calvin B. *Economic Systems of the Commonwealth*. Durham: Duke University Press, 1962.

Howson, Susan. *British Monetary Policy, 1945–1951*. Oxford: Oxford University Press, 1993.

———, ed. *International Economics*. Vol. 3 of *The Collected Papers of James Meade*. London: Unwin Hyman Ltd., 1988.

Howson, Susan, and Donald Moggridge, eds. *The Cabinet Office Diary, 1944–1946*. Vol. 4 of *The Collected Papers of James Meade*. London: Unwin Hyman Ltd., 1990.

Howson, Susan, and Donald Moggridge, eds. *The Wartime Diaries of Lionel Robbins and James Meade, 1943–1945*. New York: St. Martin's Press, 1990.

Hudec, Robert E. *The GATT Legal System and World Trade Diplomacy*. New York: Praeger, 1975.

Hull, Cordell. *The Memoirs of Cordell Hull, Volume I*. New York: Macmillan, 1948.

Hussain, A. Imtiaz. *Politics of Compensation: Truman, the Wool Bill of 1947, and the Shaping of Postwar U.S. Trade Policy*. New York: Garland, 1993.

Hutchison, Keith. *Rival Partners: America and Britain in the Postwar World*. New York: Macmillan, 1946.

Ickes, Harold L. *The Lowering Clouds, 1939–1941*. Vol. 3 of *The Secret Diary of Harold L. Ickes*. New York: Simon and Schuster, 1954.

Ikenberry, G. John, David A. Lake, and Michael Mastanduno, eds. *The State and American Foreign Economic Policy*. Ithaca: Cornell University Press, 1988.

Irwin, Douglas A. *Against the Tide: An Intellectual History of Free Trade*. Princeton: Princeton University Press, 1996.

Jackson, John H. *World Trade and the Law of GATT*. Indianapolis: Bobbs-Merrill, 1969.

James, Robert Rhodes. *Robert Boothby: A Portrait of Churchill's Ally*. New York: Viking Penguin, 1991.

———. *Winston S. Churchill: His Complete Speeches, 1897–1963: Volume VII, 1943–1949*. New York: Chelsea House Publishers, 1974.

Jeffreys-Jones, Rhodri. *Changing Differences: Women and the Shaping of American Foreign Policy, 1917–1994.* New Brunswick: Rutgers University Press, 1995.

Jessop, Bob. *State Theory: Putting the Capitalist State in Its Place.* University Park: Pennsylvania State University Press, 1990.

Johnson, Walter, ed. *Governor of Illinois, 1949–1953.* Vol. 3 of *The Papers of Adlai E. Stevenson.* Boston: Little, Brown, 1973.

————, ed. *"Let's Talk Sense to the American People," 1952–1955.* Vol. 4 of *The Papers of Adlai E. Stevenson.* Boston: Little, Brown, 1974.

Jones, Joseph M. *The Fifteen Weeks.* New York: Viking, 1955.

Kaplan, Edward S. *American Trade Policy, 1923–1995.* Westport: Greenwood Press, 1996.

Katzenstein, Peter J. *Between Power and Plenty: Foreign Economic Policies of Advanced Industrial States.* Madison: University of Wisconsin Press, 1978.

Kaufman, Burton. *Trade and Aid: Eisenhower's Foreign Economic Policy, 1953–1961.* Baltimore: Johns Hopkins University Press, 1982.

Kelly, William B., Jr., ed. *Studies in United States Commercial Policy.* Chapel Hill: University of North Carolina Press, 1963.

Kennedy, Paul. *The Rise and Fall of the Great Powers: Economic Change and Military Conflict from 1500 to 2000.* New York: Random House, 1987.

Keynes, John Maynard. *The General Theory of Employment, Interest, and Money.* New York: Harcourt Brace Jovanovich, 1964.

Kindleberger, Charles P. *Power and Money: The Economics of International Politics and the Politics of International Economics.* New York: Basic Books, 1970.

Kock, Karin. *Trade Policy and the GATT, 1947–1967.* Stockholm: Almquist and Wiksell, 1969.

Kolko, Gabriel. *The Politics of War: The World and United States Foreign Policy, 1943–1945.* New York: Random House, 1968.

Kottman, Richard N. *Reciprocity and the North Atlantic Triangle, 1932–1938.* Ithaca: Cornell University Press, 1968.

Krasner, Stephen D., ed. *International Regimes.* Ithaca: Cornell University Press, 1983.

Krauss, Melvyn B. *How Nations Grow Rich: The Case for Free Trade.* New York: Oxford University Press, 1997.

Krugman, Paul. *Pop Internationalism.* Cambridge: MIT Press, 1997.

Kunz, Diane B. *Butter and Guns: America's Cold War Economic Diplomacy.* New York: Free Press, 1997.

Lake, David A. *Power, Protection, and Free Trade: International Sources of U.S. Commercial Strategy, 1887–1939.* Ithaca: Cornell University Press, 1988.

Landes, David S. *The Wealth and Poverty of Nations: Why Some Are So Rich and Some Are So Poor.* New York: Norton, 1998.

Leffler, Melvyn P. *A Preponderance of Power: National Security, the Truman Administration, and the Cold War.* Stanford: Stanford University Press, 1992.

Loree, Robert F. *Position of the National Foreign Trade Council with Respect to the Havana Charter for an International Trade Organization.* New York: NFTC, 1950.

Louis, Wm. Roger. *In the Name of God, Go!: Leo Amery and the British Empire in the Age of Churchill.* New York: Norton, 1992.

Lowe, Peter. *The Origins of the Korean War.* London: Longmans, 1986.

McColl, G. D. *The Australian Balance of Payments: A Study of Post-War Developments.* London: Melbourne University Press, 1965.

McCormick, Thomas J. *America's Half Century: United States Foreign Policy in the Cold War.* Baltimore: Johns Hopkins University Press, 1989.

Martin, A. W. *Robert Menzies: A Life: Volume I, 1894–1943.* Melbourne: Melbourne University Press, 1993.

Martin, John Bartlow. *Adlai Stevenson of Illinois: The Life of Adlai E. Stevenson.* Garden City: Doubleday, 1976.

Matusow, Allen J. *Farm Policies and Politics in the Truman Years.* Cambridge: Harvard University Press, 1967.

Meyer, F. V. *International Trade Policy.* New York: St. Martin's Press, 1978.

Milner, Helen. *Interests, Institutions, and Information: Domestic Politics and International Relations.* Princeton: Princeton University Press, 1997.

Milward, Alan. *The Reconstruction of Western Europe, 1945–51.* Berkeley: University of California Press, 1984.

———. *War, Economy, and Society.* Berkeley: University of California Press, 1977.

Milward, Alan, and George Brennan. *Britain's Place in the World: A Historical Enquiry into Import Controls, 1945–1960.* London: Routledge, 1996.

Moggridge, Donald, ed. *Activities, 1940–1943: External War Finance.* Vol. 23 of *The Collected Writings of John Maynard Keynes.* Cambridge: MacMillan Cambridge University Press, 1979.

Morgan, Kenneth O. *Labour in Power, 1945–1951.* Oxford: Clarendon Press, 1984.

Muirhead, B. W. *The Development of Postwar Canadian Trade Policy: The Failure of the Anglo-European Option.* Montreal: McGill-Queen's University Press, 1992.

Nordlinger, Eric. *On the Autonomy of the Democratic State.* Cambridge: Harvard University Press, 1981.

Orde, Anne. *The Eclipse of Great Britain: The United States and British Imperial Decline, 1895–1956.* New York: St. Martin's Press, 1996.

Pastor, Robert A. *Congress and the Politics of U.S. Foreign Economic Policy, 1929–1976.* Berkeley: University of California Press, 1980.

Patterson, James T. *Mr. Republican: A Biography of Robert A. Taft.* Boston: Houghton Mifflin, 1972.

Penrose, E. F. *Economic Planning for the Peace.* Princeton: Princeton University Press, 1953.

Pimlott, Ben, ed. *The Second World War Diary of Hugh Dalton, 1940–1945.* London: Jonathan Cape, 1986.

Pollard, Robert A. *Economic Security and the Origins of the Cold War, 1945–1950.* New York: Columbia University Press, 1985.

Pomfret, Richard, ed. *Australia's Trade Policies.* Oxford: Oxford University Press, 1995.

Pratt, Julius W. *Cordell Hull, 1933–1944, Volume I.* New York: Cooper Square Publishers, 1964.

Rhodes, Carolyn. *Reciprocity, U.S. Trade Policy, and the GATT Regime.* Ithaca: Cornell University Press, 1993.

Ritchie, John. *The Australian Dictionary of Biography.* Melbourne: University of Melbourne Press, 1983.

Robbins, Lord. *Autobiography of an Economist*. London: Macmillan, 1971.

Rogowski, Ronald. *Commerce and Coalitions: How Trade Affects Domestic Political Alignments*. Princeton: Princeton University Press, 1989.

Rosenberg, Emily S. *Spreading the American Dream: American Economic and Cultural Expansion, 1890–1945*. New York: Hill and Wang, 1982.

Ruggie, John G., ed. *Multilateralism Matters: The Theory and Praxis of an Institutional Form*. New York: Columbia University Press, 1993.

Sayre, Francis Bowes. *The Way Forward: The American Trade Agreements Program*. New York: Macmillan, 1939.

Schaller, Michael. *The American Occupation of Japan: The Origins of the Cold War in Asia*. New York: Oxford University Press, 1985.

Shutt, Harry. *The Myth of Free Trade: Patterns of Protectionism since 1945*. Oxford: Basil Blackwell, 1985.

Snape, R. H. *International Trade and the Australian Economy*. Croydon, Victoria: Longmans of Australia Pty Limited, 1969.

Swann, Paul. *The Hollywood Feature Film in Postwar Britain*. New York: St. Martin's Press, 1987.

Taft, Robert A. *A Foreign Policy for Americans*. Garden City: Doubleday, 1951.

Tennant, Kylie. *Evatt: Politics and Justice*. Sydney: Angus and Robertson, 1970.

Truman, Harry S. *Year of Decisions*. Vol. 1 of *Memoirs*. Garden City: Doubleday, 1955.

Vatter, Harold G. *The U.S. Economy in World War II*. New York: Columbia University Press, 1985.

Verdier, Daniel. *Democracy and International Trade: Britain, France, and the United States, 1860–1990*. Princeton: Princeton University Press, 1994.

Wallace, Henry. *Sixty Million Jobs*. New York: Simon and Schuster, 1945.

Wilcox, Clair. *A Charter for World Trade*. New York: Macmillan, 1949.

Williams, Francis. *A Prime Minister Remembers: The War and Post-War Memoirs of the Rt. Hon. Earl Attlee*. London: Heinemann, 1961.

Williams, Philip M., ed. *The Diary of Hugh Gaitskell, 1945–1956*. London: Jonathan Cape, 1983.

Williams, William Appleman. *The Tragedy of American Diplomacy*. New York: Dell, 1972.

Woods, Randall Bennett. *A Changing of the Guard: Anglo-American Relations, 1941–1946*. Chapel Hill: University of North Carolina Press, 1990.

Yergin, Daniel. *The Commanding Heights*. New York: Simon and Schuster, 1998.

Young, John W. *Britain, France, and the Unity of Europe, 1945–1951*. Leicester: Leicester University Press, 1984.

ARTICLES

Beresford, Melanie, and Prue Kerr. "A Turning Point for Australian Capitalism: 1942–1952." Postwar Reconstruction Seminar: Part II. Canberra: Australian Archives, 1981.

Bothwell, Robert, and John English. "Canadian Trade Policy in the Age of American

Dominance and British Decline." *Canadian Review of American Studies* 8 (Spring 1981): 52–65.

Burnham, Peter. "Re-evaluating the Washington Loan Agreement." *Review of International Studies* 18 (1992): 241–61.

Butlin, S. J., and C. B. Schedvin. "War Economy." In *Australia in the War of 1939–1945: Series IV, Civil Volume IV*. Canberra: Australian War Memorial, 1977.

Cohen, Stephen D. "General Agreement on Tariffs and Trade." In *Encylopedia of U.S. Foreign Relations, Volume 2*, edited by Bruce W. Jentleson and Thomas G. Paterson. New York: Oxford University Press, 1997.

Coombs, Herbert C. "The Keynesian Crusade." Postwar Reconstruction Seminar: Part I. Canberra: Australian Archives, 1981.

———. "The Keynesian Crusade-International." Postwar Reconstruction Seminar: Part II. Canberra: Australian Archives, 1981.

Cornish, Selwyn. "Full Employment in Australia: The Genesis of a White Paper." Postwar Reconstruction Seminar: Part I. Canberra: Australian Archives, 1981.

Dickinson, Margaret. "The State and the Consolidation of Monopoly." In *British Cinema History*, edited by James Curran and Vincent Porter. Totowa, N.J.: Barnes and Noble Books, 1983.

Diebold, William. "The End of the ITO." *Essays in International Finance* 16 (October 1952): 1–37.

———. "Foreign Economic Policy in Dean Acheson's Time and Ours." In *Dean Acheson and the Making of U.S. Foreign Policy*, edited by Douglas Brinkley. New York: St. Martin's Press, 1993.

Dietrich, Ethel B. "Foreign Trade Blocs." *Annals of the American Academy of Political and Social Science* 211 (September 1940): 85–91.

Dobson, Alan. "Economic Diplomacy at the Atlantic Conference." *Review of International Studies* 10 (April 1984): 143–63.

Fieldhouse, D. K. "The Labour Governments and the Empire-Commonwealth, 1945–51." In *The Foreign Policy of the British Labour Governments, 1945–1951*, edited by Ritchie Ovendale. Leicester: Leicester University Press, 1984.

Finlayson, Jock A., and Mark W. Zacher. "The GATT and the Regulation of Trade Barriers: Regime Dynamics and Functions." In *International Regimes*, edited by Stephen D. Krasner. Ithaca: Cornell University Press, 1983.

Frieden, Jeffry A., and David A. Lake. "Introduction: International Politics and International Economics." In *International Political Economy: Perspectives on Global Power and Wealth*, 2d ed., edited by Frieden and Lake. New York: St. Martin's Press, 1991.

Goldstein, Judith. "Creating the GATT Rules: Politics, Institutions, and American Policy." In *Multilateralism Matters: The Theory and Praxis of an Institutional Form*. New York: Columbia University Press, 1993.

Griffith, Robert. "Forging America's Postwar Order: Domestic Politics and Political Economy in the Age of Truman." In *The Truman Presidency*, edited by Michael J. Lacey. Cambridge: Cambridge University Press, 1991.

Harper, Norman. "Australian Foreign Policy." In *Australia, New Zealand, and the Pacific Islands since the First World War*. Austin: University of Texas Press, 1979.

Hogan, Michael J. "Corporatism: A Positive Appraisal." *Diplomatic History* 10 (Fall 1986): 363–72.

———. "The Rise and Fall of Economic Diplomacy: Dean Acheson and the Marshall Plan." In *Dean Acheson and the Making of U.S. Foreign Policy*, edited by Douglas Brinkley. New York: St. Martin's Press, 1993.

Holsti, Kal J. "Politics in Command: Foreign Trade as National Security Policy." *International Organization* 40 (Summer 1986): 643–71.

Ikenberry, G. John. "A World Economy Restored: Expert Consensus and the Anglo-American Postwar Settlement." *International Organization* 46 (Winter 1992): 289–321.

Lipson, Charles. "The Transformation of Trade: The Sources and Effects of Regime Change." In *International Regimes*, edited by Stephen D. Krasner. Ithaca: Cornell University Press, 1983.

Lowi, Theodore J. "The Public Philosophy: Interest-Group Liberalism." *American Political Science Review* 61 (March 1967): 5–25.

McGowan, Pat, and Stephen G. Walker. "Radical and Conventional Models of U.S. Foreign Economic Policy Making." *World Politics* 33 (April 1981): 347–82.

MacLeod, Rory. "The Promise of Full Employment." In *War and Social Change: British Society in the Second World War*, edited by Harold D. Smith. Manchester: Manchester University Press, 1986.

Milner, Helen. "International Theories of Cooperation among Nations: Strengths and Weaknesses." *World Politics* 44 (April 1992): 466–96.

Mitchell, Timothy. "The Limits of the State: Beyond Statist Approaches and Their Critics." *American Political Science Review* 85 (March 1991): 77–96.

Murphy, Robert. "Rank's Attempt on the American Market." In *British Cinema History*, edited by James Curran and Vincent Porter. Totowa, N.J.: Barnes and Noble Books, 1983.

Odell, John S. "Understanding International Trade Policies: An Emerging Synthesis." *World Politics* 43 (October 1990): 139–67.

Pincus, Jonathan. "Evolution and Political Economy of Australian Trade Policies." In *Australia's Trade Policies*, edited by Richard Pomfret. Oxford: Oxford University Press, 1995.

Ruggie, John Gerard. "International Regimes, Transactions, and Change: Embedded Liberalism in the Postwar Economic Order." In *International Regimes*, edited by Stephen D. Krasner. Ithaca: Cornell University Press, 1983.

Sally, Razeen. "International Trade and the Conclusions of the Uruguay Round: A Liberal Critique." European Community Studies Association Convention. Charleston, S.C., May 1995.

Schatz, Arthur W. "The Anglo-American Trade Agreement and Cordell Hull's Search for Peace, 1936–1938." *Journal of American History* 57 (June 1970): 85–103.

Stein, Arthur A. "The Hegemon's Dilemma: Great Britain, the United States, and the International Economic Order." *International Organization* 38 (Spring 1984): 355–86.

Stevenson, John. "Planners' Moon? The Second World War and the Planning Move-

ment." In *War and Social Change: British Society in the Second World War*, edited by
Harold L. Smith. Manchester: Manchester University Press, 1986.

Taylor, Graham D. "Debate in the United States over the Control of International Cartels,
1942–1950." *International History Review* 8 (July 1981): 385–98.

Vogel, David. "Why Businessmen Distrust Their State: The Political Consciousness of
American Corporate Executives." *British Journal of Political Science* 8 (January 1978):
45–78.

DISSERTATIONS

Burr, William. "The Truman Administration and European Reconstruction, 1947–1950:
Corporate Internationalism and Foreign Aid." Northern Illinois University, 1987.

Murans, Francis. "Reciprocal Trade Agreements Program, 1945–1955." Michigan State
University, 1957.

Paterson, Thomas G. "The Economic Cold War: American Business and Economic
Foreign Policy, 1945–1950." University of California, 1968.

Schatz, Arthur W. "Cordell Hull and the Struggle for the Reciprocal Trade Agreements
Program, 1932–1940." University of Oregon, 1965.

Index